The Complete Colonial Gentleman

The Complete Colonial Gentleman

Cultural Legitimacy in Plantation America

Michal J. Rozbicki

UNIVERSITY OF VIRGINIA PRESS
Charlottesville and London

UNIVERSITY OF VIRGINIA PRESS
© 1998 by the Rector and Visitors of the University of Virginia
All rights reserved
Printed in the United States of America

First published 1998

First paperback edition published 2003
ISBN 0-8139-2236-4 (paper)

Library of Congress Cataloging-in-Publication Data

The Library of Congress has cataloged the hardcover edition as follows:

Rozbicki, Michal.
　The complete colonial gentleman : cultural legitimacy in
plantation America / Michal J. Rozbicki.
　　p.　cm.
　Includes index.
　ISBN 0-8139-1750-6 (cloth : alk. paper)
　1. Virginia—Social life and customs—To 1775. 2. Plantation
life—Virginia—History—18th century. 3. Elite (Social) sciences—
Virginia—History—18th century. 4. Gentry—Virginia—
History—18th century. I. Title.
F229.R86　1998　　　　　　　　　　　　　　　97-22568
　　　　　　　　　　　　　　　　　　　　　　　　CIP

To My Parents

Contents

	List of Illustrations	ix
	Acknowledgments	xi
	Introduction	1
1.	The Problem	7
2.	Gentility: A Transatlantic Aspiration	28
3.	The Curse of Provincialism	76
4.	Beautiful Order and Politeness	127
5.	Genteel Ethos on the Eve of the Revolution	172
	Notes	193
	Index	217

Illustrations

1. A gentleman socializing with common people in a coffeehouse   40
2. Daniel Defoe   44
3. Frontispiece of *The Gentleman's Calling*   53
4. The Washington family   146
5. The front parlor at Mount Vernon   168

Acknowledgments

My interest in the legitimizing process among colonial elites in British America is rooted in my own transnational background, which includes a transplantation from Europe to America, and the need to come to terms with various cultural identities and values. America, with its atypical past—never having experienced widespread starvation, mass lawlessness, devastating foreign invasions, or brutal dictatorships—seems, on the whole, to have a bit less need for history to create its cultural identity than the Old World nations (after all, exceptionalism in history has been a form of freeing Americans from the past). To a European eye, American culture is essentially popular, takes more things for granted, is less skeptical about the causal role of ideas, and is more optimistic about the present and the future. This never ceases to intrigue European intellectuals, used to their special status and their hallowed legitimacy, anchored in their still lingering monopoly of high culture. In these transatlantic encounters both sides sometimes show a species of cultural parochialism and insularity which has always fascinated me and which led to a series of questions that are the main themes of this book.

I am grateful for the initial support for my project from the Kennedy Institute for American Studies at the Free University in Berlin, Germany, and especially for the unmatched competence of its librarian, Ms. Ilse Repplinger. I am also happy to acknowledge scholarships from the Henry E. Huntington Library in San Marino, California, the Center for Seventeenth- and Eighteenth-Century Studies of the University of California in Los Angeles at the William Andrews Clark Library, and the John Carter Brown Library in Providence, Rhode Island. I am also very indebted to the Rockefeller Foundation for a fellowship at its study center in Bellagio, Italy, to write parts of this book. Portions of chapter 1 have appeared in my article "The Roots of American Culture: History and Myth," *To Be: Polish American Academic Quarterly* 3, no. 7–8 (1995): 23–25, and portions of chapter 3 were used in my article "The Curse of Provincialism: Negative Perceptions of

Colonial American Plantation Gentry," *Journal of Southern History* 63, no. 4 (1997): 1–26.

Of the numerous distinguished scholars of colonial America from whom I have learned and on whose works this essay has heavily relied, I especially admire the scholarship of Jack P. Greene, whose books have inspired all those who are interested in the cultural relationships between the colonies and Britain. I owe him my deepest respect and appreciation, as well as my original interest in early modern America. I also have a debt to many historians who have kindly provided various types of assistance in my research endeavors, especially to professors Bernard Sheehan, Walter Nugent, James Madison, J. R. Pole, Martin Ridge, Mary McGann, and Tim Wiles. Without the gracious help of Lee and William Bloomer of Pasadena, California, I would not have been able to spend the time I needed at the Huntington Library. I would especially like to thank my editor Dick Holway for his excellent insights and suggestions. And finally, without my wife Jody's patient correcting of her husband's foreign idiom, there would have been a lot more of it in the text.

The Complete Colonial Gentleman

Introduction

In 1782 the chevalier de Chastellux noted: "I wanted to speak of the virtues peculiar to the Virginians, but in spite of my wishes, I have found only magnificence and hospitality to mention. I have been unable to add generosity to these; for they are strongly attached to their interests, and their great wealth, joined to these pretensions, further distorts this vice." When Chastellux traversed Virginia in 1781 and 1782 with the French army under Rochambeau, the planter gentry received him with much enthusiasm. His diaries show he was feasted and entertained in the most generous manner Virginia had to offer a Parisian aristocrat and an acknowledged man of letters who joined the American cause. Widely honored and admired, he became a longtime friend of George Washington and Thomas Jefferson. Yet he consistently refused to concede that the American planter elite represented true gentility. The concept of generosity to which he referred—one of the prime virtues that contemporaries inventoried under the rubric of the genteel ethos—was defined by Samuel Johnson as being "of noble mind, magnanimous, open at heart," signifying a person "not of mean birth." For Chastellux, the wealthy planters' lifestyle had a parvenu tinge because it invoked a merchant's opulence, scrupulously attended to, rather than the natural affluence of a landed gentleman. Even their legendary hospitality did not signify authentic liberality, in his view, because they were too terse and lacked sufficient disinterestedness. Exceptions only confirmed the rule; on visiting Maycocks, the residence of David Meade, he found the host to be highly untypical of the local gentry, "a philosopher of a very amiable but singular turn of mind, especially for Virginia, since he rarely attends to business."[1] Jefferson, with all his respect for Chastellux, was not pleased with this judgment and suggested in a tactful response that Virginians were indeed "disinterested," but in a different sense—by being "thoughtless in their expences and in all their transactions of business." Both considered themselves gentlemen, but where the Frenchman pointed to the presence among the planters of a bourgeois materialism and a business mentality—both ungentlemanly features—Jefferson saw the main weaknesses of Virginia gentry as their excessive extravagance and lack of frugality, sins not so much against the genteel ethos as against utilitarian, bourgeois values. These two perspectives represented two different worlds—that of a new colonial gentility and that of the old European one—bound together by a common transnational model but set apart by dissimilar realities of life. The great planters, especially in Virginia, probably came closer to the lifestyle of English landed gentry than any other group in British colonial America, and yet, throughout the eighteenth century, the entrenched British and European elites denied them legitimacy and routinely labeled them as mere provincial upstarts.[2]

Chastellux's comments exemplified only that part of the long controversy over the authenticity of American gentry which related to European attitudes toward the colonials. At the same time, a far-reaching and protracted struggle for genteel cultural legitimacy was also being waged within British America, especially in the plantation region where it took on a character peculiar to the society and economy there. Questions concerning these ambitions have long intrigued historians. What use in the coffeehouses of Williamsburg would William Byrd II have had for his diligently practiced Greek and Hebrew? Why did Jefferson extol simplicity and egalitarianism while putting so much energy into living like a European aristocrat, complete with sophisticated European paintings of which sixty-three were shipped to Monticello following his stay in France? Why would Washington, leader of the revolt against monarchic corruption and a symbol of republican virtue, become involved in obtaining armorial bearings from the Herald's College in London? And why would Benjamin Franklin, not a landowner but a practical businessman, laud landed virtue and condemn the corruption of commerce? The historian is tempted to classify such divergences between rhetoric and real life as paradoxes, but when the specific rationales of these acts are examined within a broader cultural context, it becomes apparent that they all invoked contemporary criteria of legitimate gentility. The ideal of classical education as the way to cultivate a gentleman's mind was powerful enough to compel Byrd to toil daily on ancient texts in the solitude of his library. Jefferson's version of egalitarianism was grounded in gentry culture and was far from implying an equality of intellect and refinement. Franklin was using the dichotomy—central to contemporary genteel ethos—of noble virtue versus materialistic corruption. Finally, Washington's ambition to be recognized as an armigerous gentleman referred to a standard in British elite culture that outlasted even the Revolution.[3]

Controversies over Old World gentility in America have provided American historians with a topic for a relentless debate which to this day remains lively and engages some of the best pens. The themes recurring in this discussion over the last several decades may be broadly grouped in two categories, one arguing that colonial elites met all the standards of European gentility and the other claiming that while ignoring the realities of colonial life, they not only belatedly pursued an ideal which was destined for the dustbin of history but by doing so created a barrier to the development of an original American culture. In this book I offer a different interpretation. I believe that both categories are based on a misreading of the legitimizing process in culture. I argue that this process—which is the central theme of the pages that follow—enabled the colonial planter elites between the 1720s and the 1770s to develop a strong identification with the European genteel ethos. In turn, this identification not only effectively validated their identity as a dominant group but also, instead of impeding Americanization, became a cultural prerequisite of their ability to successfully invoke concepts of liberty, equality, virtue, and rights as anti-British weapons during the Revolution. The appropriation of this ethos by young American elites, heretofore the objects of metropolitan condescension, thus turned out to be a major cultural resource for legitimizing a new identity. When viewed from this perspective, colonial planter gentility emerges in a fresh light and takes on a new interest as its essentially conservative aspirations foreshadow distinctly American and democratic developments. Consequently, I see the Revolution not so much as instantly creating a radically new meaning of gentility but as an occasion for a number of concepts contained in the old ethos to acquire a new and objectively democratic meaning, as the gentry leaders propagated and effectively legitimized them through the language of republicanism for a wider population of Americans.

The interpretation offered here contrasts with the orientation of a number of major recent studies which tend to view the colonial quest for gentility as not only unrealistic, and even doomed to failure from the very beginning, but also necessarily so artificial as to border on cultural pathology. This perspective is perhaps best embodied in the comment of Kenneth Lockridge that the Virginian gentleman's "recurring need to borrow a perfect model of English gentry culture" resulted in a high price in "personal and cultural destructions."[4] It seems to me that if we accept such a perspective, we would have to conclude that had the colonial elites abandoned current English models of social advancement and prestige at the very beginning of their ascent to prominence in the early eighteenth century, they would have become culturally more stable and secure. I argue instead that their rise was taking place precisely due to, and in terms of, such models. In fact, their pursuit of gentility—despite insecurities and self-doubts—can be seen as one of the more stabilizing elements of the otherwise diverse and fluid eighteenth-century colonial cultural scene. The model of the gentleman, with its highly desirable historical sanction and its contemporary implications of improvement, cultivation, and honor, functioned as a powerful organizing paradigm, embracing a wide spectrum of behavioral patterns from aesthetic preferences, through economic choices, to ideas of civic virtue. I further contend that provincialism, contrary to what we have been often told, not only did not make this quest unduly fragile but provided it with a vigorous and sustained incentive. In this sense, gentility became a versatile and ubiquitous mirror in which the planter elite looked to verify and affirm its progress in achieving cultural, social, and political maturity "in the woods of America."

This colonial pursuit was, of course, far from smooth and unproblematic. Its drama unfolded along a perilous path between the Scylla of provincialism and the Charybdis of metropolitan condescension. The colonists found themselves doubly excluded from membership in the legitimate genteel culture, first, because their life was played out in the American wilderness on a distant periphery of Britain, far from the centers where its genteel values and styles were produced and practiced, and second, because they were seen—on account of the recent origins of their wealth—as upstarts to prosperity, lacking appropriate cultural lineage. As a result, their ambitions were accompanied by a deep-seated inner antagonism as they were torn between their zeal for elevation to gentility, defined by the criteria of British culture, and the persistent refusal to acknowledge their rank by those who were the very source of such criteria, part of a larger colonial dilemma of provincialism which Franklin described as "a deep sense of comparative weakness and inferiority."[5]

It is not possible to understand these battles for legitimacy by examining only the colonial scene. To grasp the apparently paradoxical attractiveness of European gentility in America, one cannot overemphasize, first, that its pursuit by new classes seeking validation was not peculiar to America, and second, that in contemporary Britain its model was not a static, petrified pattern but an object of lively controversy. For these reasons, this book looks at this legitimizing process across the larger British cultural scene, embracing both the metropolis and the plantation colonies, including the British West Indies, where some of the early reputation of the American slaveholding gentry had its sources. Without such rather broad territory it would not be possible to examine the cosmopolitan nature and enduring appeal of what throughout the period in question was essentially the same British standard. The core of the argument, however, is anchored in Virginia, because of its well-crystallized and sophisticated gentry class and the prominent role its members played in the early shaping of the national identity. The discussion is based on both new sources and some familiar ones read anew; some literary material has been introduced whenever it reflects the British public's perceptions of the colonial gentry.

This book is an extended essay in interpretation, written with an implicit set of rules to meet the peculiar needs of the subject. It does not undertake to trace the process of elite formation in Virginia, nor is it an internal history of genteel taste or manners; both subjects have a very sizable literature, the findings of which need not be repeated here.[6] Those themes appear here only insofar as they contribute to arguments concerning legitimacy. It is therefore not a narrative, causal account of the pursuit of the European genteel model by the provincial elites but a rather modest and rigidly circumscribed discussion of how and why certain select facets of this model made sense to them, how transnational gentility, with its ethos and aesthetics, functioned in the context of colonial provincialism, and what new conceptualizations and theoretical perspectives on this subject may be useful. Thus defined, the approach must necessarily be interdisciplinary, with the sociology of culture providing some of the necessary tools. By virtue of its topic and method, this book is not a chronological survey; it is organized around the analysis of specific components of the legitimizing process, although one of its main interests is to explore continuities within this process during the century preceding the Revolution. It shows development within the three main subject areas: the sources and ways of arbitration, the dual—both motivating and destructive—role of provincialism, and the manner of constructing rank by sanctioned taste. These developments reveal two time frames. One is linear, stretching from the decades around the turn of the eighteenth century, when the genteel model's validating role was established for the rest of the colonial period, to the Revolutionary years that brought the first American attempts to alter the sources—but not quite the essence—of the old paradigm. The other is generational—not always parallel to the linear—and reflects the differing modes of seeking legitimacy utilized by the first and the later generations of colonial elites.

The structure of the book reflects its analytical objectives. Because of the complicated nature of cultural legitimacy, chapter 1 addresses its conceptual background by first looking at its persistent manifestations in historiography and then by proposing specific methodological guidelines for its discussion. Chapter 2 correlates the first phase of the pursuit of gentility in the early decades of the eighteenth century with analogous aspirations by "new men" in England, which allows for viewing the colonial ambitions as part of a larger controversy in Britain about the cultural identity of the gentry, rather than seeing it exclusively through the prism of American experience. Chapter 3 examines aspects of the colonial syndrome of provincialism and its effects on the legitimizing process. Chapter 4 considers how attempts to command objects of approved taste and to assume genteel styles succeeded in the colonies without the need to reproduce the more complete model mandated by European elite culture. It looks at such decorum not only as a case of embracing an ideal of refinement but as the very mode of existence of gentry as a class. Chapter 5 reflects on the elusive relationship between the success of the colonial pursuit of gentility and the American Revolution.

CHAPTER 1

The Problem

> "They [Americans] certainly do not have aristocratic grace, but they have an ease that comes from space, the ease of those who have always had lots of space, and this makes up for a lack of manners or noble breeding."
>
> Jean Baudrillard, *America*

> "Charleston did its best to imitate the beau monde of Augustan London. Its leading citizens kept up with the fashions and the news of the English metropolis, and by the middle of the eighteenth century their punctiliousness of manners gave them an air of gentility hardly equalled by the English aristocracy in the same period."
>
> Louis B. Wright, *The Cultural Life of the American Colonies*

A Persistent Theme in American Historiography

One of the reasons the question of genteel cultural legitimacy is so intriguing is that it has been a tenacious theme in colonial scholarship. However paradoxical it may seem on the surface, many American historians have long operated on the assumption—explicit or implicit— that European high culture should be used as the ultimate criterion for interpreting colonial elites. In the past several decades, heavy cannon have been rolled out to prove either that colonial America was different, and this exceptionalism was a source of its own independent cultural legitimacy, or that European criteria were more than fully met among the colonial elites, and therefore any charges of provincialism were unwarranted. For the sake of argument I have simplified and reduced these two approaches to "romantic" and "exceptionalist" (there were, of course, numerous variations within

7

this spectrum). Both views, apart from showing the usual constructedness of knowledge, demonstrate how the inescapable immersion of historians in their own culture influences interpretation. The romantic approach rested on the assumption—interestingly, much resembling the views of colonial gentlemen themselves—that the criteria of European high culture were the only ones that could justify a claim to having any culture at all. The exceptionalist view assumed that such adherence to European norms by the colonial gentry was an aberration of sorts, and that, instead, the roots of any new, indigenous American culture must be found in the colonial period to legitimize such a claim.

Today, historians have widely accepted the notion that the colonies were cultural provinces of Britain, and such searches for roots are less intense.[1] But the complicated problem of legitimacy continues to exert an influence on colonial historiography in many ways. This is so, first, because in colonial America, just as in contemporary Britain, the fundamental division between the social groups of gentry and commonalty paralleled the cultural division between gentility and vulgarity. Hence, the question of the political legitimacy of the American elites in the late colonial and Revolutionary periods was closely linked with their cultural legitimacy, then still almost exclusively defined in terms of European high culture. Second, in relation to Europe, American has always been an overwhelmingly popular culture, both in its origins and in its modern character. Its identity was forged in the mobile age of industrialization, urbanization, and mass immigration, with few established highbrow traditions; in this century it also emerged as the world's first mass culture, where technology conveys standardized and largely homogeneous contents simultaneously to huge audiences, a development that only furthered its popular character. Even though certain elements of genteel culture have been widely adopted by the ever-growing middle class, gentility and cultivation as central criteria defining the ruling elites were already—to the disillusionment of Jefferson—on the wane by the early nineteenth century.[2] Third, against this popular backdrop, the high style of colonial gentry stands out all the more as a rather remarkable attempt of a social group to achieve improvement in this manner under frontier conditions. As such, it justifiably continues to hold the interest of historians, for whom at the roots of national identity there looms an intriguing contradiction between the high and the popular cultures, the former elitist and exclusive and the latter democratic. As a result, much of the historical discourse on colonial culture has revolved around attempts to resolve this apparent incongruity.

The fourth reason for interest in colonial gentry is a chapter in itself and involves European attitudes toward America and the various tensions over this issue. The Revolution did not put them to rest; throughout the nineteenth and twentieth centuries sensitivity to charges of provincialism lingered among American intellectual elites, irritated by the Europeans' application of norms of high culture to their young country but simultaneously harboring—like heroes of F. Scott Fitzgerald—a certain sense of unease in the area of the sublime and artistic.[3] A residue of both these attitudes continues to persist on both sides of the Atlantic. From Matthew Arnold, through Oswald Spengler, to some of the more recent writers, European authors have been bringing up the old charge that America, deprived of aristocratic and high cultural traditions at its roots, has been saturated by philistine materialism and lacks true refinement. A few examples from this century will suffice. The eminent Dutch historian Johan Huizinga observed in 1928 that the simplicity of American culture was an inheritance of the colonial period. Like Alexis de Tocqueville a century earlier but obviously influenced by the pessimism of European culture of his time, he linked American popular democracy with the lack of high culture. "The elements of culture which are bound to the old, traditional atmosphere of the aristocratic society," he wrote, "remain behind in the old country—not only feudal attitudes, but also refined literature. We need only think of the puritanical Pilgrim Fathers, to be sure, but the planters of Virginia also make us realize that they did not bring over much of the English Renaissance in their baggage." With Spenser and Shakespeare left behind, the country remained, in his view, provincial and petit bourgeois in spirit; "a certain small-town attitude still holds sway on an immense scale. . . . a solidarity of mediocrity . . . permeates American life."[4]

Four decades later French philosopher Jacques Maritain, a sincere admirer of America, wrote that Americans have a simplistic idea of achievement, "a very old illusion, already denounced by Socrates: mistaking external success, which depends on a great many ingredients extraneous to ethical life—good connections, cleverness, good luck, ruthlessness, and so forth—for genuine 'success' in the metaphysical sense." He left few doubts that he spoke from the vantage point of the possessor of legitimate high culture when he noted that "in France, artists are kings; everybody is interested in their doings and in the opinion of a great novelist or great painter on national affairs. Here, on the contrary, their opinions carry less weight than that of a prominent businessman." Worse still, artists in America seem suspect, and the "communion between the beholder and the artist is lacking in the very place where it should exist, namely, in that area which, though indeed larger than the small group of expert connoisseurs, is narrower than the general public, and which may be called the enlightened public."[5] In a similar vein British critic F. R. Leavis linked the deluge of mass culture, which he saw as threatening civilization as such, with "American vulgarity, moral, intellectual and social." Nobel Prize–winning Polish poet Czeslaw Milosz, in a 1982 essay, called this—as he saw it—peculiarly American torment an "ontological anemia," revealed in a "nothingness sucking from the center in, a sense of chronic hunger."[6]

It may be helpful for our understanding of the power that similar attitudes exerted on colonial Americans—especially for those today who believe that such European views belong in a museum—to refer, as an example, to a 1988 study of American culture by Jean Baudrillard. The author, a French poststructuralist thinker, became prominent on the European intellectual scene as theorist for the "death of modernity." His book reflects many attitudes—dressed in postmodernist robes—of his European predecessors who commented upon America from the pedestal of elite culture. His chief claim is that America has achieved a modernity that had eluded Europe and for that reason is a mirror of the future. This modernity is based on a lack of history, a cultural rootlessness: "America has no identity problem. In the future, power will belong to those people with no origins and no authenticity." He notes that American civility "is often, in fact, far superior to our own (in our land of 'high culture')," but in other respects "Americans are barbarians." This is because "deep down, America, with its space, its technological refinement, its bluff good conscience . . . is the only remaining primitive society." One look at Los Angeles shows "how provincial this metropolis still is." The popular character of culture precludes refinement; "everything is so informal, there is so little in the way of reserve or manners." In a truly Trollopian observation, he remarks that Americans smile, but it is not a smile of gentility; it originates "neither from courtesy, nor from an effort to charm

....Americans may have no identity but they have wonderful teeth." Good taste is scarce; America is a "society which seeks to give itself neither meaning nor an identity, which indulges neither in transcendence nor in aesthetics." Culture for him is synonymous with high culture, and America is too popular to have any. "If the term taste has any meaning," he writes, "then it commands us not to export our [European] aesthetic demands to places where they do not belong." Conversely, "when the Americans transfer Roman cloisters to the New York Cloysters, we find this unforgivably absurd." What separates Europeans from Americans is that "we [Europeans] do not have either the spirit or the audacity for what might be the zero degree of culture, the power of unculture." Incidentally, his only mention of "patrician elegance" in America refers to the "Indian summer in Wisconsin."[7] Despite Baudrillard's numerous disclaimers to the contrary, this is evidently another analysis of America in Europocentric terms of high culture, an indication that the provincial-cosmopolitan tensions over legitimacy which so vexed the colonial gentry are far from extinct.

All historians, of course, carry the heritage of their culture, ideologies, mentalities, taken-for-granted knowledge, and forms of discourse. And historians' choices have always been shaped by the values of their society. The American interpreters of colonial gentility—both romantics and exceptionalists—were not exempt from this rule. It does not take much deconstruction to reveal just how central the issue of cultural legitimacy has been in their analytical methods.

Until the last two decades, the romantics interpreted colonial gentility in the context of the then still influential definition of culture that went back to Arnold, with its stress on taste and tradition, spiritual qualities, and high moral and aesthetic standards—standards which he himself believed America, with its vulgarity of taste and manners, did not meet—as opposed to materialism, crudity, and lack of subtlety.[8] Since only genteel elites could meet such standards, it seemed desirable to focus on the evidence that early American elites satisfied such criteria of refinement, a position that logically had to follow the Arnoldian assumption, since to deny it would put in doubt the legitimacy of early American culture as such. Thus, Philip Alexander Bruce wrote in 1907 that the colonial gentry was so completely English in its lifestyle that a gentleman arriving from the mother country would "at once take the same position in the society of the Colony as he had held in his native shire, and would hardly recognize in outward customs that he had made a change in habitation."[9]

Howard Mumford Jones, writing in 1952, felt it was still necessary to refute Trollope's *Domestic Manners of the Americans*, which had greatly offended America a hundred and thirty years earlier by presenting its culture as lacking in manners and gentility. He did so by arguing for the presence of the idea of a Renaissance gentleman in early America side by side with simple, popular culture: "The Virginia or South Carolina aristocrat, the New England Brahmin, the well-bred Pennsylvanian representative of the Main Line family, and others like them are American types as characteristic as the hillbilly and the squatter, types which take away from the United States the sting of Mrs. Trollope's charge that democracy breeds boorishness and must ever do so."[10] Louis B. Wright, one of the most eminent historians of that generation, went even further along the same path. Depicting colonial South Carolina, he compared it to Renaissance Italy, claiming that "Charleston, like Venice in its heyday, was a city-state, ruled by an intelligent and cultivated oligarchy of great families," an elite more than comparable to European aristocracy. In another work he suggested that "the planter aristocracy of the agrarian colonies approximated English county families more nearly than any other group in America." In a similar vein Thomas Wertenbaker elevated the late colonial gentleman to a rank equivalent not only to European knighthood but even to nobility, suggesting that "the planter spent his life in isolation almost as great as that of the feudal barons of the Middle Ages." He de-emphasized the colonial gentleman's commercial values in order to fit him into the accepted mold of European nobility: "The gradual loss of the mercantile instinct, the habit of command acquired by the control of servants and slaves, and the long use of political power, the growth of patriotism, eventually instilled into him a chivalric love of warfare not unlike that of the knights of old."[11] These examples are not quoted to be censured for their exaggeration of the cultural standards of the colonial gentry, standards which in themselves—if viewed from proper distance and within in the colonial context—were often impressive. The point here is quite different, for it concerns the mighty pressure of culture on historians not only to reconstruct the national past but also to validate it.

A feature peculiar to American colonial historiography was that the romantic position did not necessarily contradict the exceptionalist one. Both approaches coincided when the colonial gentleman was presented as having not only adopted the virtues of British nobility but preserved them in a form that was even purer than that in the motherland, a notion which, incidentally, goes as far back as Jefferson's belief in the American elite as a true aristocracy of merit and not birth.[12] For instance, Arthur Schlesinger Jr., depicting in 1969 an idealized "colonial aristocracy," pointed to its superiority over the vain European counterpart, claiming that "its members had not . . . used their station exclusively for self-aggrandizement and worldly display, but, as a class, had considered themselves trustees for the common good, identifying their welfare with that of the community at large." This paralleled the approach taken by Wright, who declared that the "notion expressed by cynics that the wealthy planters monopolized all the civil and military power exclusively for their personal aggrandizement is demonstrably false." Charles Sydnor's interpretation attempted to combine two legitimacies— that of European high culture and that of nascent American democracy—by pointing to the centrality of a sophisticated and responsible aristocratic elite in eighteenth-century Virginia and by reconciling their role with the emergence of democracy. "Political power," he wrote, "truly rested with the people; democracy was a real and active force. . . . Virginia did not regard democracy and aristocracy as contradictory kinds of government."[13]

For the more strict exceptionalists the crucial task was to come up with a new legitimacy for America. They explored the colonial scene for that which was original and downplayed the fact that practically all of the high cultural patterns were taken from Europe. But their denials only revealed just how powerful the old sources of legitimacy were. For instance, for Carl and Jessica Bridenbaugh, the reason for the surge in late colonial Philadelphia's artistic activity was not so much the newly emergent market for English-style objects but an effort "to enable colonial society to escape from the humiliating parent-child relationship to a spiritual status more nearly equal to that of the mother land." They pointed out that "gradually the intellectuals of Europe sensed that the evident ability of the city's representatives, their absence of provinciality and their quiet self-assurance presaged the emergence of a new kind of society." As Philadelphia came of age, it "had shaken off its early allegiance to Old World standards and conventions," freeing itself from the "mistaken faith in Old World canons." The authors acknowledged the dominance of British cultural patterns in the colonies but treated it as an aberration. Such a viewpoint could only lead to their condemning Benjamin West and John Singleton Copley for choosing Europe over their native America and to presenting these episodes as unfortunate accidents rather than a consequence of the lack of public support for the "high" artistic ambitions of the two painters. Similarly, in the area of applied art, stubborn eighteenth-century American cabinetmakers "failed to develop a style of their own" and persistently copied fashionable English models, innocent of the supposedly impending Americanization of taste.[14] The modesty of colonial literary achievement had to be validated in a like manner. As one historian put it, "If too little of the literary production of the seventeenth and eighteenth centuries in America has the capacity to hold our interest, that fact does not indicate a lack of imagination or mental capacity on the part of the writers. They usually had objectives much nearer to their immediate concerns than Milton's noble dream of writing something that the world would not willingly let die."[15] This validating impulse introduced an essentially anachronistic perspective. By focusing on the new achievements of colonial culture—sometimes presented as objectively existing but not yet realized by the colonists as their own—these authors often inadvertently reversed the legitimizing criteria to which the colonial gentlemen wholly subscribed.

In the process they sometimes raised what they must have felt to have been certain weaknesses of colonial culture to the status of virtues. For instance, the spontaneous, simple, and natural aesthetics of Americans was contrasted with British formality and contrived style. From such a perspective, the colonial gentleman, with his attachment to English taste, appeared only to slow down the inevitable Americanization and represented the "forces of convention and tradition." The usual suspects were "the gentry, whose wealth, conservatism, and considerable stake in the society of the British Empire bred in them a great reluctance to experiment and a timid devotion to the status quo." By "worshipping" English culture, the gentry "hoped to impose upon the magnificent distances and complex social and racial patterns of colonial America the tight little stylized culture of Georgian England." This craving for British genteel attributes was only a kind of temporary delusion, for "actually, these Anglophile gentlemen were more American than they knew." Similarly, we have been told that in the awkward imitations of Hogarth drawn by the otherwise tasteful Alexander Hamilton of Annapolis, "the very amateurish quality of the drawings gives them a greater realism than the imaginative subtleties of Hogarth."[16] Daniel Boorstin, in his engagingly written book on the American colonial experience, felt it was necessary to make a vigorous, almost Thomas Paine–like effort to argue that European standards of high culture should be rejected as measures of early American cultural legitimacy and that its roots should be sought in the colonies. In doing so, he ingeniously turned some of the limitations of provincial life into cultural achievements: "The older culture traditionally depended on the monumental accomplishments of the few, while the newer culture—diffused, elusive, process-oriented—depended more on the novel, accreting ways of the many."[17]

Such interpretations of colonial American history have now been largely rejected by colonial historians, as a broader concept of culture, no longer treated as equivalent to its high variety, has removed the urgency to authenticate colonial American culture historiographically. No longer pressed by what has aptly been called the "logic of validation," we should be able to take a fresh look at the pervasive influence of the issue of cultural legitimacy in colonial history.[18] In the rich and rapidly expanding scholarship on colonial America, validation is being replaced by discovery, and the interpretation of culture is increasingly being removed from the realm of intuition, although the constructedness of historian's knowledge is, of course, not likely to disappear.

Despite these profound changes, the issue of legitimacy remains very close to the surface; it often emerges in the shape of a newer interpretation, which seems to have evolved out of the two older schools, and which can be clearly discerned in the current works of some of the most distinguished American colonial historians. It portrays the colonial gentry's quest for British high culture as a sort of mild aberration, a childhood disease which needs to be explained away as a transitional phase of immaturity on route to an original American culture. The question at the heart of this approach is no longer whether pre-Revolutionary America had a legitimate culture, but why did the colonial gentry strive so relentlessly to achieve the English model of landed virtue. Why did it not create a new style, better attuned to the realities of life in America? This question—which inspired the main theme of this study—was posed by Jack P. Greene in his seminal essay on the

American search for identity. Greene was especially intrigued by what he called the colonists' relentless "imitation" of British tastes and their "refusal to construct a new system of values that would correspond more closely to conditions of life in the colonies." Like earlier scholars, he drew attention to the apparent contradiction between the gentry's tenacious Anglophilia and the reality of colonial life, stressing that its members were remarkably "dependent" for their normative values on an idealized image of English society and culture. The result, in his view, was that the development of American identity was stifled, or at best delayed, and that the colonists were thus subjected to psychological insecurities. In his most recent works, one finds continued emphasis on the role of European culture in the colonial mind as an obstacle that "operated powerfully to prevent observers from developing a fully positive identification of the societies of colonial British America during the first three quarters of the eighteenth century."[19]

This approach presented in Greene's influential studies was subsequently taken up by a number of other leading historians. A recent example is Kenneth Lockridge's book on William Byrd, in which British culture, and specifically its model of the gentleman to which Byrd—like so many of his Virginian contemporaries—intensely aspired, is compared to a "cage." The model is depicted as culturally restrictive and its pursuit as resulting in an artificial and rigid gentility, incompatible with the emerging democratic society in America. A similar approach to colonial gentility is taken by Stephanie G. Wolf in her study of everyday life in eighteenth-century America. Writing about the rise among the great southern planter gentry of a "pseudo-dynastic family type," she calls it "an almost grotesque transmogrification of the English model" because "eighteenth-century slaveholders saw nothing false or inappropriate in their identification with the medieval/Christian ideal." Richard Waterhouse, in turn, follows Greene's paradigm in his examination of the planters of South Carolina, who "chose to base their lifestyle on an exaggerated imitation of the 'culture' of the English gentry" and sought "to impose their idealized version of English hierarchical society in their own colony." The inevitable outcome of this American "caricature" of the metropolitan elite was that the colonists "failed to establish a society based on the values to which they adhered." A prominent colonial historian referred to fashionable consumption that became "an exaggerated symbol of personal worthiness and a dreadful instrument of social control." Another study pointed to the planters' "ahistorical aristocratic ideal" and "the fantasy" of people engaged in what was essentially capitalist enterprise while identifying themselves with "residual aristocratic values."[20]

All this was true, to a varying degree, but the discussion here pursues a different path, focusing on the ways this model functioned among new aspirants to gentility. What may appear to us as a profound tension between inherited cultural patterns and the realities of life in America need not be seen as primarily a paradox. It also seems unlikely that the ideal of a landed gentleman had the power to act as a "barrier." One reason is that this model's complex appeal was partly located at the precognitive level of the contemporary British mind-set. The model was reproduced in America not so much through purely conscious imitation but because many of its building blocks had been acquired from the historically established repertoire of culture's values, standards of behavior, concepts of social advancement, hierarchy, and prestige, and as such were taken for granted. Another reason was that gentility's central attraction was rooted not so much in empty sentiments for the English past as in its potent social and political uses as a tool of constructing and authorizing order, identity, and power. Without proper acknowledgment of these functional aspects it is difficult to fully appreciate the fact that for the colonial elite, meeting metropolitan criteria of legitimacy was the only culturally viable means of succeeding in their ambitions. Suggesting that the colonial gentleman declined to build a new system of values and resisted the reality of American life implies that adopting a different, local model was open to him, if only he had not been restricted by these self-imposed barriers. Yet if the nouveaux riches adhered so passionately to English genteel style, doing so must surely have made sense to them. Maintaining that the colonists were trapped by a set of ineffective values comes very close to assuming that the criteria of effectiveness present in the colonists' world were more compatible with post-Revolutionary, modern developments rather than with the culture from which the earliest generations of gentry emerged, a culture to which certain meanings of gentility were intrinsic. Overemphasizing "barriers" appears to be methodologically just as risky as another not uncommon approach in American historiography, preoccupied with the roots of democracy: overstressing the element of free choice in the colonists' "selection" of lifestyles, to the neglect of the elements delimiting such choice. For instance, a fine recent study of colonial Maryland culture claims that most of those who indentured themselves to the Chesapeake had a "range of options," "elected their lot," and struck a "bargain" with the recruiters. To take such a perspective is not only to overestimate the historical bargaining power of the propertyless and the unemployed in early modern Britain but to make a philosophical assumption that they voluntarily elected to free themselves from the liberty of not accepting the recruiter's offer of a job, room, board, and a future in America.[21]

In sum, the importance of the continuing influence of exceptionalism is threefold. First, when viewed from the perspective of cultural legitimacy, exceptionalism clearly has been in itself a product of the legitimizing impulse. As such, it has inspired historians—even those who adopted a transoceanic viewpoint—to ask certain kinds of questions of the colonial past (such as why the colonials did not develop cultural values more closely reflective of the reality of America), rather than others (such as why did they so intensely pursue English patterns). Second, the exceptionalist-inspired "either-or" approach sins against the very essence of cultural behavior, which as a rule involves not choices between culturally "inherited" dispositions and current confines of life but improvisations between the two. Third, at its very core the exceptionalist question contained an erroneous assumption that American colonial culture was not merely unique but that its development fundamentally differed from some supposed regularities of development elsewhere. Both orthodox and, more recently, milder forms of this core question tend to distract us from the fact that colonial culture could be both British and American and both mimetic and unique.[22] Indeed, it appears that in the specific case of the colonial gentry's impact on the identity of American culture, some of the most socially radical and original aspects of this influence—to be felt especially from the Revolution onwards—were grounded in its otherwise conservative quest for Englishness.

Interpreting Cultural Legitimacy

Because cultural legitimacy is such an amorphous subject, pertinent methodological postulates must be carefully identified. The dilemmas of navigating in this field were well expressed by Pierre Bourdieu when he advised scholars involved in it "to be ready to be always dealing with things that are complicated, confused, impure, uncertain, all of which runs counter to the usual idea of intellectual rigor."²³ Since much of the evidence is limited and oblique and firm generalizations are rarely possible, the most viable path for a cultural historian is interdisciplinary, and it often leads, in a somewhat eclectic manner, through scattered and not always compatible kinds of sources, such as behavior, correspondence, diaries, or economic and demographic data. Most would agree, however, that whatever the obstacles, cultural history must be studied. The approach here is a simple one, distanced from the classifications of grand theory and positivist paradigm and focused on asking questions about the various, sometimes not very visible, ingredients out of which colonial gentility was being forged and about the mechanism of this construction.

As to the concept of culture itself, it seems best defined as a framework of socially established and inherited practices, ideas, and institutions shared by members of a particular society. Its ethos, in turn, may be understood as the general orientation of a given culture, a hierarchy of accepted values and ideas, either explicitly formulated or such as can be abstracted from the behavior of its members when they tend to behave in particular ways. Clifford Geertz calls it, equally precisely but somewhat more poetically, "the moral and aesthetic style and mood of a culture."²⁴ Most current definitions of culture emphasize interrelationships and multiple, intertwined systems rather than watertight boundaries and coherent organic cores; the latter are now mostly seen as abstractions taken out of a larger context. The cultural life of any society thus involves a number of heterogeneous orders of things—for instance, legal, aesthetic, or religious—mutually influencing but not reducible to one another. Its texture is loose, and individuals must meet the demands of often conflicting and even contradictory pressures. Understanding this keeps the historian from putting undue stress on the consistency of cultural patterns. Contradictions, of course, have always existed, especially between the inner ideals and the external theater of life. Historical actors usually behaved "paradoxically" because they saw sense in different behaviors separately, in their particular contexts. It is these specific rationales that the cultural historian should pursue. As Norbert Elias observed, culture as a form of social order is neither "rational," in that it is intentionally designed, nor "irrational," in that it happens incomprehensibly. Instead, it emerges from an interdependence of three elements: preexisting "restraints" or internalized norms, planned change, and a complex web of concrete actions.²⁵

Thus, our gentleman possessed some socially inherited, preexisting norms of elite lifestyle, he consciously planned to enact some of them, and he had to reconcile all this with the realities of colonial life.

Values, as part of a culture's ethos, are something toward which we take a position of acceptance or rejection. Most scholars today agree that in the history of knowledge there are no concepts that are entirely valueless; they all have some uses. But the process of assigning value and meaning is not arbitrary. People are historical products and see the world through their culture; the meanings and values they assign to reality involve the earlier experiences of their society. For the seventeenth-century Virginian William Fitzhugh, a coat of arms carried an immense value that was placed on it by preceding centuries of British culture, and we should not expect him to have rejected its meaning in favor of future American egalitarianism.

For this study, some of the theoretical propositions of Pierre Bourdieu have been particularly useful. His conceptualizations of the ways that cultures as systems of symbolic meaning are made legitimate for social groups or classes provide the historian with many effective tools. Especially productive are his notions of the arbitrariness of legitimate cultural forms and of their ability—once they had been claimed by the arbiters—to reproduce power relations. Similarly valuable is his proposition that culture is both a means and an end in the struggles for social position, as well as his approach to social and cultural practice, which he sees, much like Elias, not as a conscious or unconscious application of some rules but rather as an improvisation and adjustment between the particular limitations of life and the cultural dispositions of people. His economic metaphor used to describe how all discourse is assigned value and meaning by the "market" in which it circulates has been increasingly in use; it has recently been adopted in Stephen Greenblatt's influential New Historicism, which also stresses the continuum between author, text, and social context.[26] I do not, however, share Bourdieu's view that culture and taste can be reduced to relations of power and, consequently, that gentility's ultimate goals were singularly a function of power relations. Such reductionism disembodies cultural phenomena from the sociohistorical context through which they acquire meaning. For instance, objects of taste may signify genuine desires for dignity, refinement, and order in a chaotic environment—all facts that for a cultural historian have autonomous significance, outside the network of power relations, even if the criteria of taste are defined by the ruling class and serve their domination. Culture may be restrictive, but it allows a range of choices considerably broader than that defined by conditions of material existence and social interaction. Bourdieu's concept of symbolic violence in culture leads us to an almost sophistic conclusion that historical actors—because they are not aware of the mechanism of domination—may be "enslaved" by a belief in the freedom of choice. It is much more likely that a culture "imposed" upon actors by a power group may become the subject of authentic, autonomous experiences. Such was apparently the case with the model of gentility, culturally "imposed" by the old British ruling elite on the colonial planters but ultimately becoming a source of genuine and autonomous experiences for some provincials. I do not think it is the task of the historian of culture to discover neo-Hegelian grand plots and patterns which determine human choices or to play the part of an omniscient narrator in pursuit of unified reality. It is to reveal subjectivity and meaning.

The genteel model itself, although it continues to exert power over our historical imagination, was not homogeneous; in fact, it has never existed in pure form. It only thrives in the somewhat gray area—one of special interest to us—where the ideal meets actual life or, more precisely, where dispositions encoded in culture meet concrete existential situations. Ideals as models of aspirations have, of course, been an integral part of all endeavors to improve the human condition; any thought that plans for the future is simultaneously engaged in a sort of utopianism because it assumes and directs its reflection toward some future state of perfection. In this sense, an ideal motivates people to real action and thus is not a synonym for the impossible. An ideal may be a helpful tool in the construction of hypotheses and in discussing cultural expectations and evasions, but one needs to be cautious in applying it because—as a model of what ought to exist—it is not a description of reality. An ideal type only assembles various individual phenomena into a homogeneous mental image, without empirical reality. Max Weber cautioned that ideal types as scholarly tools have no value-content, they have little to do with perfection, they are not statistical averages, nor are they some deep and permanent "essence" of things. He was also careful to point out that not all attributes of an ideal type are present in each of its real-life exemplifications, and therefore it is never definitive. It cannot be true or false; it can help us understand the colonial gentleman, but we should not measure him against some supposedly perfect matrix—which existed nowhere in Britain either—to discover if he "complies" with or "deviates" from it.[27]

After all, the contemporary British image of the country gentleman was far from uniform and internally coherent. Henry Fielding's *Tom Jones* popularized two different images, that of the hot-tempered, drinking, foxhunting Squire Western and that of the generous and good-natured Squire Allworthy. Yet comparisons with perfect prototypes have been quite frequent, leading historians to infer inaccurately that incomplete colonial renditions of this model were also ineffective. The eighteenth-century Virginian gentleman, one recent study notes, was surrounded with "an air of artifice." Another author points to the "exaggerated imitation of the culture of the English gentry" among South Carolinians.[28] This difficulty fades if we view the problem through local experience, in terms of what was available to the actors. The same genteel styles and rituals or even only their partial execution often had different meanings in the colonial environment from those in the Old World, involving such new ingredients as slavery, Indians, and frontier wilderness. Cultural phenomena as objects of historical reflection had already been objects of somebody's experience and actions, so we can only know them in relation to the experiences of the people who used them.[29] In any given culture there is no such thing as the ultimate, core reality; many systems are possible, and each is equally rational within that culture. Even if we treat the early modern Anglo-American world as one culture, we should be wary of applying to members of the American gentry any criteria of behavior from outside their own environment and their local "rationality."

If people in their behavior usually do not consciously imitate an ideal model, they are often guided by cultural predispositions, sometimes called "common sense" or "taken-for-granted knowledge." This usable residue of the past in collective memory plays a major role in our cognitive process. For instance, presuppositions of rank, elegance, ugliness, or rules of conduct help to translate everyday life into a familiar, sensible world and, consequently, to formulate goals and ambitions. Played out in the complex dialectic of human contact with the world, they are inseparable from the very process of experience. As James Ostrow observed, they are like the eyes that we do not "know" as eyes when we see the world, unless they hurt or unless we consciously refer to them specifically as eyes.[30] This epistemological aspect of experience is crucial in the study of cultural history because it enables us to peek into how reality—that is, that which was taken by the colonists for real, objective, and having a meaning on its own—was constituted. It also goes a long way toward preventing what Joyce Appleby has called a reversed human encounter with time, when "men and women are examined in relation to future developments unknown to them," a syndrome that has plagued the study of American colonial gentility. And finally, it enables us to better understand that the colonists could not easily or rapidly abandon old, ingrained presuppositions for new, American ones.[31]

These prereflexive forms of knowledge were no less historical facts than buildings and carriages. One consequence of recognizing this should be more attention given to language. Ernst Cassirer, who pioneered explaining the cultural role of language, saw it as a symbolic form of cognition providing us with an a priori construction, a prism through which we organize our notions of reality. It was also in this sense that Edmund Husserl wrote about the subjective, commonsense conceptions of the world, in which particular objects are assumed to have a "natural" existence outside of our experience, and where the constitutive role of our culturally conditioned consciousness is simply ignored.[32] The one cultural pattern that all British colonists, regardless of rank, transplanted with them was their language, which mediated heavily in the reproduction and construction of social order and worldviews. For instance, words pertaining to social ranks commonly used in early eighteenth-century Britain, such as "true-bred gentleman," "meaner people," "ancient families," "gentry rank," "inferior persons," "persons of rank and dignity," "ancient houses," "person of quality," "mechanicks," "the mob," and "plebeians," all restricted conscious choice and structured reality for users—British and colonial—as preexperiential filters including presuppositions of hierarchic order.[33] When the Virginia council, alarmed at petitions against new tobacco regulations in 1715, blamed the attorneys for initiating the movement "by their evil practices amongst the ignorant & illiterate people . . . in order to persuade the Vulgar into an opinion," the words used not only presupposed the existence of a lower order, but construed it as incapable of understanding matters of government and being essentially irrational. Similarly, in 1774 when Philip Fithian wrote in Virginia that "the lower Class of People here are in Tumult on the account of Reports from Boston," he knew exactly what social group he was referring to—the nongenteel.[34]

The notion of legitimacy provides a convenient link between the diverse aspects of cultural reproduction and change. What makes legitimacy so pivotal is that the power of culturally encoded concepts and symbols to structure social reality does not reside in them but in the relationships of acceptance. For instance, gestures and rituals of deference conveyed appreciation—and status—to a recipient only when he or she was also considered as legitimately deserving of such recognition.[35] This pattern worked well in England where the cultural environment corresponded to, or reflected, habitual presuppositions; participants easily used them to communicate with reality. But America was not a miniature replica of the mother society and its cultural configurations, so the old taken-for-granted knowledge was applied to a different experience. Specifically, when the genteel model migrated, it had left in England a whole system of reference points which produced it and gave it meaning. Whatever the efforts to fully reproduce this model in America, the only way it could survive and succeed was by adjusting to the tensions between those metropolitan reference points and provincial realities. This colonial dilemma has long absorbed historians, but a closer focus on legitimacy allows us to look beyond it and seek a different perspective. The key to this perspective is in the fact that one crucial cultural ambition remained identical, serving the same purpose in America and in Britain: control over the symbolic power of gentility. For the young planter elite it was just as critical as for the old gentry in Europe because only such control—not even economic or physical power—was capable of providing legitimacy and thus ensuring an effective acceptance of its members' authority, as well as confirming their hard-earned self-identity as gentry.[36]

Any understanding of how legitimacy functions must therefore include the notion of arbiters. Legitimacy involves status conferred or confirmed by some authority. Samuel Johnson's *Dictionary* defined it as "genuineness, not spuriousness," and gave a phraseological example that well reflected the indispensable hierarchical component: "It would be impossible for any enterprize to be lawful, if that which should legitimate it is subsequent to it, and can have no influence to make it good or bad."[37] For genteel style, taste, literary and architectural forms, manners, dress, or virtues to be recognized as authentic and reputable, they had to carry the mark of approval by an authority qualified to declare such standards legitimate. In other words, there must first exist an authority with a title to do so. For colonial gentry there

The Problem 25

was practically only one available source of such arbitration, the metropolis that not only defined what was polite and refined but also controlled this precious capital by assigning it to the anointed. Although the transatlantic designation of taste was a one-way street for Americans, the case was less clear with assigning legitimacy within the colonial market, which the planter gentry dominated by the later eighteenth century and where its members functioned locally as practical arbiters, despite being persistently rejected as such by the metropolitans.

Once they achieved the status of arbiters of genteel lifestyle and values locally, they became capable of practicing exclusion and inclusion (good taste is, as a rule, partly defined in terms of bad taste), ingredients crucial to constructing social order, and inherent in the struggles for winning and maintaining legitimacy, but at times underestimated by those historians who tend to view gentility as primarily a "desire for refinement" and "an ideal toward which wealth and power gravitated."[38] Tensions between established legitimacies and alternative propositions need not be caused by conscious programs of opposition to authority; often the mere existence of an alternative is seen as a threat to the old order. In the early modern period, the lines between social, political, legal, and cultural rank were often fine or even invisible. For instance, the legitimacy of the cultural capital accumulated by certain groups was sometimes sanctioned by law or right, as in the case of sumptuary legislation that prohibited the possession of certain stylistic objects not appropriate to the order of precedence and rank.[39] It is well then to bear in mind that legitimacy is not a state of things but a constant struggle, a dynamic that cuts across the network of cultural, social, and political relationships. One may safely assume that there is, at any time, a legitimate hierarchy of culture, but it is equally evident that at any time there is also an ongoing battle for changes in this hierarchy. Cultural legitimacy is not fixed; it constantly fluctuates—rapidly, as with dress fashions, or slowly, as with architectural styles. In fact, it must change, so that styles that have become vulgarized by too wide a usage among the nonelite can be replaced by new, exclusively high ones. Change also takes place when a new aspiring group attempts to undermine the old legitimacies and to authorize new genres, styles, or values. This contest of definitions itself must be seen as part of the process of legitimization; the parallel struggles for gentility by eighteenth-century slaveholding colonial elites and by commercial groups in Britain provide vivid testimony to this mechanism. Those who are able to define the legitimate culture as absolutely and naturally theirs—and, consequently, to define their own affiliation within the hierarchy of culture—are usually those who win in the larger power relations between groups. It is in this context that cultural legitimacy—providing it is considered in the framework of larger social and economic realities—may yield some answers to questions that have for long puzzled us about the behavior of the American planter gentry.

Finally, let me point to a few potential consequences of all these analytical assumptions by referring to a study of the origins of Virginia gentry by Martin H. Quitt. He has argued persuasively that the first generation of this elite consisted of mostly younger, dispossessed sons or sons of trading families, many of whom shared an experience of London, commercial occupations, and a business ethic. As a result, the lifestyle and values of landed gentry were not an inherited part of their cultural baggage and were only re-created by the subsequent generations in the eighteenth century who "synthesized a genteel style with the competitive, commerce-oriented ethos that they inherited from their immigrant fathers." The effect of this happy blending was a "common gentry culture without the divisions and resentments that existed in England between city and country, and between eldest and younger sons," in other words, a new model of gentry culture, nonexistent in Britain. While agreeing with the general thrust of this interpretation, my methodological perspective puts a different light on a number of problems. First, the Virginia gentry's struggles and frustrations in its battle for legitimacy indicate that the cultural synthesis was not smooth and unproblematic, nor did it quite harmonize the two ethoses into an integrated new one. In fact, it is hard to speak of achieving a specific "model" or even its "refraction" where there was constant struggle for validation, with sizable confusion and unsettled cultural configurations, both in England and in the colonies. Second, we need a more complex explanation of why and how the planters adopted elements of the genteel model than a "self-conscious pursuit of gentility," that is, voluntary, deliberate imitation. Instead, we need to look more closely at both their encoded dispositions and at the wide variety of practical uses of such gentility within the plantation society. Third, one must address the fact that since the immigrant leaders had mostly commercial and city backgrounds, they already carried a powerful cultural stigma—

exclusion from gentility—that needed to be overcome. One may be skeptical whether it was being defeated by embracing both the genteel and the commercial ethos, when the latter was the very source of such a stigma. Fourth, Quitt's study dismisses the colonists' quest for genteel attributes defined by the metropolis as mere "snobbery," an assumption which leads him to interpret William Fitzhugh's desire for a coat of arms as simply a mere "conceit" of a man who did not really crave recognition in terms of the Old World criteria.[40] But the view that the colonial gentry was somehow more American and different than it knew—an echo of the exceptionalist approach—underemphasizes the real power and the practical functions of such apparently conservative cultural yardsticks. The next chapter explores these problems of interpreting colonial gentility by putting them in a transatlantic perspective which makes it possible to grasp the cultural mechanisms of the legitimizing process involved.

CHAPTER 2

Gentility: A Transatlantic Aspiration

> "For where there are two in a noble mans house ... as soon as it is knowne that the one is a Gentleman borne, and the other is not, the unnoble shall be much lesse esteemed with everie man, than the Gentleman, and he must with much travell and long time imprint in mennes heades a good opinion of himselfe, which the other shall get in a moment, and only for that he is a Gentleman."
>
> Castiglione, *The Book of the Courtier*

> "All Great things begin in Small, the highest Families began low, and therefore to examine it too nicely is to overthrow it all.... the tallest Tree has its Root in the Dirt."
>
> Daniel Defoe, *The Compleat English Gentleman*

New Elites and the Parvenu Gap

The first three-quarters of the eighteenth century saw a rapid emergence of two new social groups, divided by the Atlantic but linked by the same aspiration to achieve recognition as gentry: the urban, commercial class in England and the upper crust of the slaveholding planters in Virginia. Despite major differences, the guiding star in their pursuits was the same cultural model of European gentility. To understand that the aspirations of planter elites were neither eccentricities nor barriers to modernization, it is essential to take a transatlantic perspective and concurrently view the problem through the eyes of the colonists and their contemporaries in England, engaged in a similar legitimizing process. This has been a rather neglected approach in studies of colonial gentility, which tend to be American-oriented despite the fact that colonial British America was British rather than American, and that the planter gentry was a part of the larger British cultural world. Such an international viewpoint is indispensable if we are to assess more fully the sources of the cultural dispositions involved in their pursuit and the mechanism of arbitrating its legitimacy.

The efforts of both new elites must be viewed as part of broader socioeconomic and cultural developments in Britain in the late seventeenth and early eighteenth centuries. The substantial number of manors changing hands indicates mobility within the gentry class. Propertied urban elites, increasingly annoyed with the limitations of their political liberties by aristocratic government, were growing in economic power; as Lawrence Stone has shown, elites of power and prestige in early modern England were not necessarily synonymous with elites of wealth.[1] Clashes between the "Court" party and the "Country" opposition provided a forum for public polemics over the links between money and personal quality.[2] Especially after the death of Queen Anne in 1714 and the domination of the political scene by the Whigs, much more favorably disposed to mercantile interests, ambitious members of commercial classes were encouraged to look for new avenues of realizing their social ambitions. Having already secured wealth and lifestyles that competed with those of the landed gentry, they now sought to establish their social respectability. There were tactical routes to this goal, such as obtaining positions that carried the label of gentility or marrying into landed families, but the strategic game was about cultural acceptance into the club of gentility. Despite these attempts, Mr. Profit was at this stage a long way off from membership. Genteel writers still widely associated business interests with such distasteful ideas as republicanism, usury, utilitarianism, and pretension. Although only a marginal number of merchants were able to become fully assimilated into the gentry, the blurring of lines between "true" gentlemen and those who "styled themselves gentlemen" and a growing wave of protests from the old gentry against infiltration by outsiders were rapidly becoming major facts on the cultural scene.[3]

It is perhaps due to the wide influence of J. G. A. Pocock's seminal studies that much of the recent scholarly debate on elite values in this period has been dominated by the concept of civic virtue, defined essentially in political categories. But there was also at the same time a serious cultural revolution taking place in Britain—and affecting the colonies—as a major struggle went on over the identity of the gentleman, the control of the sources of its legitimacy, and the meaning of the link between personal quality and social rank. Perhaps the most prominent voice in the early eighteenth century representing the ambitions and frustrations of those in England who aspired to gentility but faced a wall of cultural resistance was Daniel Defoe (1660–1731). His were some of the most consistent early attempts to redefine the idea of genteel legitimacy in order to accommodate newcomers. For this reason I have chosen him as a case study to illustrate the English aspects of the same legitimizing process that so engrossed the American gentry. The comparison is facilitated by the fact that his struggles were chronologically parallel to those of his colonial contemporary William Byrd II (1674–1744), who epitomized such aspirations of the young colonial elite in the early phase of the process under consideration here. Defoe was a particularly good witness of cultural change. Equipped with an acute sense of observation and tirelessly active, he produced a steady stream of publications and engaged in diverse public polemics, sometimes with devastating effects, as in the case of *The Shortest Way with Dissenters*, for which he paid with time in the pillory. He had a journalistic ability to present issues convincingly, even if his writing did not have the sparkling lightness of style expected in the literary salons of London. His writings, especially *The Compleat English Gentleman* written in 1729, gave eloquent expression to the ambitions of "new men," of commoner background, to gain cultural approval for admission into the ranks of the gentry.[4]

Gentility in eighteenth-century Britain was not merely an open model of refinement; it was developed and tailored exclusively for the elite. The gentry as a social class treated land ownership as the basis of its rank but, unlike the aristocracy, had no inherited titles (since I believe that socioeconomic class is only one of many possible clusters of social relations, I use *class* here in the simple sense of a class of people, as employed by eighteenth-century writers; I use the term *gentry* simply because the colonists themselves used it, and because it accurately reflected their ambitions). The notion of gentility, however, was perceived as an attribute of both the gentry and the peerage, cutting across the dividing line. The point is well illustrated by the reputed comment of King James I who, when asked by a petitioner that her son be made a gentleman, replied that he could make him a nobleman, but even God Almighty could not make him a gentleman.[5] A claim to gentility was thus a claim to membership in the ruling classes—the gentry and nobility. Even late in the century, with the rise of the middle class and mass production of objects of genteel style, the genteel ethos remained primarily exclusionary. New groups emulated it mainly for social elevation and not equalization; the grand bourgeoisie imitated the court, and the petite bourgeoisie aspired to style that would raise them above ordinary commoners. Because from the early decades of the century both the rising urban middle class in England and the emergent colonial gentry had embarked on a major effort to appropriate gentility, it is convenient to treat them as new elites. Since this is primarily an examination of a cultural process, it is necessary at this point to briefly delineate the evolution of the colonial elite, in order to establish a base for such an analysis.

Since New History—properly giving voice to previously silent groups—has shifted our attention to nonelites and cultural pluralism, few would postulate that the gentry determined the evolution of Virginia culture.[6] There are, however, good reasons to take a new look at the planter elite—without the burden of exceptionalist or romantic validation—and to reassess its impact on the roots of American cultural identity. First, this elite produced in the first three-quarters of the eighteenth century—in Virginia and in other plantation colonies—a distinct subculture; that is to say, its life experience was markedly different from that of the rest of colonial society. It is this specificity that should be the context of our inquiry rather than some universal framework, so dear to the consensus view of history. Second, the elites—whether we like them or not—set many patterns against which others defined themselves; boyars, mandarins, rajahs, or European nobility and gentry concentrated power and wealth which in turn gave them the ability to make cultural decisions that profoundly affected whole societies. Third, some scholars have credibly argued that societies tend to reproduce themselves primarily at the highest level, by re-creating elites. This theory has interesting implications for British plantation colonies; once established, elites in Virginia, Maryland, South Carolina, Barbados, Jamaica, and St. Kitts, despite regional differences, showed remarkable similarities in their quest for gentility.[7]

Just as exceptionalism needlessly imposed validating priorities on colonial historiography, the hostility of American culture to the very notion of elites may unintentionally produce other distortions. It is undeniable that elites have always been with us and that the need to construct them seems to be written into the makeup of humans as social animals. As Fernand Braudel put it, "All societies are diversified pluralities. They are divided against themselves and such division is probably intrinsic to their nature."[8] But the term *elite*, as Kenneth Prewitt and Alan Stone have observed, not only "grates on the ears of most Americans" but "comes close to denying that all men are created equal." What ensues is a certain reluctance to visualize societies highly stratified by ranks or to accept that the early modern gentry not only excluded large parts of the population from civic roles and the right to refinement but held them in contempt. American historians are well aware of this tendency. Gordon Wood, writing about the universally accepted division of colonial American society into gentlemen and commoners, stressed that "since this distinction has lost almost all of its older meaning . . . it takes an act of the imagination to recapture its immense importance in the eighteenth century." And yet even he, having acknowledged the remarkable power of honor among the British-American gentry, commented that "there was, of course, something old-fashioned, even feudal, about this gentlemanly concern with reputation and honor." It is no wonder that the notion of equality has sometimes been extended retrospectively to colonial times. One recent study stated that the "antidemocratic facts of our history are the matrix out of which the gentleman emerges," as if the very existence of early modern predemocratic elites contradicted some larger, inevitably democratic course of development.[9] In other words, our notions of elite and privilege are now divorced from their early modern taken-for-grantedness, making it hard to grasp eighteenth-century hierarchic perceptions of social reality—among all classes. In Britain at the beginning of that century, the distance, both economic and cultural, between the elite and the commoners was immense. Carole Shammas has calculated that the average yearly expenditure on food was £319.5 for the gentry and nobility, £45 for small farmers (those with incomes under £50) and freeholders, and £6.75 for day laborers and paupers.[10]

Furthermore, group identity and often a sense of dignity were closely linked to one's rank. Both patricians and plebeians condemned those among them who exhibited symbols of a group to which they had no legitimate

Gentility: A Transatlantic Aspiration 33

title. A 1741 history of British America illustrates this servile-free dichotomy in perceptions of society: "The People of Virginia are, as in England, distinguished by the Names of Masters and Servants. The Distinction of the Masters are by Office or Birth, and of the Servants, by such as are for Life, and such as are for a Term of Years; tho' Negroes and their Posterity are all servants for Life; the white Men and Women for as many years as they bind themselves."[11] Deference of inferiors toward their betters was an inherent part of both elite and popular views of society. William Darrell's popular 1723 courtesy book advised the gentleman to "converse not ordinarily with Persons above your Rank, nor with those that are below it; that will endanger your Estate, this your Breeding." Similarly, "stoop not below your Station, nor set them on equal Ground; if once you make 'em Companions, they'll usurp the Authority of Masters." Dr. Alexander Hamilton, who saw himself both as a Marylander and a member of a larger British culture (referring to the country in which he now lived simply as "our colonies"), noted in 1752 that "the mind of the multitude" was so different from that of the gentry that it was incapable of independence and therefore dangerous for liberty.[12] It is our own cultural distance from such distinctions that is in part responsible for the treatment of colonial American gentility as something manufactured and unnatural.

Virginia provides a good example of certain characteristics peculiar to a planter elite in its mature form. After the early formative period, stretching roughly from the turn of the century to the 1740s, this elite emerged as a group peculiarly homogeneous socially, economically, and politically when measured in relation to British elites (court, country gentry, aristocracy, merchants). I would argue that a major indicator of such homogeneity was the fact that its members' institutional positions and functions usually interlocked and overlapped. There was much less role separation than in Britain; members of the group could shift from one function to another in each of the following institutional orders: the colonial assembly, other governmental offices, economic enterprise, or cultural activity. William Byrd, Landon Carter, George Washington, and Thomas Jefferson could easily move between the roles of militia officer, merchant, legislator, judge, scholar, surveyor, or even architect. In Europe the landed gentry had to face pressures from peasants revolting against conditions of their life and from the wealthy bourgeoisie who increasingly challenged the gentry's monopoly of power and prestige, but in the plantation colonies, once slavery was well established, there were fewer sources of such opposition. There were also relatively fewer clashes of interests within the group. Although mainland planters were ever fearful of slave rebellions, they faced relatively few of them. All this gave them a more unquestioned position of power—from the plantation microcosm to assemblies and offices—than many of their European counterparts could enjoy, a situation that deeply affected their mentality and explained their legendary low tolerance for those who doubted or challenged their title to such a position. John Adams was well aware of this southern mentality when he wrote that "these Gentlemen are accustomed, habituated to higher Notions of themselves and the distinction between them and the common People, then We are."[13] Finally, the late colonial planter gentry also came to represent a remarkable concentration of educational capital. Thomas Jefferson, Landon Carter, William Byrd II, James Madison, George Mason, Charles Carroll, Edmund Randolph, and George Wythe were people of remarkably broad cultivation and, perhaps unlike in any other period of American history, embodied a rare combination of both intellectual and political leadership.[14] If we apply the traditional three criteria of defining elites—power, wealth, and prestige—to the planter oligarchies of the eighteenth century, we find that within the colonial context they had all to a large degree been met. This is notable, because in Europe these attributes were at times separable, as in the case of British merchants of the early eighteenth century, who controlled immense wealth but were not yet accorded prestige or political influence equal to that of the gentry and aristocracy.[15]

This power of the planter gentry must be viewed as a means to obtain future goods: wealth, social rank, education, and prestige. But these prerogatives in turn become powers: wealth breeds wealth, prestige adds to position of influence, while education, style, and taste add to the ability to maintain domination by controlling cultural capital. The process by which the elite defines the legitimate cultural standards of its membership—the requirements of wealth, social background, lifestyle, education, and refinement—is in itself an integral part of the exercise of power. Thomas Hobbes referred to this pattern in his astute observation that "the nature of power, is in this point, like to fame, increasing as it proceeds; or like the motion of heavy bodies, which the further they go, make still more haste." Modern elite theory confirms it by showing that elites, if unchecked, tend to accumulate power and become self-perpetuating because they control the use of the resources: finances, influence, prestige, legitimizing rituals, dependents, apparatus of coercion, legislation, and inside knowledge.[16] To a significant extent, the gentry in Virginia and other established mainland plantation colonies was by the mid–eighteenth century such a largely unchecked group, a pattern all the more visible after 1763, when London attempted to impose checks and restrictions on it.

As for the concentration of wealth and power in the hands of the planter elites, a few examples will suffice here. For instance, as early as the last decade of the seventeenth century in Maryland, only 1.5 percent of probated estates were valued over £1,000 sterling while 96.3 percent were under £500, a polarization greater than in Jamaica where at this time 9.4 percent were worth over £1,000 and 72.1 percent under £500.[17] Concentration remained a constant throughout the century, reaching striking dimensions in some areas. In the district of Charleston, South Carolina, the 1774 per capita wealth was £2,337.7, that is, four times that of the Chesapeake region and almost six times that of New York and Philadelphia.[18] Power followed suit; the local gentry established close political networks and extensive control of local offices, from the vestries to county government. In Maryland in the 1680s about 80 percent of the delegates to both houses of the assembly owned over one thousand acres each, and by the beginning of the eighteenth century it became highly unusual for a provincial officeholder to own less than a thousand acres. Patronage in filling offices of profit or honor was widely practiced, creating networks of influence that further cemented the elite's position.[19]

Kinship networks, in the case of Virginia strengthened by the replacement of primogeniture by partible inheritance, contributed hugely to the homogeneity of the elite as children of the gentry married within the group and as family ties were used to fill offices, increase fortunes, and exercise political pressure. In Virginia nine family names in the pre-Revolutionary century accounted for about one-third of the councillors, and fourteen others for another third. Proportions were similar with the justices of the peace. William Fitzhugh's five sons all married into major planter families: Lees, Masons, McCartys, and Cookes. Landon Carter's five sisters married into the Burwell, Harrison, Page, Braxton, and Fitzhugh families, and two of his brothers into the Hills and Churchills, while Landon himself acquired substantial landholdings through his three marriages. Bernard Bailyn aptly called the colony's gentry elite on the eve of the Revolution "one great tangled cousinry," and Jack P. Greene and Allan Kulikoff have discussed its prominence. It is important to realize that these kinship networks were not only a result of conscious, encouraged matches; the subtle working of culture was a more powerful influence than parental pressure. Men and women born into the gentry families also were born into similar backgrounds, lifestyles, expectations, contacts, education, values, and notions of rank and prestige—all elements that brought together members of the same group and worked against forming associations and contacts with members outside or, in their view, "below" their group. These family links continued well into the Federalist period and often provided the glue for political party connections within the states. This, for example, was the case with Maryland and such gentry families as the Carrolls, Taneys, Keys, Goldsboroughs, Hansons, Ridgelys, Steretts, and Platers.[20]

Matrimony accelerated entry into the elite for those who were not born into it. Thomas Sumter, a prominent colonial leader in South Carolina, was a man of very humble origins born in the Virginia backcountry in 1734; jailed for debts, he escaped to South Carolina where he founded a store and tavern, becoming a slaveholder established well enough by 1767 to marry wealthy widow and plantation owner Mary Cantey. George Washington gained access to large-scale wealth by marrying the widow of Daniel Parke Custis and thereby acquiring 15,000 acres, 200 slaves, and $100,000. Edmund Randolph, Virginia lawyer and future member of Washington's cabinet, greatly increased his wealth by marrying a granddaughter of Robert "King" Carter. By the late colonial period these networks dominated the local scene. For example, in South Carolina a tightly knit political and economic oligarchy controlled much of the power; the most prominent families were the Pinckneys, Rutledges, and Middletons. Thomas Pinckney (later Washington's ambassador to Britain) was a law partner of Edward Rutledge (later chief justice of the Supreme Court) who was a business partner of Charles Pinckney (Thomas's brother); the latter two both married daughters of Henry Middleton, owner of 800 slaves and 20 plantations.[21]

The republican rhetoric coming from members of these groups during the Revolution expressed disgust with European pedigrees and hereditary privileges, but its authors were very accustomed to the sanction of kinship and family on their own ground. If plantation gentry could be categorized as an elite, it was a new elite and not a historical class; it was even less a historical class than the metropolitan commercial groups in England—also aspiring to genteel respectability—which often had at least a tradition of pride in their occupation. In the case of eighteenth-century Virginia, the great planters rarely represented more than the second generation of wealth and rank. In many cases the original basis of wealth was created by the success of the first immigrants; both William Byrd II, born in 1674, and King Carter, born in 1663, inherited land accumulated by their fathers. Less common were swift first-generation success stories like that of Daniel Dulany, who emigrated to Maryland without any property, but through patronage and connections established a lucrative legal practice, and ultimately became a slaveholding planter.[22]

The seventeenth century, whether in the Chesapeake or in the Caribbean, did not produce stable and cohesive societies and cultures; wealthy Virginia families in the 1680s and 1690s were not always the same that dominated the scene in the following century. It was the relative rapidity with which—after the introduction of slavery on a larger scale—wealth and power were concentrated in the hands of the planter gentry that played a key role in creating a demand for gentility. While in England around 1800 the gap between the groups of lower wealth and those with medium to high wealth was increasing considerably, the Chesapeake planters, with very few exceptions, still lived in relatively unsophisticated and impermanent settlements. Even in the 1720s, 80 percent of the wealthiest residents of Virginia lived in single-story, one- or two-room houses, and possibly only 10 percent lived in houses with more than one room. Consumer goods were scarce; not until after 1730 do Chesapeake probate inventories show a definite increase in the ownership of such more sophisticated home amenities as clocks, books, tableware, and linen. Only in this period did clear variations in the value of consumer goods relative to wealth, an unmistakable sign of strong socioeconomic polarization, become prominent. Only then did two-story houses, with halls and dining rooms as areas for public and social functions, become more frequent.[23]

The rise of the southern planter gentry to prominence meant that it attained so much control of power and wealth in relation to the rest of the colonists that membership in this group now defined specific life opportunities such as the supply of goods, living conditions, and the character of personal life experiences. The group's relatively rapid emergence produced radical changes in three major indexes of its earlier lifestyles: the amount of leisure time increased greatly with the growth of slavery; consumption rose high enough above subsistence levels to become expressive of a group lifestyle; and work now assumed a clearly distinguishing supervisory character, well distanced from that of the small and medium planter. A distinctive feature of this swift rise of the slaveholding elite was that it propelled its first two generations into what may be called a parvenu gap, a situation where affluence was often acquired sooner than the cultural prerequisites to use it in a way they aspired to—according to the genteel model. Their new position had to be made socially visible, translated into effective cultural symbols of distinction, and placed within an ethos that would provide a larger raison d'être for the group. Gentility provided a remarkably versatile formula not only for validating new power and prestige and forging a workable identity for the elite but also for providing a sense of personal improvement and refinement as an antidote to provincial life and for creating existential order in a chaotic world.[24] The elite's ambition, however, had few solid roots in time; its members had neither the luxury of a long line of forebears standing behind them nor a consciousness of a long tradition sanctioning their power. As a group they could not look to a historical solidarity of interests for confidence. Genteel style and ethos were rarely passed on from the earlier generation; they had to be painstakingly acquired and reconciled with a practical, utilitarian worldview. This process extended from about the 1720s to the 1770s. Essentially, the elite had already emerged as an objective social and economic group, but it still needed to be forged as gentry by acquiring appropriate cultural capital. This was why bridging the gap of legitimacy became such an imperative at this stage.

An Iron Curtain between the Genteel and the Vulgar

At the time when both the rising English commercial middle class (which for the sake of this discussion I shall call the Defoeans) and the emerging colonial slaveholding planter class were embarking on their quest for gentility, there extended in British culture a virtual iron curtain between the polite and the vulgar, the gentleman and the commoner. It was guarded by innumerable ritualistic devices and by jealous adjudicators of established norms. To understand the nature of this obstacle is to gain an insight into the larger battlefield for legitimacy and, consequently, to grasp the differences between the metropolitan and colonial routes to the same target.

Although recognition as a member of the genteel class was the coveted goal, there was no one homogeneous model of gentility on the British cultural market, which, if satisfied, would automatically validate a gentleman. There was a whole spectrum of variants, with a set of core values differently emphasized, stretching from the liberal approach of Joseph Addison and Richard Steele to highly elitist versions such as that of Defoe's contemporary, the earl of Shaftesbury. While the editors of the *Spectator* were flexible enough to admit select merchants into their genteel club, Shaftesbury's model, rooted in the culture of aristocracy, represented the other extreme of the spectrum. One may conjecture that a refined colonial planter such as William Byrd II could hold at least a slim hope of being invited to the Spectator Club but certainly could not—and probably would not even attempt to—meet Shaftesbury's criteria (fig. 1).

Nevertheless, the two models differed mainly in the degree of demands rather than in the essence of what was demanded of a gentleman. Shaftesbury's model—with all its stress on the sublime and the aesthetic—well reflected these essential requirements and provides a good mirror for this discussion. Aimed at enlightened and leisurely elites, it put its main stress on the gentleman's intellectual and moral independence. According to Shaftesbury, this vital liberty was threatened by enthusiasm, that is, by passions and prejudices that perverted the indispensable detachment of a gentleman. Enthusiasm was attributed to the vulgar commoners; dependence on passions rendered them incapable of being free and independent (yet the earl also believed they required a degree of that vulgar emotion known as fear to keep them in their place). This was one of the most historically durable ingredients of the model. Baltasar Gratian, a classic authority as a theoretician of gentility since the mid-seventeenth century, wrote that the singularity of the gentle few "takes its Rise from a greatness of Soul, and an Elevation of Sentiments; in which the true Nobility and Excellence of Man consists; to wit, such a Nobility as exempts us from the Passions and Imperfections which the Vulgar are enslav'd to."[25]

1. A gentleman in a coffeehouse, improperly—according to the *Spectator*—fraternizing with simple folk, "filling common people's heads with ... senseless ambitions, and inspiring them with ... absurd ideas of superiority." From *Harrison's British Classicks* 3 (London, 1786).

Gentility: A Transatlantic Aspiration

Typically, Shaftesbury's idea of genteel virtue presupposed a fixed, hierarchical society where "the superior, easy sort" were obliged to devote themselves to refinement and reflection, and where the "vulgar" were "by necessity confin'd to Labour." This separation was reflected in a world of affections divided into the "Soft and Harsh, the Agreeable and Disagreeable." He was thus able to blend a "moral sense" and an aesthetic sense, the latter being a taste for the beautiful and the harmonious. One might add that he was immensely influential in defining high gentility among polite European society in the first half of the eighteenth century, and his impact included the American colonies. One colonial journal referred to Shaftesbury in 1758 as the ultimate authority on "good breeding," the essence of which he defined as "much the same as Politeness and (among the Romans) Urbanity," with a stress on the principle that "the Conduct of the well-bred Man is formed according to the most perfect Ease and good Entertainment of Company." It is well to bear in mind that the emphasis on ease—consistently central to the model—had its genesis in the comfortably established status of the old gentry. Bourdieu has pointed out that such claims to aristocratic virtue—with its disinterested dispositions to refinement—were so easily accepted by the social mind because the link between them and the freedom from economic necessity that made them possible often tended to pass unnoticed and thus effectively made them appear natural.[26]

For newcomers to gain entrance to the fortress of gentility guarded by such cultural requisites was a formidable and often hazardous task. Even before one could argue about the criteria of virtue, one had to show an entry ticket that was rather hard to obtain—pedigree, a qualifier that retained its validity throughout the eighteenth century. Samuel Johnson's definition of a gentleman was short: "a man of ancestry," although he was careful to distinguish the gentry from aristocracy, defining the former as a "class of people above the vulgar; those between the vulgar and nobility." And birth was not merely a formal sanction of rank and privilege but also a cultural code for the possession of what were supposed to be certain naturally superior qualities, a notion at the time still largely taken for granted. Francis Markham, another seventeenth-century classic authority on gentry and nobility, defined a gentleman by birth as a person both of whose parents were of noble pedigree, and whose nobility went back at least three generations, with no "Mixture or base Match."[27]

This definition had not changed much by the early eighteenth century. The arguments of Defoe's opponent Jonathan Swift, whose sharp pen was widely celebrated in Britain's literary circles and political establishment, epitomized the mechanism by which such notions of natural excellence were constructed by the arbiters of gentility. He linked certain practical facts of life, such as family, wealth, educational opportunity, independence, and distance from necessity, with a more fuzzy, if not mythical, concept of ancestry in order to create the composite of virtue:

> Suppose there be nothing but Opinion in the Difference of Blood; every Body knows, that Authority is very much founded on Opinion. But surely, that Difference is not wholly Imaginary. The Advantages of a liberal Education, of chusing the best Companions to converse with; not being under the necessity of practicing little mean Tricks by a scanty Allowance; the enlarging of Thought, and acquiring the knowledge of Men and Things by Travel; the Example of Ancestors inciting to great and good Actions. These are usually some of the Opportunities, that fall in the way of those who are born, of what we call the better Families; and allowing Genius to be equal in them and the Vulgar, the Odds are clearly on their side. Nay, we may observe in some, who by the appearance of Merit, or Favour of Fortune, have risen to great Stations, from an obscure Birth, that they have still retain'd some sordid Vices of their Parentage or Education, either insatiable Avarice, or Ignominious Falsehood and Corruption.

Where Shaftesbury saw uncontrolled emotions, Swift saw corruption by circumstances of "necessity," but both expressed an assumption deeply embedded in the genteel ethos that virtue was by definition associated with the wellborn and independent. Even the grand bourgeoisie could not escape the stigma of vulgarity linked to its members' origins as commoners; according to Swift, their position was, after all, often gained only "by the appearance of Merit" or "Favour of Fortune." There was no talk here of the possibility of genuine talent and ability as equivalent means of attaining a high station. Swift was, of course, too sophisticated a mind not to allow such a likelihood, but he did so as a strict exception that in itself supported the general rule: he conceded that "a Pearl holds its Value tho' it be found in a Dunghill; but however, that is not the most probable Place to search for it."[28] In such a

Gentility: A Transatlantic Aspiration

context, his solidly practical middle-class values as well as the assumption—incorporated into his rendition of the model of a gentleman—that virtue was achieved primarily by merit situated Defoe at the very opposite extreme of the spectrum in relation to the aristocratic Shaftesbury, indeed practically beyond legitimate territory.

The Irresistible Allure of Heraldry

Clearly, an open and total rejection of birth as a criterion of noble virtue was not an option for anyone seriously aspiring to be admitted into the genteel ranks. Neither the Defoeans in Britain nor the colonial gentry in America—both having little use for the antiquity of families—brought themselves to make such a radical and ultimately self-defeating move. Alternative models more reflective of their real-life values were simply not viable if the primary goal was to join the ranks of the existing elite that controlled the legitimizing process. If we keep in mind that legitimacy is indivisible in that there are no agencies legitimizing the legitimacy-producing agencies, choices on both sides of the Atlantic were very limited.

In these circumstances the temptation of claiming the right to a pedigree in order to corroborate one's new gentility was immense and clearly cannot be explained—and discarded—as mere snobbery. Defoe—son of a London tallow-chandler and butcher—may have considered himself a gentleman by virtue of good breeding and may have often argued theoretically against restrictions by ancestry, but he nevertheless found the lure of pedigree stronger than his revulsion for the exclusiveness of lineage. In a number of his publications, he alluded to his own supposedly ancient descent from a noble family. In one book he implied that he was related to an "ancient Norman family of the name of De Beau-foe" which had retained only the "latter part of their sirname." On other occasions he hinted that he was related to Sir Walter Raleigh. After 1706 he signed his works with the more elegant name of "Daniel De Foe, Esq." From 1703 he published his works with a portrait engraved by Michael Van der Gucht and a coat of arms he probably devised himself (fig. 2).[29] The heraldic substance was of secondary importance here. The struggle for validation dictated its own priorities, and this particular sign from the arsenal of symbolic codes of gentility was relatively accessible and carried potent cultural meaning.

It can be argued, however, that the American colonist, and not Defoe and others like him in England, provided the most striking examples of the legitimizing power of pedigree. It would seem that the young planter gentry, living in a distant periphery under frontier conditions, should be the last to pay attention to such niceties as coats of arms. But facts point to the exact opposite; in Virginia nearly all of the prominent gentry families sooner or later made claims to coats of arms. Highly coveted throughout the eighteenth century, they were obtained by various means from Britain and as a rule prominently displayed on coaches, seals, and silverware. The significance of armorial bearings among the planter gentry has been underestimated in recent American historiography; the long exceptionalist tradition of projecting the more democratic and egalitarian culture of post-Revolutionary America back into the colonial period made the colonial appetite for heraldry seem only a fanciful whim of vanity. This, however, confuses the narrow question of actual lineage—indeed, in itself of little significance to the colonists—with the larger issue of legitimacy, for which there was an intense demand. Coats of arms were used not so much as indications of noble birth—for which in many cases there was little ground—but as cultural signs of genteel legitimacy, much in the way Defoe employed his.

2. Portrait of Daniel Defoe by Michael Van der Gucht, from *A True Collection of the Writings of the True-born Englishman* (London, 1705).

Instances of such colonial uses of heraldry abound from the late seventeenth century to the Revolution, and well after. William Fitzhugh—son of a woolen draper and grandson of a maltster in the town of Bedford, England—had ascended to the status of a prominent tobacco planter and gentleman in Virginia. In 1687 he was showing signs of a pressing need to display a family coat of arms, writing several times to his brother in England to ask that one be sent "fairly and rightly drawn." Once he received it, he intended to have his servant engrave it on his silverware. This last step was crucial, of course, for arms were essentially an item to exhibit as a sign charged with meanings of respectability. Fitzhugh also used the arms on his seal; he wrote to Nicholas Heyward in 1688 that "the Inclosed is Impression of my seal & Coat of Arms, the seal is lost, therefore I request your favour to supply me with another steel one." It appears that the coat of arms he used properly belonged not to his family but to that of Baron Fitzhugh of Yorkshire, to whom he was not related. That the baronial extraction was assumed by the Virginian family was manifested by the fact that his descendants named his Stafford County plantation Ravensworth, after the seat of the English aristocrats. Of course, what really matters here is not whether the Virginia Fitzhughs knew they were not entitled to the arms, but that possessing and displaying them carried such legitimizing power. Major Robert Beverley the elder, one of the most prominent Virginians of his time and father of Robert Beverley the historian, possessed several pieces of silver plate engraved with the family crest. Ralph Wormeley II accumulated many pieces of silver plate at his Rosegill plantation and also had them marked with his coat of arms. In 1774 Robert Carter III of Nomini Hall ordered as a gift for his son Ben a "gold seal . . . with a Coat of Arms price five Guineas."[30] A visit to the well-preserved Shirley plantation in Charles City County in Virginia—built in 1738 for John Carter, son of King Carter, and his wife Elizabeth Hill Carter— makes one realize the role such symbols played in elite life. Almost all the displayed colonial pieces of family silverware, from the large to the smallest, were meticulously engraved with the Carter family coat of arms, something that must have been conspicuously noticeable to the numerous guests the house has seen.

Perhaps one of the best examples of the persistence of this pattern was George Washington in the years immediately after the Revolution. It was already obvious that he was sensitive to the social value of pedigree when he ordered from London several hundred bookplates with his coat of arms printed on them for his library. But in 1792 he entered into a correspondence with Sir Isaac Heard, the Garter King-at-Arms, who was to verify his pedigree and family coat of arms. He supplied Heard with a genealogical account of the Washington family since "the year 1657, or thereabouts," when two of its members emigrated from England and settled in Westmoreland County in Virginia. Unfortunately, he noted, "from whom they descended, the subscriber is possessed of no documents to ascertain," nor was he able "to give a satisfactory account" of the "lateral Branches of the family." Heard had undertaken appropriate research in several counties and even obtained coats of arms from the tombstones of some of the Washington ancestors at Sulgrave near Banbury, but he was never able to uncover enough evidence to prepare a complete genealogy. One reason was that Washington himself could not provide sufficient information. He admitted to Heard that studying the details of his ancestry was "a subject to which I confess I have paid very little attention," because of a "busy and active" life, "even if my inclination or particular circumstances should have prompted the enquiry." Regretting that he was unable to fill in the sketch of family connections that Heard had sent him, he complained that "we have no office of Record in this Country in which exact genealogical documents are preserved." He could only say that he had "heard" from family members "that our ancestors who first settled in this Country came from one of the Northern Counties of England, but whether from Lancashire, Yorkshire, or one still more northerly I do not precisely remember." He had already been using a coat of arms on his seal well before this correspondence took place; these arms, as the letter indicated, were not exactly the same as what Heard sent him from England. He nevertheless thanked Heard for his search and ended by underscoring once again that, despite the difficulties, he would be "glad to be informed of the result and of the ancient pedigree of the family." The continuing power of such an "ancient pedigree" to validate gentility becomes all the more evident when it is realized that Washington became involved in these heraldic pursuits after he had already been elevated to the presidency of the United States and was enjoying a greater degree of prestige and eminence than any other person in the country.[31]

Jefferson, too, like other Virginia gentlemen, attempted to trace his father's lineage. His search in Wales was not successful, and he found only two minor references to it, not adequate to establish a viable pedigree. Years later,

Gentility: A Transatlantic Aspiration 47

in his autobiography, he made an acerbic remark about the family of his mother, the Randolphs, who could trace their origins far back into England and Scotland, commenting: "let every one ascribe" to that family's genealogy "the faith & merit he chooses." Such rationalist and intellectual disdain for the authority of lineage was a position Defoe would have heartily approved, though probably not publicized.[32]

The roots of this allure of heraldry clearly lay not in the colonies but in England, where, despite the ongoing struggles for legitimation by new men, very few dents had been made on the old metropolitan British model of gentility, with its link to lineage. It was widely known, of course, that ever since the early Tudors wealthy tradesmen had been purchasing coats of arms with money, while patronage opened the doors to nobility for affluent commoners.[33] As a result, false heraldry became a frequent object of attacks, gradually shifting the stress of the public debate from genteel pedigree to genteel virtue. In 1666 George Alsop used his description of the Chesapeake Indians to make a point about English upstarts who purchased coats of arms to disguise their low origins and lack of virtue. In contrast, among Indians no such false dignity was possible, he claimed, as there was "seldom any creeping from a Country Farm, into a Court Gallantry, by a sum of money; nor feeing the Heralds to put Daggers and Pistols into their Armes, to make the ignorant believe that they are lineally descended from the House of Wars and Conquests; he that fights best carries it here." For Maryland gentleman Alexander Hamilton nearly a century later, the purchasing of titles was annoying, but by then he was equally irritated by the precedence of lineage over quality. He blamed King James I, who disturbed the order of ranks by creating "knights Baronets . . . a rank, which makes a cement, or fills up a gap, between the lowest of the nobility and the highest of the Gentry." This move had confused true nobility with empty pretensions; "that Shitten Monarch's motive was sordid avarice, and a desire to fill his coffers, and support his extravagance, by means of the fees, which certain Rich fools gave him for these caps and feathers."[34]

Despite the lively discourse on virtue, the old model of gentility functioned as the legitimizing yardstick for the whole British cultural area throughout the eighteenth century. Unfortunately for the colonists, it was routinely applied by members of the metropolitan ruling class to colonial claims of rank and quality. A good sample of this pattern is provided by one of Defoe's contemporaries, writer and historian of England and the American colonies John Oldmixon, himself a member of a very old family. He was willing, as an exception, to acknowledge the planter elite of Barbados as gentlemen, but only because many of them could document some sort of genteel ancestry. "This Island," he argued, "was the soonest peopled of all our Colonies; the Riches of the Planters produced by that of the Soil, tempted Gentlemen of good Families and moderate Estates, to transport themselves thither to improve them." The rest of British America was, in his eyes, populated by an inferior sort of people, even though many of them rose to great wealth. "Indeed whoever will look over the Map of Barbados will find, the Country is not possessed by such a set of Men as inhabit the other Plantations; the Walronds, the Fortescues, the Collitons, the Thornhills, the Farmers, the Pickerings, the Littletons, the Codringtons, the Willoughbies, the Chesters, the Kendals, the Dimocks, the Hawleys, the Stedes, the Prideauxes, the Alleyns, the Quintines, the Bromleys, and others, whose Families are of the most ancient and honourable in England."[35]

Another member of the British elite, Lord Adam Gordon, writing a few years later, noted that the planter gentry of Virginia had impressed him very favorably as possessing a whole register of genteel qualities. They "far exceed in good sense, affability, and ease, any set of men I have yet fallen in with, either in the West Indies, or on the Continent," and were "conversable and accomplished people." Searching for an explanation of such unexpected refinement in the provinces, he offered two reasons that to him seemed the most obvious: genteel birth and the education of at least some of the planters "at home," that is in England. "The first Settlers," he noted, "were many of them younger Brothers of good Families, in England, who for different motives chose to quit home in search of a better fortune, their descendants, who possess the greatest land properties in the Province, have intermarried, and have had always a much greater connection with, and dependence on the Mother Country, than any other Province." In other words, when the genteel qualities of the colonists were acknowledged as genuine, the only credible exegesis was that they satisfied traditional metropolitan criteria. Gordon, in fact, illustrated further consequences of this logic by suggesting that those who had achieved positions and quality nearest to those of the English landed gentry should return to the greater civility of the mother country; he had little doubt that "the most opulent planters, would prefer a home life."[36]

We have long been told to expect to find that the planter gentry ignored pedigrees. Admittedly, there were some good reasons for this view, reasons other than the exceptionalist emphasis on the early democratic character of America. After all, the situation of American elites, who were in a much more comfortable position with regard to this issue, was very different from that of Defoe, who from the start had to openly face the barrier of birth. There was no significant local old gentry or nobility on the colonial scene, able to act as a coordinated group with anything resembling the cultural power and influence of the old classes in Britain. As a result, the colonists enjoyed a luxury of sorts: they rarely had to confront such an established class, either in a direct power struggle or in rival lifestyles; by the second half of the eighteenth century, they themselves were the elite that dominated the political and the cultural scene. Westover did not have to compete with Hampton Court, nor did the *Virginia Gazette* employ a Swift to attack a Byrd. The sources of cultural legitimacy were in distant Britain, but then so were its arbiters who could oppose the ambitions and undermine the positions of colonial "upstarts" as effectively as they contested Defoe's. The second-generation colonial gentlemen could now take their own rank for granted; in Virginia by midcentury it was already being inherited together with wealth and family names. But the history of their prominence was short, and, even more than in the case of the Defoeans, their acquired economic, political, and educational capital did not yet outweigh the demand for a cultural validation of their authority.

We are often struck by the apparent inconsistency on the part of the late colonial and Revolutionary gentry, who were so often members of well-established American families, and sought lineages to enhance their membership in the Virginia patriciate, but led the country in bitter attacks on Britain's "patrician order." Part of this bitterness can be explained not so much by the power of democratic ideas—which did not, after all, affect the emergence and practice of family privilege in the plantation colonies—but by the same kind of resentment as that felt earlier in the century by Defoe, at being excluded from gentility by the tenets of genealogy. From this perspective, the apparent incongruity between the two attitudes loses much of its contradictory nature.

A Modified Model of Virtue

To pursue further the frequent argument that the colonists need not have chosen to adhere so zealously to a conservative, landed model of gentility, and that they could have adopted one more suited to the realities of American life, we should now take a closer look at the model articulated by Defoe, one which was never embraced by the planter elite but seems to fit such a prescription well. Although it had little chance of being accepted by contemporary English arbiters of culture, today—with our hindsight—it appears remarkably suited to colonial American experience.

Defoe was well aware of the inertia of culture; nowhere did he openly reject the birth criterion. Instead, he argued that the bred gentleman and the born gentleman can be reconciled in the notion of a "compleat gentleman." This new path to virtue by its very design undermined the requisite of birth by postulating that even a person of "mean" origins—if possessed of sufficient breeding, education, and personal qualities—was entitled to genteel rank. He knew that a total rejection of pedigree would deeply antagonize the very circles he wished to enter; he hoped instead that a shift of emphasis to merit would make ancestry gradually irrelevant. As a concession to genteel opponents who, like Swift, would recoil at the iconoclasm of his proposals, he conceded that gentility should not be claimed by the first generation that by "unheard summs of money amass'd in a short time" raised itself to "a stacion in life." After all, he admitted, "the word gentleman is understood to signify men of ancient houses, dignify'd with hereditary titles and family honours." But at the same time he made a new and radical claim: "When I say I thus giv up the founder of the house, I must yet open the door to the politer son, and the next age quite alters the case." The son, having accumulated "a stock of personal merit," would now qualify to be a gentleman "not upon the money only." He offered historical evidence for his claims, pointing to "an abundance of the mansions and parks and estates and inheritances of the most ancient extinct families bought by citizens, merchants, lawyers," who "rise up as new families of fortune and make new lines of gentry in their stead." Thus, "soon the posterity of such establish themselves among the gentry, and are accepted among gentlemen as effectually as if the blood of twenty generations was running in their veins."[37]

For the commonsensical Defoe, to place the essence of genteel quality in "a long Descent of Blood" implied both irrationality ("defeated Reasoning")

Gentility: A Transatlantic Aspiration

and ahistoricism. His contentions unmistakably anticipate the Enlightenment arguments against heredity, so commonplace later during the Revolution in America. Reason shows, he claimed, that if we examine ancestry deep enough, we will "strike at the Root of both the Gentry and nobility; for all must begin somewhere." To him, the much mythologized antiquity is "like a Rope of Sand, if it be stretched out too far it separates and falls back into the Mass or Heap of the meanest Individuals." While for the genteel Swift such examinations of the "parentage" of certain gentlemen were a way to unmask "assuming upstarts," Defoe's rationalistic analysis showed that pedigrees carried no power to exclude anyone.[38] In his polemics with Andrew Fletcher, he observed that liberty and virtue were modern phenomena and thus did not require antiquity to legitimize them. In 1700 Whig pamphleteer John Tutchin wrote a satirical poem in which he complained about King William's foreign favorites and made a larger point about upstarts, birth, and virtue:

> In vain is Blood, or Parentages, when
> Ribbons and Garters can ennoble Men.
> To Chivalry you need have no Recourse,
> The gawdy Trappings make the Ass a Horse."[39]

Defoe, in *The True-Born Englishman*, reacted predictably by ridiculing pedigree-proud gentry and pointing out with delight that even the "ancient" Norman nobility had low origins as mere French "musqueteers" given land by bastard king William I ("The Rascals thus enrich'd, he call'd them Lords, To please their Upstart Pride with new-made Words").[40] In sum, by suspending the legitimating role of "family antiquity" in the establishment of one's gentility, he was advocating the elevation of personal merit to the role of the primary criterion.

This was a shift of emphasis rather than a change of content. It is particularly interesting for this discussion because half a century later Revolutionary American gentry would use exactly the same cultural device. The belief that ancestry alone did not guarantee virtue and that true nobility also required adequate merit was an inseparable part of the old genteel ethos. A contemporary guide to conduct declared that it was "a Madness to take the Measure of our Deserts by the Parts of our Forefathers" because "their personal Worth adds not one Hairs-breath to our Stature. We may enter upon their Estates, and perchance upon their Titles, but not upon their Virtues." This closely echoed Gratian, who asserted that "after all, the solid Basis and Foundation of the Superiority we are speaking of, which rendered us truly superior to other People, is real Merit; and this Merit consists in a perfect Knowledge of the World, the Affairs of the Times, some certain Sciences, Employments, and Business, and the whole Conduct of human Life."[41] Defoe extended this claim even to a "son of a mean person," who could be admitted "into the rank of gentleman" if he possessed "wit, sense, courage, virtue, and good humour" and was "set apart by a liberall education for the service of his country" (fig. 3).[42]

But if we look more closely at Defoe's concept of education for merit, it was far from the genteel, classics-oriented ideal. For him, the distaste of the traditional noble ethos toward "professional" knowledge only led to ignorance. The English gentleman "educates his sons at the stable door, instead of the Grammar School, and his huntsman is the Head Tutor." An heir to an estate "must not go to school; no, his father scorns to put him to school, because he is, or rather is to be, a gentleman." How could such a gentry acquire the expected public virtue, he asked. "Shall he that may be suppos'd to share the government with his sovereign, to represent his country in Parliament, to be cloth'd with commissions of the peace, and, perhaps, of war, he that is by birthright a magistrate and a man of quallity, should he alone not be allow'd to choose whether he shall be a man of sence or a fool?" Defoe, who had "never found a mannor held in England by the weight of the brain," was clearly implying that a new gentleman who achieved his success through learning and knowledge could be a more valuable citizen.[43]

To encourage such change he sought to alter the hierarchy of educational values by removing classics from the center of the stage and by disputing the genteel canon that any learning over the dilettante minimum implied professionalism or material necessity befitting only commoners. He ingeniously reversed the values attached to the traditional curriculum: the academic focus on classics "throws the English tongue entirely out of use" among the gentry, and modern science has "exploded the Ancients" in many things, so English and practical subjects such as "Experimental Phylosophy," "astronomical knowledge," "Geography," and "naturall history" should be promoted. He used the traditional cultural rhetoric to make a new point: "We must distinguish between a man of polite learning and a meer schollar; the

3. Frontispiece of *The Gentleman's Calling* (London, 1705), attributed to Richard Allestree. (Courtesy, William Andrews Clark Memorial Library, University of California, Los Angeles)

first is a gentleman and what a gentleman should be; the last is a meer bookcase, a bundle of letters, a head stufft with the jargon of languages."[44]

Interestingly, some contemporary voices in Virginia with a view to colonial realities suggested similar adjustments. Hugh Jones, who taught at the College of William and Mary and was chaplain to the House of Burgesses, in his observations upon the education of Virginian planters' sons suggested comparable changes toward the useful and the practical in order to reflect the specific mind-set of the average colonist. He too found the focus of the formal curriculum on grammar and classics ineffective because the students saw it as bearing no relation to the reality of colonial life, and he too proposed that all subjects be taught in English.[45] But Jones's comments did not signify a radical redefining of gentility. He only attempted to face some of the practical problems of teaching colonists, while Defoe was expressly questioning the domination of classical schooling as a means of excluding commoners.

The belief that a gentleman's learning should not be too professional, lest it smack of useful knowledge which is born of necessity, was still solidly established in high culture. George Washington—a self-made man without formal education, whose successes depended on his unrelenting efforts at personal improvement—was using the same conceptual framework and language when he wrote in his comments on the education of Jacky Custis that he did not think "becoming a mere scholar is a desirable education for a gentleman." He did, however, concede that Greek and French, as well as other bookish knowledge, form a necessary "basis upon which other knowledge is built." Ambitious planter gentlemen told themselves that without the classics, their knowledge would be too exclusively practical and utilitarian and, consequently, ungenteel. The classics were consecrated as the cultural capital of gentility and as such also served as a criterion of exclusion (and not just for some men; because the classics were supposed to prepare one for public service, an exclusive sphere of gentlemen, women were barred from classical education, both in England and the plantation colonies). The immense legitimizing power of this standard was manifest in Byrd's dogged—though apparently joyless and unreflective—insistence on everyday readings of Latin, Hebrew, and Greek and in Fitzhugh's orders from his Bristol tobacco merchant, which included—side by side with the coveted silverware—intellectual supplies such as "Virgil in English, Horace in Latin & English Juvenal & Perseus in Latin & English."[46]

Although Defoe's revised model of gentility was against the grain of his time, one cannot escape a reflection that for a Fitzhugh, Byrd, or Washington, its general thrust would have offered a more feasible cultural path than the one they chose. Stress on merit was a precept which operated widely in practice among their class. Eliza Lucas Pinckney, writing to a friend in England from her South Carolina plantation in 1762, asserted that she cared for "few Intimacys and no friendships but with those whose real Virtue and Internal merrit (abstracted from every external advantage and consideration) attracted and fixt my Esteem." Hamilton—member of the lower house in Maryland and husband of Margaret Dulany, daughter of Daniel Dulany the elder—openly took a position identical to that of Defoe, but he was a notable exception. Pedigree for him had no significance since both commoners and gentlemen were equally capable of being virtuous or corrupt. Personal qualities and noble principles, he believed, "give a juster claim to the titles your honor and honorable Sir, than all the foppery of Stars and Garters, golden fleeces, Georges, St. Andrews crosses, Thistles, and such like farsical trash and Trumpery." Like Defoe, he appealed to common logic, arguing that "it is a Certain truth, which will be granted by every man of plain Sense and understanding . . . that the noblest and most eminent marks or Signatures, which can dignify or decorate men or distinguish human Societies, are Virtue, honor and Integrity."[47] But unlike Defoe, who was trying to facilitate access to the genteel sphere, Hamilton, already an acknowledged gentleman before arriving in America, was only reacting to the colonists' heraldic enthusiasm when he decried "late upstarts, having some badge or Symbol, which they call their coat of arms, and which they wear upon their furniture coaches and equipage, with which they adorn their houses by way of picture, and which they engrave upon their plate." All this only served "to distinguish and render conspicuous, certain families and persons, who have no other quality in nature."[48] In this sense he was a lone voice, for until the Revolutionary decade such views were not frequently articulated as a cultural agenda for aspiring colonial gentry.

It is important to note that the debate on the essence of genteel virtue, and specifically on the relative significance of ancestry versus merit, did not begin with Defoe; it is only that—under the pressure of social and economic changes—new answers were beginning to be given in the early eighteenth century. The problem had already been raised in 1561 in Castiglione's *Courtier*. The question asked was why noble birth rather than qualities should be the criterion of legitimate superiority, since some have been "borne of most noble bloud, yet have they been heaped full of vices," while many unnoble people "have made famous their posteritie." It also appeared a "strange opinion that the parents of our Courtier being unnoble, his good qualities should be defaced." Castiglione's response was a customary one from his caste and would later be echoed by Shaftesbury. Birth was indispensable because it nourished quality; "it is a great deale lesse dispraise for him that is not borne a gentleman to faile in the actes of vertue, then for a gentleman." It is "natural," he claimed, that noblemen "resemble their ancestors."[49] The idea of personal virtue as primary requisite of nobility may have been registering some gains among intellectuals in contemporary Europe but not in practical social usage. Thomas More, for instance, insisted that true nobility springs not from inherited possessions but from learning and virtue. By the seventeenth century such arguments were increasingly being picked up by those whose economic prominence led them to aspire to higher cultural status. Oudard Coquault, a merchant from Reims, expressed much vexation in 1650 that many "gentlemen who say they are of high birth . . . are good only for berating and devouring the peasant in their village," while "the honourable bourgeois of the towns and the good merchants are more noble than them all; for they are more gentlemanly, live better lives, and set better examples" and yet receive nothing but contempt from the gentry. Defoe did not go this far; he rejected only that part of the old ethos that dismissed commercial talents as entirely nonvirtuous. Ignoring trade was simply impractical, he argued, pointing to the Spaniards as an example of the old precept's uselessness:

> Too Lazy and too Haughty to be Rich.
> So proud a People, so above their Fate,
> That if reduc'd to beg, they'll beg in State.
> Lavish of Money, to be counted Brave,
> And Proudly starve, because they scorn to save.[50]

Gentility: A Transatlantic Aspiration

Defoe was well aware he was touching a dangerous subject when he proposed a new model of gentility. In the introduction to his *Compleat English Gentleman*, he anticipated the "clamour . . . from idolators who worship escutcheons and trophyes." Yet the cultural scene was ripe; moral essays in the *Tatler* and *Spectator* in 1711 deliberately aimed to adjust the social ideal of virtue by introducing to their high society reading public the notion that certain members of the moneyed classes could be considered respectable. This novelty was symbolized by the socializing of two fictional characters in the essays, Tory country squire Sir Roger de Coverley and London merchant Sir Andrew Freeport. But just as the public of Defoe and of the *Spectator* were different, so was their manner of presenting arguments for change; the former had the eagerness of a neophyte, while the latter tried to smuggle the new ideas to its readers indirectly and unobtrusively. For instance, Addison attempted to persuade the gentry subtly that gardening may be a more creative and practical occupation than hunting. "Many of our Country Gentlemen in their busie Hours," he wrote, "apply themselves wholly to the Chase. . . . Exercises of this kind, when indulged with Moderation, may have a good Influence both on the Mind and Body." But he pointed out that "the Country affords many other Amusements of a more noble kind. Among them I know none more delightful in it self, and beneficial to the Publick, than that of PLANTING. " To ensure that he was not understood as advocating "mechanical," commoner occupations for the landed class, he invoked the authority of Virgil to emphasize that he did "not only recommend this Art to Men of Estates as a pleasing Amusement, but as a kind of Virtuous Employment."[51]

Compared to these attempts, Defoe's redefinition of genteel virtue was manifestly iconoclastic. It expressed the objective interests and values of his class and was intellectually prophetic, foreshadowing the direction in which culture would develop, but because of its radicalism it could not achieve its intended objective. It was too early for that. Clearly, the American colonists were making the only choice that carried practical legitimizing power—high on their cultural agenda—when they adopted the orthodox landed model of gentility. Only during the Revolutionary conflict half a century later, when this model had developed into an established way of life for them, could the American gentry afford to begin evolving a new cultural model for its members. When this model did appear, it was labeled "the aristocracy of merit," and it uncannily resembled the Defoean one.

Safeguarding the Balance between Patricians and Plebeians

Had the new colonial gentry attempted to pierce the iron curtain by questioning the basic structural rules of the old legitimacy, its members would have brought on themselves a backlash of the sort that Defoe had to face from London high society for his proposals, but exacerbated by their even weaker position as provincials. When Defoe began his campaign, he was not a nobody; already a well-known author of a political journal, the *Review*, he enjoyed the patronage and protection of the powerful Robert Harley, Speaker of the House of Commons. Many charges were made in political polemics involving Defoe's defense of moderate Tory positions, a subject that can be left aside in order to focus on their cultural dimension.

All the attacks were linked by one common theme: they questioned the legitimacy of Defoe's title to gentility. This was usually done by bringing up two arguments: his lack of proper manners and education and his ungenteel social origins. These happened to be the same accusations as those routinely leveled at American colonials; for Defoe, however, their immediacy was probably more bitter than what a Byrd or a Fitzhugh would suffer in the colonies. Political polemists repeatedly used one specific cultural device to discredit him: they pointed to his low pedigree as a "mechanic" and claimed that as such, he could not have had an adequate education, no doubt being ignorant of Latin, the benchmark of genteel learning. Defoe was compelled to devote much space in his journal to repudiating such invectives. "Those Gentlemen," he wrote, "that Reproach my Learning to Applaud their own, shall have it proved, I have more Learning than either of them—Because I have more Manners." He was also forced to declare that he had "never been a Hosier, or an Apprentice," a label that had been condescendingly pinned on him. This charge must have been particularly slighting because he strongly believed that trade should be treated as an honorable occupation and was proud of his own financial successes. His background in classics was obviously weaker than that of Swift or other antagonists from the genteel circles, and his writing—including his stylistically unpolished but didactically effective poetry and his realistic prose—gained wide popularity among a middle-class audience rather than among the classically educated. At the dissident academy of Newington Green, he had received a relatively good education, not just for a butcher's son. He was close enough to meeting the criteria of genteel merit to be a threat to the genteel elite's cultural monopoly.[52]

This is particularly evident in the 1710 assaults by Swift in the *Examiner*. In an outburst against his opponents, he called Defoe and George Ridpath of the *Observator* "two stupid, illiterate Scribblers, both of them Fanaticks by Profession." He ascribed to them a whole assortment of ungenteel attributes, none connected with the political argument in question but all imputing vulgar social rank. "I cannot but suspect, that the two Worthies," wrote Swift, "have in a degree done Mischief among us; the mock authoritative manner of one [Defoe] and the insipid Mirth of the other, however insupportable to reasonable Ears, being of a level with great numbers among the lowest of Mankind." It was this outrage, he continued, "that moved me to take the matter out of those rough, as well as Dirty hands, to let the remote and uninstructed part of the Nation see, that they have been misled." This attack is a perfect instance of cultural arbitration in action. First, he classified Defoe as belonging to the nongenteel, even laboring, class and therefore by definition—in accord with Shaftesbury's paradigm—driven by emotions and not reason. Second, Swift's response dismissed Defoe as an unequal partner without even taking up the argument of the polemic.[53]

Questioning power in cultural terms was a recurrent theme whenever accelerated social mobility was taking place, a point particularly pertinent to the colonies. Over two decades earlier this pattern could easily be detected in the sharp exchanges between Governor Berkeley and the rebellious Nathaniel Bacon in Virginia. Berkeley, as a member of the established elite, felt entitled to label his challengers "the lowest of the people" and "rabble." Bacon used the very same device in castigating Berkeley's oligarchy for accumulating illicit privilege as people of low birth, without "learning and virtue."[54] But if the weapon was the same, in Virginia the lines of social hierarchy were less transparent, while in the English debates it was the rigidity of such divisions that was most striking. Swift's rank was taken for granted, while Defoe, a new gentleman, constantly had to justify his, thereby often producing new pretexts for censure. For instance, in his *Review* polemic

Defoe gave much space to asserting gravely that he had adequate genteel manners, but he lost his control toward the end of the article and compared his opponent Tutchin to a barking dog on whom Defoe, as a dog with dignity, "holds up one leg, pisses upon him, and so goes on about his business."[55] The irony was that if anything this unmannerly was accidentally uttered by a "true-born" gentleman, it sometimes was forgiven because his supposedly inalienable honor could not be damaged. Unfortunately for Defoeans, this cultural doctrine did not apply to a mere "hosier."

That English cultural reactions—whether at home or in distant colonies—to the ascendance of upstart gentry involved questions of power and order, and not merely the quality of refinement, was well illuminated in Swift's comments on the various risks to state, society, and liberty ensuing from ambitions of this kind. He blamed such aspirations of the "vulgar" for major historical catastrophes, claiming, for instance, that the "entire Subversion of the Roman liberty and Constitution, was altogether owing to those Measures which had broke the Balance between the Patricians and Plebeians." "Of all the Heresies in Politicks," he noted in reaction to *The True-Born Englishman* and especially to Defoe's reservations about the link between ancient ancestry and genteel virtue, "none ever displeased me more, or seemed to have more dangerous Consequences to Monarchy, than that pernicious Talent so much affected, of discovering a Contempt for Birth, Family, and ancient Nobility. All the Threadbare Topicks of Poets and Orators were display'd to discover to us, that Merit and Virtue were the only Nobility; and that the Advantages of Blood, could not make a Knave or a Fool either honest or Wise."[56] Such assumptions did not represent some waning, outmoded attitudes of the British elites; on the contrary, they remained in force for a long time to come. Charles Lamb, commenting in 1822 on *The Complete English Tradesman*, expressed essentially the same contempt for Defoe's "pompous detail, the studied analysis of every little mean art, every sneaking address, every trick and subterfuge (short of larceny) that is necessary to the tradesman's occupation, with hundreds of anecdotes." The only way for a refined reader to find it "amusing," suggested Lamb magnanimously, would be to "read it in an ironical sense, and as a piece of covered satire."[57] The iron curtain of high culture was now more porous but still far from demolished; a century had passed, but Defoe was still an object of distaste for those who saw themselves as agents of high culture.

Commercial Roots, Landed Ideal

In the context of Defoe's attempts to incorporate certain commercial values—expressive of his class of origin—into the genteel paradigm, a fair question to ask is why the colonial gentry, mostly of urban or commercial roots, did not attempt to attach honor and dignity to such values but adopted the traditional landed ethos wholesale, complete with its anticommercial bias.

The opposition between commercial and genteel values was one of the central themes in the cultural dynamics of eighteenth-century Britain. In 1711 Swift associated "avarice," "falsehood," and "corruption" with commercial and urban occupations. William Penn sanctioned the same view with religious authority, writing in his 1706 book on the proper conduct of human life that "the country life is to be preferred, for there we find the works of God, but in Cities little else but the works of Man." Commercial pursuits were categorized along with laboring occupations as "vulgar." Aphra Behn, in her 1690 play, portrayed a Mrs. Ranter who rose from an indentured servant to a wealthy Virginian lady and member of the county gentry but carried the crudeness of a commoner like an albatross around her neck. A contemporary tract on gentility, published in Britain as well as in America, took for granted that the town was a source of corruption when it complained that "contention for Gain, which had begun in Town, spread itself by Degrees into the Country."[58] These views were rooted in the entrenched concepts of genteel honor, which was assumed to be based on immutable foundations of land and birth that financial problems could not damage. By contrast, a "citizen" whose respectability was founded on the quality of commercial operations within ever-changeable markets would be disgraced if such transactions failed. In one of Richard Steele's plays, Mr. Sealand, an "India Merchant," complained about the morals of Sir John Bevil's son. Sir John, a landed gentleman of ancient family, exclaimed: "Sir, I can't help saying, that what might injure a Citizen's Credit, may be no Stain to a Gentleman's Honour." Sealand countered with a bold argument that "Merchants are a Species of Gentry, that have grown into the World this last Century, and are as honourable, and almost as useful, as you landed Folks, that have always thought yourselves so much above us."[59] The enduring cultural power of the commercial-landed opposition is perhaps best manifested in the judgment of Benjamin Franklin—no landed gentleman himself—expressed only eight years before the Declaration of Independence on the three possible paths to wealth: "First is by war, as the Romans did, in plundering their conquered neighbours. This is robbery. The second by commerce, which is generally cheating. The third by agriculture, the only honest way." "People of the Trading Towns," he wrote, "may be rich and luxurious, while the Country possesses all the Virtues."[60]

That it was not feasible for ambitious rising Englishmen to turn to the commercial ethos in search of legitimacy becomes clear upon taking a second, closer look at the issue of the *Spectator* in which Addison and Steele introduced their model merchant, Sir Andrew Freeport, to the genteel reading public. Their effort has been interpreted as an acceptance of the bourgeois into the gentry. It is true that his "indefatigable industry" was presented as a positive quality, but the overall tone used toward him was strikingly patronizing. "A General Trader of good sense," they said, "is pleasanter Company than a general Scholar; and Sir Andrew, having a natural unaffected Eloquence, the Perspicuity of his Discourse gives the same Pleasure that Wit would in another Man." Thus the merchant's attraction—even for these most sympathetic of editors—still remained essentially exotic: his common sense and plain style were merely entertaining, while refinement and wit were not even to be expected from a trader.[61] An instructive example of the depth of such cultural classifications—in this case applied to the colonies—was Oldmixon, one of those rare members of the old English gentry who conceded that commercial activities, providing they were "honest" and "industrious," may represent some virtue. He was, however, willing to apply such a categorization only to the safely remote American colonies. Virginia, in his view, was one such part of the empire where the elite was essentially commercial but could be accepted as honorable because of its contribution to the wealth of Britain and because at least some of its members derived from gentry stock. "Men of good Families and small Fortunes removed to Virginia, thrived and grew great by their Industry and Success," he noted, but "there is no need as yet of an Herald-Office to be set up at James Town." He concluded that "the honest Merchant and industrious Planter are the Men of Honour in Virginia." Barbados received similar treatment; its great planters, by virtue of their "Possessions, equal to many of our Nobility and Gentry," were portrayed as deserving honor even without the ancestry to back it up. He thus expanded the notion of genteel honor but explicitly lim-

Gentility: A Transatlantic Aspiration 63

ited its scope to the colonies, implying a lesser sort of virtue reserved for their elites.[62]

Colonial planter gentry and the Defoean group shared not only the newness of their rise to prominence but also the commercial roots of their wealth. Even if we look at Virginia only, and even if we accept assertions that more eighteenth-century elite of that colony derived from armorial families than of any other region of mainland America, the fact remains that most of the original immigrants were in commercial occupations before leaving England, and that their genteel status in the colony emerged through commercial success.[63] Many major gentry families—to mention only the Ludwells, Spencers, Steggs, Byrds, and Bollings—descended from merchants and tradesmen. Instead of sending his son to study at a university, William Byrd I sent him to Holland to learn commercial transactions and later to London to the countinghouse of Perry and Lane for the same explicit purpose—to study business methods. It was only in the second generation that the ideal of a country gentleman began to replace that of a successful businessman. Old mentality, of course, still overlapped the new. William Byrd II scrupulously noted in his diary the exact sums of money he lost playing cards, and the letters of King Carter, whose successful commercial activities included trading in slaves, reveal meticulous attention to business. For instance, Carter complained to Barbados merchants about a delivery with "boys and girls so very much exceeding all manner of proportion to the men and women" and was pleased with the "seven pounds which the unsold negro fetched more than she was valued at." One of the wealthiest and most polished Virginia gentlemen, Robert Carter III was in reality a successful entrepreneur, able to run efficiently an extensive network of economic undertakings, including ironworks and other manufacturing. Eliza Lucas Pinckney experimented successfully with indigo production and effectively managed her father's plantations in South Carolina, rising every day at five o'clock to "take a walk in the garden and field" to "see that the servants are at their respective business."[64]

The utmost practicality of Landon Carter was another case in point. He recorded in his diary that he had personally moved a slave from the "hindmost" to the fourth place in the line of workers in the field, with the result that "it made him quicken the motion of his arm." When Carter found he could save on repairing his carriage by employing slaves instead of a professional, he precisely calculated the value of the loss of their labor at their previous assignment, "fixing my waste dam and pier heads to my mill." He lectured an overseer about a minute loss of corn, claiming that "truth and justice have no virtue if it does not shine in a farthing as well as in a million." Although this noble principle could have come from a courtesy book, his actual behavior resembled less the magnanimous attitude of a gentleman than that of a petty shopkeeper.[65]

The commercial mind-set was also quite visible in attitudes toward work. The planter gentry was never quite far from it, nor did its members share the prohibitive attitude toward it so typical of the old landed classes of Europe. Since their status derived both from the pioneering experience of their parents or grandparents and from their own entrepreneurial business activities, traditions of work remained, while genteel leisure and consumption had few ready patterns. Of course, a visitor to Charleston from Philadelphia in 1760s would have been struck by the slow and leisurely lifestyle of the South Carolina elite. In the words of one, "They live in these towns in opulency and ease great part of the summer, taking a ride once in a fortnight more or less as any urgent action requires, sometimes taking their Ladies with them and children in a chair; so that there is not the appearance of as much business carried on here as in Philadelphia where the people live immediately by their own industry, as trade and manufactory, and generally by their own labour."[66] But this observation by a northerner should not mislead us; unlike old European landed gentry, these leisurely planters had business calculations and plantation management very much on their minds.

Yet, once established, first- and second-generation colonial gentry disavowed the very commercial virtues and rationale that brought them to prominence and preferred to be identified with the more respectable designation of "planter," implying landed rank. In South Carolina, Joseph Kershaw, Robert Goudey, LeRoy Hammond, Alexander McIntosh, and Thomas Sumter attained prominence by running stores, gristmills and sawmills, indigo works, distilleries, tobacco warehouses, and Indian trading posts, but they all ultimately invested their profits into land and slaves, thus identifying themselves with the status of the British landed class.[67] Certainly by the last four decades of the colonial period, prominent planters manifestly considered themselves landed gentlemen and looked upon their British business partners as tainted by commerce. Byrd referred indignantly to his English factor Micajah Perry in 1736 as a "hungry magistrate" and chafed at being "in the gripe of that usurer." When on another occasion he proudly declared that in Virginia he had no use for money, it was not just a rationalization of the colonial barter trade but a clear reference to the landed ethos, which associated financial operations with corruption. There is little question about the continuity of this view well into the 1770s. T. H. Breen has shown how the colonists were offended—on the grounds of genteel honor—by the increasing urgings of British merchants for debt payments. In 1764 Washington was clearly affronted when a factor pressured him for payments; he strongly believed his honor as a gentleman ought to have been sufficient guarantee that the debts would ultimately be paid.[68] Landon Carter, with all his practicality, unquestionably identified himself with landed virtue and condemned commercial vices: "I have lately read in some author that them as in the trade generally has too much of the theif in him; and I hardly see an instance much to the Contrary." This to him was only rational, "for by profession a broker is a villain in the very engagements he enters into. He must buy and must sell as cheap and as dear as he can which is the very trade of a Jockey. . . . I intend to preserve Honour." Of course, even the courtesy-book gentleman had to deal with some business matters, but never on par with the businessman. As the *Tatler* advised, a true gentleman "acts with great ease and Freedom among Men of Pleasure, and acquits himself with Skill and Dispatch among the Men of Business."[69]

In England a gentleman was defined as a person "above the Assistance of Trade and Employment to help out his Subsistence." The colonial dilemma was that for ambitious planters material wealth was both an end in itself and a means to the coveted landed status. But being associated with trade—which produced much of the wealth—canceled the validity of genteel rank. Contemporary cultural authorities would point out that to teach Latin to a child from a commercial sphere was "ridiculous" because "there are Attainments of a meaner nature that will serve him most, such as will turn him best for Business and are requisite for a Man of trade and Commerce."[70] The link between wealth and gentility was elusive but firm. Only property provided the independence necessary to be a free and enfranchised citizen (and to have a stake in the public good), but only landed, not commercial, wealth was associated with virtue.[71]

Evidence that in plantation America—more so than among the urban

Defoeans—the landed model was taking hold and displacing the older commercial identifications among the elite may be found in attitudes taken toward the issue of luxury. In early eighteenth-century British discourse, attacks on luxury were a commonplace weapon in the cultural confrontation between commercial and landed values. The genteel and landed elite pointed to the "unmerited" extravagance of the newly wealthy commoners and to the ill effects of the expansion of trade. Defoe's nemesis Fletcher believed that European liberty, thus far kept stable by landholding subjects, was collapsing as people were becoming trapped in a "perpetual Change of the Fashions in Clothes, Equipage and Furniture of Houses." Commerce, new products, and the diversity of cultural choices were presented as incompatible with virtue.[72] These attacks were framed by putting the anticommercial attitudes of the old landed ethos to new use as weapons against early capitalism and against new groups aspiring to respectability and power. This argument was also widely used in Britain to discredit the genteel ambitions of wealthy colonial planters. Defoe's contemporary, bishop of Cloyne and philosopher George Berkeley, specifically linked commercial mentality and extravagance with what he saw as the corrupt nature of the colonial slaveholding gentry when he argued against founding a missionary college in Barbados, "a place of so high a trade, so much wealth and luxury, and such dissolute morals."[73]

Commercial groups responded by assailing the extravagance of old elites and pointing to the need for such urban middle-class values as frugality, thrift, and modesty. Joseph Morgan, whose tract on riches Franklin printed and admired in 1732, saw the landed gentleman spending most of his time "pampering Horses and Dogs" and living a "useless life" on rents. We must note, however, that these new commercial aspirants to gentility had conspicuously double standards when it came to luxury. Defoe, in order to criticize landed interests, invoked the vain indulgence of the old gentry who cared about "no thing but to glut themselves in plenty, wallowing in wealth and in the grossest part of what they call pleasures, not capable of enjoying the sublime and exalted delight of an improv'd soul." But when he defended commercial interests, he justified luxury as largely beneficial for trade ("a Vice in Morals may at the same time be a Virtue in Trade"). It is also noteworthy that he was careful to condemn luxury among those below him—the common and the poor—as leading to idleness and vice.[74]

In the early decades of the eighteenth century, the Virginia gentry already was showing unmistakable signs of its identification with the landed model. In 1698 Fitzhugh invoked the modesty of a landed gentleman by requesting that his Bristol merchant George Mason, who was overseeing William's eleven-year-old son Henry while he was at school in England, furnish his son "with what is fit & decent, as befits an honest Planter," and not "with what's rich and gawdy."[75] But by 1729 Byrd, writing to his English factor, conspicuously manifested a landed ethos and assigned low materialism to tradesmen. He observed with indignation that the shopkeepers supplying him with articles he ordered had grown vain through new commercial wealth and abandoned "their frugality, and their spouses must be maintained in splendor. . . . Luxury is bad enough amongst [peo]ple of quality, but when it gets among that order of men that [stand] behind the counters, they must turn cheats and pickpockets."[76] What was merely unsavory in a gentleman was corrupt in a tradesman. Byrd had already relegated his own commercial background to irrelevant prehistory. He now saw himself a representative of landed order and virtue, and it is likely that had he met Defoe, he would have looked down on him as a mere hosier. It is essential to understand this shift to genteel values in the first half of the eighteenth century in order to grasp the American gentry's readiness to denounce the alleged corruption of such values among European aristocracy during the Revolutionary period.

Tensions between landed and urban-commercial values were often expressed in a gendered rhetoric which identified materialist pressures with "effeminacy," seen as a result of the decline of the ancient, simple landed virtues in favor of luxury, defined in Johnson's *Dictionary* as "voluptuousness; addictedness to pleasure." Such definitions were commonplace in the process of constructing an identity for the young gentry, a large subject in itself that can only be touched on here. Poet and author John Brown, in a study familiar to both British and American readers, criticized contemporary culture for replacing inner (masculine) virtue with what he called superficial and vain (feminine) external style. He blended this contrast with the traditional genteel opposition between city and country. "The first and capital Article of Town-Effeminacy is that of Dress," he noted, "yet in this must every Man of every Rank and Age employ his Mornings who pretends to keep good company. The wisest, the most virtuous, the most polite, if defective in these exterior and unmanly Delicacies are avoided as low People whom nobody knows."[77] Practical Defoe contrasted true elegance with "effeminate" courtly styles; he believed a gentleman should be able to write in a "masculine and manly stile . . . without foolish flourishes and ridiculous flights of jingling bombast." Byrd satirized the "Female fluency" of tongue and the irrationality of a woman's mind, characterized by excessive "Faith and Imagination." Landon Carter much respected his friend Richard Henry Lee but believed that for a gentleman, "this McVain" succumbed to far too much feminine-like narcissism by being "always open to flattery" and allowing himself to be "eternally wounded by . . . sycophants." And Hamilton, who consistently wrote from the position of the old genteel ethos, asked: "Did not the Greeks, a wise and warlike Nation, after having for several ages, maintained their honor and dignity, in arts and arms, and Integrity of Morals, sink by degrees into Softness and effeminacy, by which the Persians overcame them?" Similarly, the Romans, "once a wise honorable and warlike people, who ruled the world," had become "a parcel of Singers, dancers, fidlers, pipers, effeminate catamites." Closer to home, "the worthy knights of old were defenders and champions of virtue," but contemporary gentry, "instead of Swords, helmets, and coats of mail, the ponderous and manly badges of heroes, wear delicate soft silks, velvets, Ribbons, garters, Stars, Jewels, Golden fleeces, crosses and other gewgaws, just enough emblems of their Softness, effeminacy and cowardice."[78]

By rejecting its commercial heritage and embracing landed values early in the century, the young American gentry laid a foundation for the next generation, which would come already well equipped with the economic and social base of a plantation lifestyle. Defoe only in his late years was able to purchase an estate and finally realize his lifelong dream of becoming a landed gentleman; the planters knew nothing but a rural existence, which made the landed lifestyle an attainable model, complete with horses and dogs. Washington, like Jefferson, for most of his adult life showed considerable passion for breeding horses. He duly noted in his diary every new offspring of his mares and stallions—and hounds, an interest he picked up from Lord Fairfax, his youthful model of elegance. How deeply this identity—hostile to business values—operated among the southern gentry may be judged by Thomas Jefferson's peculiar version of the landed model, which he democratized and extended to the whole American society when he wrote that "those who labour in the earth are the chosen people of God," while denouncing "the mobs of great cities" and those living off commercial activities who depend on "the caprice of customers." At the heart of his vision was independence linked to land; it always remained a condition crucial to his ideal republic, for "dependence begets subservience and venality, suffocates the germ of virtue."[79] It was precisely this concept that had been—long before Jefferson—at the very heart of the old landed ethos.

A Conservative Model

This landed model was thus essentially conservative, despite the fact that it was used to gain cultural access into a well-established and hermetic British elite. The ascendant elites did not intend to undermine it but to become acceptable members. In the early eighteenth century, the Defoeans and the colonials pursued parallel but separate paths, ultimately guided by the same cultural paradigm of upward social advancement but operating in different environments. This is why similarities and contrasts between them help illuminate a number of questions about the legitimizing process among colonial gentry. They shared important common traits. Both groups embraced the same source—the model of a gentleman—as a passport to cultural validation as members of the dominant class. Both groups had emerged relatively recently to wealth, education, leisure, and prominence. Both lacked a historical background of elite membership. Both were compelled to struggle actively for the affirmation of their title to membership in such an elite, and neither side could realistically hope to attain this goal without accepting a canon of ethical and stylistic attributes defined by the arbiters of old legitimacy in England. Both were routinely treated by these very arbiters as cultural dunces from Grub Street. When Defoe redefined the concept of gentility to ease access to it, he was giving voice to the pressing interests of his group; but his concept, precisely because it opened new doors, was rejected and even vilified by the old elite. The colonists took the more common and realistic path to genteel legitimacy of identifying with the current model rather than questioning it.

There is, however, a link between the two which throws an interesting light on the struggles for legitimacy on both sides of the Atlantic. The American colonies were historically a land of opportunity for English commoners who often hoped to achieve landed rank and who sometimes did, as affirmed by the rise of many from commercial origins to gentry. This prospect provided much of the motivation that led people to emigrate. John Harrower from Lerwick in Scotland indentured himself to Colonel William Daingerfield in Virginia as a tutor to his children with the explicit hope that he would ultimately achieve gentility by owning a plantation and living a landed lifestyle. In 1774 he wrote to his wife in Scotland, "I yet hope (please God) if I am spared, some time to make you a Virginian Lady among the woods of America." Defoe gave what probably was the most popular public expression of such ambitions in his time; he was explicit that America was where his new model was to come fully to life. He believed that an expansion of the plantation region in British America would create vast opportunities for commoners by opening a route to gentility that in England was practically closed, but for infrequent exceptions. He saw such success possible through the exercise of the commercial virtues that he championed: industry, enterprise, and practical ability to create wealth and profit. His popular novels *Moll Flanders* and *Colonel Jacque* made plain that in America even people of low rank, such as servants or convicts, would be able eventually to acquire wealth and independence. The promise of the colonies saw Molly and Jacque raised from their position of thieves and convicts to that of planters in Virginia and Maryland and then, by acquiring merit through learning, to the rank of gentry. Jacque, once established as a prosperous landowner, obtained an education appropriate for a gentleman, complete with Roman history and Latin learned from one of his indentured servants who tutored him so that the "foundation" of his new life might have a "superstructure" of virtue, which alone made men "rich and great."[80]

Obviously, such gentility was sought less for refinement in itself and more for the status it provided for "new men." Beautification and improved taste were certainly among the motivations, but to focus primarily on them, as so many studies have done, underemphasizes the structuring power of these efforts. The guiding gentry model could be found not only in courtesy books but in the vocabulary of rank, hierarchy, and power. One can only grasp this latter motive in the context of contemporary perceptions of a naturally well-ordered society. "Tis evident," claimed Defoe, "God Almighty in peopling the Earth acted with the same Wisdom, and with the same excellent Order, as he did in peopling the sky, nay even the Heavens themselves. In the firmament he placed glorious lights; glorious indeed they are in all their Degree, but of different Magnitude." Societies and nature reflected the same order: "Here we see a Sun, an immense and amazing globe of Fire shining in its full strength. . . . There the humble Moon and her Sisters the Planets with their Satellites, the Plebeii of the Skies, dark and opake in themselves, shine by Reflection only, and borrowing beams from the Patrician Sun."[81] A 1705 edition of an Anglican guide for gentlemen stressed that "God, in his wisdom, discerning that Equality of Conditions would breed Confusion in the World, has ordered several states, design'd some to Poverty, others to Riches." A year later Penn offered a similar view of God's design: "For tho' he has made of one Blood all nations, he has not rang'd or dignified them upon the level but in a sort of Subordination and Dependency. . . . Planets have their several Degrees of Glory, and so the other Stars of Magnitude and Lustre. If we look upon the Earth, we see it among the Trees of the Wood, from the Cedar to the Bramble; in the Waters among the Fish, from the Leviathan to the Sprat; in the Air among the Birds, from the Eagle to the Sparrow; among the Beasts, from the Lion to the Cat; and among Mankind itself, from the King to the Scavenger."[82]

Chesapeake gentry had early adopted this hierarchical concept of social order—including its built-in contempt for the vulgar—as part of its group consciousness and notion of honor. When William Fitzhugh sheltered George Brent in his house during Protestant unrest, he did so not to support Catholics but out of "civility" to a gentleman who was at risk of "being plundered by the Rabble." A glimpse into such assumptions of order may be gained from a dialogue between a judge and a poor planter published in Williamsburg in 1732 and probably written by the popular and respected Virginia leader William Gooch. Intended to appease the lesser planters, unhappy with quality regulations imposed on tobacco, its chief argument was based on the notion of the cultural superiority of the gentry. The author, speaking through Judge Love-Country to poor farmer Tom, explained patiently that small planters did not possess sufficient understanding even to assume that members of the assembly could have made a wrong decision. "Consider the Persons concerned in making this Law," he argued. "Are they not all of them Gentlemen of probity and great Integrity. . . . And have they not by this very Act of theirs, sufficiently testified their Regard for the Public, and their Concern for the poor Planters?" Tom responded in a desirably humble fashion: "I am resolved never to quarrel for the future with what I don't understand; and whenever they din any idle Reports against Laws in my Ears, that are beyond my Capacity, if Your Worship give me Leave, I will wait on your Worship with them." The judge, in parting, advised, "Live as become honest Men, minding only your own Business; Fear God, honour the King, and meddle not with those that are given to Noise and Violence."[83] Similarly, Hamilton saw his society strictly through the gentry-commonalty dichotomy; describing a political gathering in 1744, he observed that "there was a rabble of about 4,000 people in the street, and great numbers of ladies and gentlemen in the windows and balconies." Referring in 1752 to his service in the Virginia House of Burgesses, Landon Carter distinguished between serious business discussed among gentlemen and speeches made "only to please the humour of the Plebeians."[84]

This powerful cultural predisposition to see society as inherently hierarchical would explain why planter elites did not attempt to level and democratize this hierarchy by identifying more fully with a utilitarian ethos and instead chose an essentially conservative concept of gentility. Even the seemingly leveling thrust of Defoe's arguments was in reality aimed more at achieving exclusiveness for his group than at equalizing society. We have been told since Marx that Defoe was primarily a modern, a radical in his times, a voice of the rising bourgeoisie, and that his vision of Robinson Crusoe's island entailed capitalist enterprise.[85] But that is clearly far too simplified an image. Apart from a number of truly iconoclastic ideas—for example, the rejection of ancestry—Defoe emerges from the debates on gentility as a deeply traditional and conservative mind, strongly royalist, far from wishing to replace the gentry and nobility with the bourgeoisie. However closely one may examine his little model kingdom of Crusoe, it does not show the slightest signs of a Lockean voluntary union or a republican agreement of the people. Instead, the author was happy to put Crusoe in absolute dominion over the slaves and other inhabitants of his island, and—much like William Byrd and later Landon Carter—expected from them full servitude and subjection to his authority. In the concluding pages of the book, speaking to a Russian prince, Crusoe explained his concept of domination and power in no ambiguous terms:

> I told him, I had the absolute Disposal of the Lives and Fortunes of all my Subjects; that notwithstanding my absolute Power, I had not one

Person disaffected to my Government, or to my Person, in all my Dominions. He shook his Head at that, and said I out-did the Czar of Muscovy. I told him, that all the Lands in my Kingdom were my own, and all my Subjects were not only my Tenants, but Tenants at Will: That they would all fight for me to the last Drop; and that never a Tyrant, for such I acknowledged myself to be, was so universally belov'd, and yet so horribly feared, by his Subjects.

His notion of mastery over his island plantation was emphatically seigneurial. "I pleased myself with being the Patron of those People I placed there," reflected Crusoe, "and doing for them in a kind of haughty majestic Way, like an old Patriarchal Monarch; providing for them, as if I had been Father of the whole family, as well as of the Plantation."[86] There can also be little doubt that Defoe's hero dreamed of owning land and slaves and of playing before them the role of an absolute lord. One cannot fail to note that whenever Crusoe acted toward them in a charitable way, it was visibly because of the immense satisfaction of being a benevolent master, the perfect landed gentleman for whom he had so much genuine reverence and admiration. There is a notable similarity here to the strict and authoritarian Virginian Landon Carter, who nevertheless sincerely believed he was "a very kind Master" to his slaves.[87]

It should strike us how closely this conceptualization of the patriarchal, ideal gentleman matches the self-description provided by Defoe's American contemporary William Byrd:

> Besides the advantage of a pure Air, we abound in all kinds of Provisions without expence (I mean we who have Plantations). I have a large Family of my own, and my Doors are open to Every Body, yet I have no Bills to pay, and half-a-Crown will lay undisturbed in my Pocket for many Moons together. Like one of the Patriarchs, I have my Flocks and my Herds, my Bonds-men and Bonds-women, and every Sort of Trade amongst my own Servants, so that I live in a kind of Independence on everyone but Providence. . . . I must take care to keep all my people to their Duty, to set all the Springs in motion, and to make everyone draw his equal Share to carry the Machine forward. "[88]

Byrd's vision of his dominion over the plantation was just as free of any symptoms of republicanism as that of Defoe. It was equally conservative in its recourse to the traditional landed ideal, with the authoritarian but benevolent master as the axis, responsible for setting the mechanisms of the plantation microcosm in motion, with the large "family" of servants, slaves, and other dependents gravitating around him and with his own independence limited by no one. This traditional model—quite far from embracing any equality other than that among the gentry themselves—became a paradigm for plantation elites in the following half century. As late as 1785 Ralph Izard wrote from his plantation in South Carolina to Jefferson lamenting the emergence of excessively egalitarian views among the common people, which he believed undermined the authority of the established planter gentry. "Our governments," he complained, "tend too much to Democracy. A handicraftsman thinks an apprenticeship necessary to make him acquainted with his business. But our back countrymen are of opinion that a politician may be born such as well as a poet."[89]

In this light, it becomes clearer why the colonists would not seriously consider commercial values as equal to the genteel ethos or trading occupations as equal to the landed status, and why the businesslike patterns of their daily practical behavior did not effectively displace the old model. It was possible to relegate these patterns to the cultural back burner because the old model of respectability coincided in a highly effective way with their roles as masters of their little kingdoms. It would therefore be anachronistic to expect the emergence in the plantation colonies of some novel, peculiarly American cultural ethos, with sufficient legitimizing power of its own to supplant the traditional one. Precognitive epistemology may help here to explain the persistence of old, internalized values, continuing to affect society and behavior through their ability to classify reality; a long view of history may enable us see that a certain cultural delay often takes place during major social and economic shifts, a lag occasioned by the inherent inertia of social consciousness.

Without the British dimension of the early legitimizing process among the colonists—who together with the metropolis were part of one British civilization—it would be impossible to explain the mechanism of cultural arbitration involved in the advancement from commoner condition to genteel

Gentility: A Transatlantic Aspiration 75

respectability, as well as the consequent adoption of the same model of such advancement by new groups in both countries. It would be difficult to grasp the peculiar dilemma of those who attempted to surmount the iron curtain of exclusion in order to establish themselves as an exclusive class. It would also be harder to show that they were justified in following a traditional path of legitimation because it effectively provided them with the precious fruits of respectability, a title to ruling class status, and a desirable social order. Both the Defoeans and the slaveholding planters aimed at change, aspiring to cross the demarcation line upwards. They did not do so in order to replace the gentleman but to become one. In historical hindsight, Defoe's method of expanding the old notion of virtue at first failed but then became successful in the nineteenth century as forms of gentility rapidly spread among the rising middle classes. The colonists' more orthodox method was defeated in British eyes from the start, but in the plantation region it was more than successful in meeting its goals.

CHAPTER 3

The Curse of Provincialism

> "Wee are here att ye end of ye World, & Europe may be turned topsy turvy ere we can hear a Word of itt."
> Colonel William Byrd I to Daniel Horsmanden, 1690

> "Our Estates here depend altogether upon Contingencys, & to prepare against that, causes me to exceed my Inclinations in worldly affairs, & Society that is good & ingenious is very scarce, and seldom to be come except in books. Good education of Children is almost impossible, & better never be born than ill bred, but that which bears the greatest weight with me . . . is the want of spiritual help & comforts, of which this fertile Country in every thing else, is barren and unfruitfull, which last Consideration bears the greatest weight in my Desires of Exchange & removal."
> William Fitzhugh to Nicholas Heyward, 1686/87

> "How hard the Lot of any Gentleman in this Part of the World!"
> Charles Woodmason on Carolina, *Journal*, 1768

The Evolution of Negative Stereotypes of the Colonist

Condescension and patronizing stereotypes directed at the New World colonial elites by the metropolitan high society were so persistent in English culture that we can only survey here some of these themes to show their stubborn continuity throughout the eighteenth century. This phenomenon—which, although recognized, has not received much systematic attention—affected the cultural ambitions of colonial elites in more ways than we have thus far acknowledged. Its sharp edge was often aimed at all colonists, but in the plantation region it significantly affected only the wealthy slaveholding gentry. Its members had already achieved adequate decorum and even deference within their communities, but as a new class that had attained such recognition through appropriating European genteel style and values, they could not afford to distance themselves from the need for metropolitan approval. This is why the process of their legitimization cannot be fully explained without a deeper understanding of the syndrome of provincialism.

Discussing provincialism is also important for another reason. American rusticity was not an invention of metropolitan polemicists; it was real. Two powerful and inescapable facts of life confronted colonists on all rungs of the social ladder. First, they were exiles from the mother country, and second, their lives were played out in the situation of the frontier. An acute awareness of both generated particular discomfort among the ambitious and educated planters, as evidenced by their continuous craving for information on current events and developments in Britain. Letters, journals, books, and news of all kinds arriving from Europe were eagerly devoured but could not relieve the sense of isolation that combined not only physical remoteness but also a cultural distance from Britain.[1] To understand this eagerness as well as the unfulfillment inherent in their situation is to grasp how provincialism, instead of undermining the ambitions for refinement, was a powerful mobilizing force to pursue the genteel model.

As the first generation of great planters was emerging on the scene in Virginia and elsewhere in the mainland colonies in the early decades of the eighteenth century, the English elites already had fairly well crystallized ideas about the colonial gentry. At their core lay the belief that it was virtually inconceivable that such a class could have legitimate claims to gentility. In 1741 John Oldmixon, one of the most influential voices shaping public opinion on the colonies at the time, observed simply that it was unimaginable that "Men of Quality and Fortune" would settle in the colonies. "Men of Estate would not leave their native Country, of which the English are of all Men most fond, to seek an Habitation in an unknown Wilderness: And what deterred such from going thither at first, will always deter them."[2] The key word was "always." The generalizing categorization here was that all colonists were tainted by inferior social origins, and consequently, those among them who did climb to wealth and power could not but be upstarts.

A glimpse of the adverse power of such cultural classification may be gained from a "character"—a genre then fashionable in literary culture—written in 1723 by William Byrd on himself. It reveals how a colonial in London struggled with both his own shortcomings as a first-generation gentleman and the stigma of provincialism. Entitled "Inamorato L'Oiseaux" (*sic*), it was sent to "Minionet," a woman he was then courting, with assurances that it was a frank portrayal. And frank it was, for it revealed a strong ambition mixed with a pervasive sense of inadequacy. Although "Nature gave him all the Talents in the World for business," he felt he did not exhibit enough "Industry" to rise up the social scale. He tried to turn weaknesses into virtues by emphasizing deeper qualities as the cause of his problems: he had attempted a legal career but was "taken off by the rapine and mercenariness of that Profession"; he then tried to become a courtier but found at St. James's "falseness and treachery, the envy and corruption in fashion that quickly made him abandon that pursuit." He emphasized that he was "easy, sensible, and inoffensive" in conversation, and that he demonstrated his respect for true virtue by paying "Court more to obscure merit, than to corrupt Greatness." Despite these assurances the text breathes a lack of leisurely confidence. As the son of a middle-class immigrant to Virginia, he was wanting in the secure ease that comes with old gentility, the "life and gaiety, that freedome and pushing confidence which hits the Ladys." His attempts to show refined gracefulness only caused him to be "all form and constraint when he shou'd have the most freedome and spirit," giving him a pedantic appearance and "a certain cast of pride." Viewed against Byrd's very reserved and impersonal diary, this was an unusually frank admission of both his ardent ambition and his awareness of the barriers separating him from sanctioned gentility.[3]

For all his efforts, to the polite society of London he remained a mere colonial. How condescendingly his provincial origins were treated may be seen from his letter to John Boyle, where he wrote of "fine ladys" in England who thought of those who lived in the colonies as "being buried alive."[4] He had suffered the humiliating impact of this attitude in London when he courted Mary Smith, daughter of the powerful John Smith, commissioner of excise. No promises and arguments about his wealth would make the Virginian acceptable to the father, who finally gave his daughter's hand to another suitor both titled and rich. In his letters to Mary, Byrd invoked the prospect of her being "chain'd to a Booby with a great Estate," although he admitted that money was "necessary to live & appear with the best People." In the end he had to concede that although he owned a very substantial estate in America, he was still treated as an inferior because he was a colonial. Arguments of reason could do little to change this stereotype, and he could only bitterly acknowledge that his "misfortune is, that this Fortune lys abroad. That is true, but for Gods sake where's the difference between its lying in Virginia or in Berkshire as long as I receive Profits of it in London?"[5]

His story was only the tip of an iceberg. Both the first and second generations of colonial gentry had to endure a painful paradox; having accumulated considerable power, wealth, and sophistication, they nevertheless found themselves continually treated by the metropolitan elites as rustic and boorish usurpers to gentility at best and as an inferior, vulgar sort of Englishmen at worst. Much more so than the Defoean group in England, they became a frequent object of ridicule, satire, and contempt from the refined British public. By the mid–eighteenth century a whole gallery of such negative British stereotypes of the colonists had emerged in a wide variety of publications, from journals, travel literature, political pamphlets, and scientific treatises to novels, drama, and poetry. It is important to realize two things. One is that many of these stereotypes emerged in the English cultural marketplace even before the rise of the eighteenth-century mainland planter elites, as a result of more generalized opinions on the nature of colonists in British America. The second is that the conventionalized English image of a slaveholding planter had its source more in the West Indian colonies than in the mainland American scene It was in the sugar islands that the legend of plantation wealth, greed, and corruption was initiated, well before it could be applied to Virginia or Maryland elites, who only approached a comparable status in the early eighteenth century (in the case of Carolina, extravagant lifestyles were actually introduced by younger sons of West Indian gentry who emigrated to the colony in the late seventeenth century). As a result of this chronology, when the mainland American planter-gentleman entered the transatlantic cultural stage, he had to confront an already well-established reputation for certain provincial traits.

Early stereotypes of immigrants to America were most often associated in the elite public mind with the poor, the dependent, and the illiterate, as well as with convicts and vagrants. Descriptions of the colonies routinely stressed the vast cultural distance between the English beau monde and the rustic Americans. One satirical tract published at the turn of the century declared that in the colonies 'tis difficult to find a Woman cleanly enough for a Cook to a Squeamish Lady, or a Man neat enough for a vallet to Sir Courtly Nice. I am sure that a Covent Garden Beau or a Bell-fa would appear to them much stranger Monsters, than ever were yet seen in America."[6] Up to the 1720s there were few references to any meaningful social hierarchy in the colonies; their society had been portrayed as a mostly unvarying one of simple commoners, with a rare few aspiring to some refinement. As early as 1629 Richard Thornton, describing to the earl of Pembroke his voyage to the British outpost in Guiana, referred to the "perverse and debayst behavior of many passengers usuallie sent into those and such like parts."[7]

Among the recurring constituent traits of these images were crudeness, lack of education, corruption of morals, materialism, alcoholism, and cruelty to servants and slaves. Life in the colonies was often painted as having a deanglicizing effect on the settlers. In his London pamphlet on Maryland, George Alsop referred in 1666 to the already popular belief that the very environment of the colonies had a corrupting influence. He accordingly warned English merchants that "the people of this place (whether the saltness of the Ocean gave them any alteration when they went over first, or their continual dwelling under the remote Clyme where they now inhabit, I know not) are a more acute people in general, in matters of Trade and Commerce, than in any other place in the World; and by their crafty and sure bargaining, do often over-reach the raw and unexperienced Merchant. To be short, he that undertakes Merchants imployment in Mary-Land, must have more of Knave in him than Fool."[8] In 1680 another narrative warned travelers to this colony that its inhabitants were a "godless and crafty people." Even promoters of emigration had to acknowledge that the belief in colonial corruption was widespread. Dalby Thomas, in the introduction to his 1690 tract championing British colonies in America, regretfully admitted that even "Men of Excellent Understanding . . . take for granted that the American Collonies occasion the decay of both the People and Riches of the Nation."[9] Eleven years later another author, commenting on Barbados, revealed that "it has grown a Proverb with the English Merchants that tho a Man goes over never so honest to the Plantations, yet the very Air there does change him in a short time. And it is certain that they have too much ground to complain of the universal Corruption of Justice among them." The cause, according to him, lay in the necessarily low social origins of judges who were recruited from "Planters, Merchants, Custom-House officers, Shopkeepers or other inhabitants of the Island who were never bred to or otherwise versed in the Law."[10] These views, of course, were not limited to the plantation region, although that was where the sharpest edge was pointed; a 1699 description of the New England colonies also referred to well-established negatives, noting that "it is a Proverb with those that know them, whosoever believes a New England Saint, shall be sure to be cheated; and he that knows how to deal with their Traders, may deal with the Devil, and fear no Craft."[11] By the mid–eighteenth century, opinions about the colonists' corruption were also being supported by news of their widespread smuggling, often presented by London as an American practice undermining a legal order that had been "always looked upon as the Bulwark of English Commerce" and "destructive of the national interest of this Kingdom."[12]

It was a harsh, unflattering, and often unjust image, but it was there to stay. For my argument it is important that these condescending stereotypes, coming from elite quarters, had a distinct class flavor. British-American society was characterized as essentially made up of commoners, people "of no rank," as Samuel Johnson put it. This classified them culturally with the servile class and therefore with very limited title to independence and liberties of the free, a major obstacle for the legitimation of a potential colonial gentry.

Sir Josiah Child, an influential writer on economy and twice governor of the East India Company, who may be considered representative of the views of well-informed and educated English elites at the turn of the century, helped popularize the view that American settlers were mostly of the vulgar sort, if not rejects of British society. In his celebrated *Discourse about Trade*, he wrote of the colonists: "These I say were such as had there been no English foreign Plantation in the World, could probably never have lived at home to do service for their country but must have come to be hanged or starved or dyed untimely of some of those miserable diseases that proceed from Want and Vice." Mindful that at least some of them derived from the gentry, he nevertheless maintained that they, too, although for different reasons, were useless to the society, "some never bred to labour, and others . . . unfit for it by the lazy habit of a Soldier's life." The theme that those who went to the American colonies were failures in Britain was a recurring one in the following decades, in both factual and other literary forms. A 1700 tract described Jamaica as "the Receptacle of Vagabonds, the Sanctuary of the Bankrupts, and a close-stool for the Purges of our Prisons" and called the colony "as sickly as an Hospital, as Dangerous as the Plague, as Hot as Hell, and as Wicked as the Devil." Thirty years later Ebenezer Cooke depicted Maryland planters as a "Race, who, when they cou'd not live at Home, For Refuge to these Worlds did roam" and generalized that they were "Scotch, English and Hibernians wild, from Sloth and Idleness exil'd."[13] The *American Magazine* reacted with outrage when Jonathan Swift caustically wrote that the colonists scrupulously hid the truth about their miserable life in America, and that the eagerness of the Irish to emigrate there could only be explained by even more wretched circumstances in Ireland itself. In his words, "It is remarkable, that the Enthusiasm spread among our Northern People of sheltering themselves in the continent of America, hath no other Foundation than their present insupportable Conditions at home." One of his own acquaintances who had emigrated was "finding all Things directly contrary to his hopes." The magazine countered that the Irish were quite content in America and that there was less violence there than in London or Dublin.[14] Not infrequently, even opinions about the plantation South coming from Britons in the Middle and New England colonies bolstered these stereotypes. A Pennsylvanian spoke of Maryland's "immorality, drunkenness, rudeness, and immoderate swearing," and a New Jersey colonist about to move to Virginia expressed much fear of "being corrupted, or carried away with the Vices which prevail in that Country," which he fully expected to be "sickly" and its people "profane, and exceeding wicked."[15]

A fairly common figure included in the image of the colonies was that of the fallen woman. For instance, one author writing in 1700 about English women in Jamaica observed that "they are such who have been Scandalous in England to the utmost Degree, either transported by the State or led by their vicious inclinations; where they may be wicked without shame, and whore on without punishment. . . . In short, Virtue is so Despis'd and all sorts of Vice Encouraged by both Sexes, that the town of Port-Royal is the very Sodom of the Universe." Half a century later, an authoritative history of the colonies confirmed that the emigration of women of ill repute to America was widely familiar to Englishmen: "Of late Years, it has been customary for young Women, who are fallen into Disgrace in England, or are ill used by their Parents, to transport themselves thither, and, as they say, Try their Fortunes."[16]

Prominent churchmen concerned with the state of colonial religion contributed to the early establishment of such images. In 1725 subtle philosopher and graceful stylist George Berkeley expressed the lowest opinion about the generality of British colonists. It was widely acknowledged, he noted, "that there is at this day, but little sense of religion, and a most notorious corruption of manners in the English colonies settled on the continent of America, and the islands." As a remedy, he proposed sending more qualified clergy "to reform the morals and soften the behaviour of men," since the current colonial churches were just a "drain for the very dregs and refuse of ours." Isaac Maddox, dean of Wells, who believed that the fabled colonial corruption sprang mostly from the luxury pursued by newly enriched elites, worried that the majority of emigrants, being of the lower sort and driven by economic urgency, would be trapped by this same mechanism of greed combined with upward social ambition. In a 1734 sermon he claimed that "the Generality of them . . . carry abroad a slender share of knowledge, which must soon be lost in their circumstances; where necessity closely engages so many in providing for their Subsistence, and the eager Desire speedily to raise a Fortune and return Home, engrosses the Thoughts of others."[17]

Lack of knowledge and education early became a part of the colonists' stereotype and endured as such throughout the eighteenth century. There was some objective ground for it since illiteracy in the plantation region remained high; as late as 1754 Governor Sharpe described the candidates for membership in Maryland's lower house as "the lowest of Persons" and "men of small fortunes no Soul & very mean Capacities." Many jurors, lay attorneys, even commissioners were illiterate, although few of them were poor. It was a fact that economic success enabled a number of uneducated ex-servants to obtain county offices that implied genteel status.[18] In addition, few cultural refinements were available; even in 1772, despite economic success, members of the Georgia gentry were complaining that they had "no Plays, Operas, or public Exhibitions, either in point of Literature or Amusements, to animadvert upon." Richard Waterhouse's study of Charleston has shown that the planter elite's priorities clearly involved accumulating wealth and living elegantly, but relatively little importance was attached to local institutions of learning or art; public theatrical performances were rare and took place in only eight out of the thirty-five years between 1735 and 1770.[19]

Planters' hostility to learning was a feature frequently stressed in British publications on mainland American and Caribbean colonies. A 1740 description of Jamaica claimed that in the colony "the Office of a Teacher is look't upon as contemptible, and no Gentleman keeps Company with one of that Character; to read, to write, and to cost up Accounts, is all the Education they desire, and even these are but scurvily taught." On the local gentry's estates, "a Man of any Parts of Learning that would employ himself in that Business would be despised and starve." Exceptions only confirmed the rule: "There are indeed here several Gentlemen that are well acquainted with Learning . . . but those are few; and the Generality seem to have a greater Affection for the modish Vice of Gaming than Belles Lettres, and love a Pack of Cards better than the Bible." The planter was portrayed as an anti-image of the gentleman proper, since "to talk of Homer, or a Virgil, of a Tully, or a Demosthenes, is quite unpolite." It was all attributed to the corrupting influence of plantation life; even when the wealthiest sent their sons to England to obtain a truly "polite generous Education," many "are spoil't and make such an inconsiderable Figure ever after, that they are the common Butt in every Conversation." "What knowledge from a winter's evening at Cards, or a long summer day's conversation about Cattle, horses and dogs?" wondered a British visitor in 1769 about the intellectual qualities of the Virginia gentry. Writing of North Carolina at the end of the colonial period, Charles Woodmason claimed that a teacher—not a very elevated occupation but nevertheless a genteel one—could not expect even a modicum of respect in this colony where "People despise Knowledge, and instead of honouring a learned Person, or any one of Wit or Knowledge, be it in the Arts, Sciences, or Languages, they despise and Ill treat them—And this Spirit prevails even among the Principals of this Province." A gentleman from Britain could only feel isolated there; "as for Society and Converse," he wrote, "I have not yet met with one literate, or travel'd Person—No Ingenious Mind—None of any Capacity."[20] Edward Kimber, in turn, pointed out that in Maryland freed servants who had some education were in great demand as teachers and for "keeping books for their illiterate Neighbours." As a result, a "clever Servant or a Convict that can read and write tolerably . . . is a tip-top Man in his Parts." He presented local gentlemen as equally lacking; in one of his novels there appears a family of "worthless Carters" who have a son that everyone knows "will be the richest man in the province, though a lad of bad principles, unlettered, and of coarse manners."[21]

Alcoholism, a specific vice commonly ascribed in British publications to the colonial planter gentry and encompassing other ungenteel attributes such as corruption, vulgarity, and lack of self-control, throws some light on the peculiar distorted-mirror effect taking place between colonial reality and metropolitan image. The foundations of the stereotype of plantation drunkenness were laid in the sugar islands of Barbados and Jamaica. As early as 1684 English moralist and humanitarian Thomas Tryon appealed to the "Gentlemen Planters" there to eradicate the ever-present habit of drinking. According to him, the "fountain of Reason" in their minds had long been obstructed by "your rum-pots, your Punch-bowls, your Brandy bottles, and the rest of your intoxicating Enchantments." He blamed the frequent diseases that decimated the colonies on the weakening of the inhabitants' bodies caused by the "frequent tipping of that Pernicious Drink called Punch."[22] In his two volumes of scientifically detailed observations on the life and character of these islands (1707–25), Sir Hans Sloane, secretary to the Royal Society and physician to the governor of Jamaica, the duke of Albemarle, included reflections on the gentlemen planters' heavy drinking as an inseparable part of the social ritual. Libations were integral to the local elite's entertainment, lasting for several hours after dinner. Although some brandy or Madeira were imported by the wealthiest Jamaicans, the staple drink was punch—rum mixed with water, fruit juices, sugar, and nutmeg.[23]

In the literature of this early period, drinking was already portrayed as inseparable from the American planter's way of life. In Aphra Behn's *Oroonoko*, it was a cultural canon in the English colony of Surinam that on Sundays "all whites were overtaken in drink." Satirical publications invariably made use of this colonial custom. One such work on Jamaica noted that what most struck a newcomer from England was that the planters were "for the most part . . . hard drinkers" who measured their time by the number of punch bowls, and that the most common of all patients requiring doctor's treatment was "a Gentleman, his stomach . . . always out of order, because of his excessive drinking, especially Brandy and Sugar by way of Dram." Another author ridiculed this custom with a heavy Renaissance humor: "They have this Pleasure in Drinking, that what they put into their Bellies they may soon stroak out of their fingers Ends; for instead of Exonerating, they Fart, and Sweat instead of Pissing." Ebenezer Cooke's references to punch are too numerous to list; he offered his readers an image of the Maryland gentry whose chief way of keeping themselves busy was by "replenishing their thirsty souls with Lemon Punch," and he declared that the provincial court was routinely "full of drunken Worships."[24]

This reputation continued well into the last decades of the colonial period, reinforced in no small part by reality. Henry Hulton, in 1756 appointed comptroller of the customs in St. John's, Antigua, found at least some polite gentlemen among the local elite but was unpleasantly struck by the rituals of drinking and the intense social pressure to participate in them. He recalled in his diary one such visit to the residence of the "Chief Justice, Col. Blizard," who "seldom went to bed sober" and whose "sense and spirit seemed to shine forth the more as he grew in liquour." After partaking in some "Punch of Arack" at his house, Hulton noted that "for hours of the next morning I was tortured with the most violent head and eye ache imaginable. I bound up my head and eyes and rolled upon the bed in agony. The Doctor put Plaister of opium to my temples, but the pain returned each day for three succeeding mornings."[25] Colonial literature corroborated this prominence of drink in the culture of the planter elites. Rum was one of the main characters of *The Candidates*, a play written about 1770 by Colonel Robert Munford of Mecklenburg County, Virginia, a gentleman planter and member of the House of Burgesses. Its protagonists begin drinking heavily as the play opens and gradually become more intoxicated until some lose consciousness. A telling reference to the reality behind such portrayals can be found in the play's depiction of one of the characters: "Drunk as ever Chief Justice Cornelius was upon the bench." This was an allusion to the proverbial alcoholism of Munford's contemporary Cornelius Carghill, a Lunenburg County magistrate.[26]

The colonial propensity to drink is substantiated by statistics. Annual alcohol consumption per capita was 3.5 gallons by 1770; in that same year 4 million gallons of rum were imported into the colonies, and another 5 million were distilled locally.[27] It is important to realize, however, that for the local gentry drinking had few of the corrupt characteristics so eagerly highlighted by writers in Britain. On the contrary, it played an unequivocally positive role as a lubricant at polite society's gatherings and as one of the not-so-numerous attractions of living on the cultural periphery. Planters drank regularly on election days, at militia musters, during court sessions, in taverns—which were centers of local life, where business transactions and political debates often took place—and in private drinking clubs for gentlemen such as the Tuesday Club of Annapolis. Imbibing itself was rarely criticized as most believed that alcohol was not only an enjoyable and relaxing diversion but also brought medical benefits.

A separate source of patronizing views of the provincials lay in British perceptions of the Indians. These opinions played very different roles for the colonists and for the elites in England. For the former, the Indian presence—much like the presence of slaves—served the construction of their identity through a process scholars have come to call "othering," that is, by means of negative contrasts with other culturally different groups. It had clear effects on the genteel aspirations of provincials.[28] Bernard W. Sheehan has demonstrated how the doctrine of savagism provided an ideological framework which allowed the colonists to place the Indians at the bottom rungs of staged development from barbarism to civility. The Indians' perceived lack of such attributes of civility as responsibility, gentle nature, refinement, elegance, and virtue—all considered as belonging in their most perfect form to the European gentleman—effectively helped to highlight colonial gentry's own qualities. Well before slaves could play this role, Indians replaced the European vulgar poor and rustic peasants as cultural antimodels of gentility, and by the late eighteenth century this view became commonplace. Kimber in 1744 saw Indians as people frozen in time, "much like the former uncultivated Inhabitants of Britain, whom Tacitus mentions," with "little in their common Behaviour above the Brute Creation." In the 1770s Woodmason considered Indians to be "in many Respects but one degree removed from Brute Creation" and asked: "Would we wish to see any of our own Complexion, Descendants of Freeborn Britons in such a State of Barbarism and Degeneracy?" A guide to good taste published in Philadelphia in 1790 asked readers "to reflect on the progress of human understanding—to compare the refinements of philosophy with a state of savage nature—a Newton with an inhabitant of New Holland—we should almost conclude some supernatural power must have contributed to give the former so infinite a superiority in the scale of beings."[29]

The problem with creating such a dichotomy was that it functioned not only in the colonies but in England as well, and observers there were often tempted to use the Indian as a metaphor for the cultural inferiority and corruption of the colonists. Such a use even surfaced in America; Cotton Mather seriously feared in 1696 that the English would "Indianize" and thus acquire "Indian Vices of Lying, and Idleness, and Sorcery, and a notorious want of all Family Discipline." When Byrd was reproaching the settlers of Carolina "Lubberland" for their sloth and laziness, he wrote that they were "just like the Indians."[30] In England, however, the edge of this metaphor was more often directed at all the colonists. Oldmixon, writing about the Anglican Church in Virginia, noted that "it were to be wish'd that Care was taken to supply them [parishes] with such Divines as might, by their Example as well as by their Preaching, invite People to a religious Life; the Indian Darkness being not more gloomy and horrid than what some of the meaner sort of Virginians live in." Bishop Berkeley also argued for an improvement in the quality of churches in British America, to help in "purging away the ill manners and irreligion in our colonies . . . where many English, instead of gaining converts, are themselves degenerated into Heathen." [31] In 1753 James MacSparran, referring to North Carolina, claimed that "upon a whole, this Province may still pass for a pretty wild and uncultivated Country, and excepting few of the better Sort, its white inhabitants have degenerated into a State of Ignorance and Barbarism not much superior to the native Indians." Kimber considered the backcountry settlers in Virginia and Maryland as "little more civiliz'd than the Indian Natives of those Regions."[32]

If we link such views to other negative labels, it becomes apparent why in eighteenth-century British pictorial images representing the colonies the Indian was one of the most frequent symbols of America. It underscored the cultural inferiority of British America by invoking the very same contrast between the savage and the civilized that in the New World was used to elevate the colonists. Such use culminated during the Revolution when the Indian became the single most common representation of all of British America in metropolitan political prints; it served to portray Americans as both alien and by nature subordinate to Britain. But even before the conflict with London, such labels offended not only the planter gentry's deeply held belief that it deserved the same respect as its British counterparts but also its concept —clearly discernible from Nathaniel Bacon to Thomas Jefferson—of its members as being vastly different as well as superior to Indians. To suggest that it was somehow alien was offensive to gentry in all regions of America, as evidenced by James Otis's angry remark that the American colonies "are well settled, not as the common people of England foolishly imagine, with a compound mongrel mixture of English, Indian and Negro, but with freeborn British white subjects." Such discontent with the Indianizing labels was evident when a print from the *Oxford Magazine* was altered to remove the figure of an Indian representing the colonies before it was published in 1775 in the *Royal American Magazine*. But in Britain, by this phase of the conflict, the image of America as a barbaric Indian, wielding a dagger or a tomahawk, scalping Loyalists, and engaged in an ungrateful war on Britain, had come to symbolize the colonial descent into anarchy and savagery.[33]

The message of provincial inferiority was conveyed by various other contemporary British graphic and artistic representations of the colonies. A patronizing attitude clearly emanates from a Derby porcelain figure made circa 1766 (now in the Victoria and Albert Museum) portraying the elegantly attired Lord Chatham looking down with the smile of a benevolent master at America, represented by a simply robed, dark-skinned woman kneeling before him. Another image—both pictorial and rhetorical—was that of America as a child of Britain. It was widely popular and was also used in the colonies. For instance, during the 1752 debate in the Virginia House of Burgesses on convict transportation, the argument was made that England would be a "a very U[n]natural Parent" if it insisted on the practice, contrary to "the interest of his Eldest Daughter." But in the late colonial period the image came to be widely utilized in Britain to indicate its patriarchal relationship to America and to underscore the colonists' immaturity. A letter from Loyalist Thomas Moffat to Ezra Stiles, written at the request of the marquis of Rockingham after the repeal of the Stamp Act, was full of parental phrases about the "conduct of the colonies," which had stubbornly "embarrassed" London even though it was "full of the tenderest and most benevolent sentiments toward America," and about England's hope for appropriate "future behaviour of the British American Colonies," especially that they would demonstrate a "dutiful Sense and Spirit of Gratitude" as well as "Submission."[34]

It was against this rhetorical practice that Thomas Paine railed so fervently in his *Common Sense* when he claimed that "the phrase parent and mother country hath been jesuitically adopted by the King and his parasites, with a . . . design of gaining an unfair bias on the credulous weakness of our minds." In British publications after 1775, the child became rebellious and ultimately parricidal, a savage behavior that coincided with the concept of the Indian. It is important not to imagine that these representations were born solely of Revolutionary disputes. They were a continuation of much earlier cultural stereotypes, now applied to current political ends. Lester Olson has concluded that "the single most salient use of the image representing the British colonies in America was to portray colonial culture as foreign and therefore inferior to British culture." A number of other contemporary images depicted the colonies as beasts of burden—barnyard or exotic animals, whose functions were primarily servile and utilitarian in relation to Britain.[35]

A Land of Exile and Penance

An early and ubiquitous perception of British America that gravely affected the planter's quest for gentility was that of a dumping ground for the poor and criminals. This view had a long tradition in British elite culture well before the rise of an established colonial gentry. Colonization as a form of poor relief was a concept already popular on the eve of British expansion into America. Population increase and economic displacement of people from rural areas had boosted the numbers of the unemployed and the homeless. Often labeled "masterless men," these people did not belong to any defined sphere of the social order, and their dismal existence was seen as predisposing them to undesirable activities. The Levellers were vocal proponents during the English Revolution of an equalitarian social order, separation of wealth from privilege, and care for the unemployed, but even such radicals did not acknowledge the poor and servants to be citizens and excluded them from the popular franchise because as a servile category, they were thought to depend too much upon the will and charity of other men.[36]

This class of people were regarded by the ruling elite as pariahs, a marginal group whose members could be forcibly impressed into the navy, sent overseas to the colonies, or put into workhouses. This contempt for the poor was a trait that did not substantially change during the whole period under discussion here. When Sir Edwin Sandys argued in 1620 for a hundred poor boys "from their superfluous multitude, to be transported to Virginia," so that "under severe masters . . . they may be brought to goodness," he was irritated when they proved reluctant to go and petitioned Secretary of State Robert Naunton for permission "to transport those children against their will." Almost exactly a century later, Hugh Jones was demanding new legal devices to force greater numbers of indentured servants to emigrate to Virginia. "There can be no Injury," he wrote, "in such moderate legal Compulsion as forces People to be honest and industrious, though it be contrary to their Inclinations or their false Notions, which ought to be subject to publick Good and Opinion of the Community."[37] The Protestant ethic reinforced such attitudes by offering a religious sanction for work and usefulness and making an idle man "a kind of Monster in the Creation," as one writer noted in 1744. Samuel Johnson claimed that money spent on almsgiving only supported the lazy, for "now that the poor can find maintenance for themselves, and their labour is wanted, a general undiscerning hospitality tends to ill, by withdrawing them from their work to idleness and drunkenness."[38] To sense the depth of such attitudes in elite culture we need only consider the serious demands made in the mid–eighteenth century for a formal enslavement of the poor as a class. Bishop Berkeley asked "whether other nations have not found great benefits from the use of slaves in repairing roads, making rivers navigable, draining bogs, erecting public buildings, bridges and manufactures," and therefore, "whether all sturdy beggars should not be seized and made slaves to the public." Enlightenment reformer Andrew Fletcher proposed that all 200,000 idle rogues in Scotland be made the slaves of free citizens. Francis Hutcheson, professor of philosophy at the University of Glasgow and author of an intricate system of moral philosophy linking aesthetic beauty and virtue, argued for a modern slavery as forced lifetime servitude for those who were a "publick burden." "No law could be more effectual," he claimed, "to promote a general industry, and restrain sloth and idleness in the lower conditions, than making perpetual slavery of this sort the ordinary punishment of such idle vagrants."[39]

As early as 1646 the famed reformer Samuel Hartlib appealed to Parliament to solve the problem of the poor and idle, arguing that "in case some will not be reformed, neither in work-houses nor houses of correction, . . . then the Magistrate may have to send such persons to sea that are fit, to the fishing trade or otherwise, or to the Plantations," in order "to rid the land of such Brambles, and this is better than to suffer them to live in mischeif, and hang them at last." The idea of deportation was already popular. The few opposing voices included Francis Bacon, who warned that it was "an unblessed thing to take the scum of the people with whom you plant: not only so but it spoileth the plantations," and John White, who thought it to be a gross error if colonies were made "sinckes for States to drayne away their filth." By the end of the century, Sir Josiah Child expressed a popular opinion among the ruling classes when he not only strongly supported deportation but added to the list of desirable emigrants the "Malcontents in the State," with their subversive potential to disrupt the "body politick." Against this backdrop a connection was being made in the public mind between these "lower conditions" and distant America as a place suitable for such social elements. One class of undesirables, not the most numerous but receiving much publicity, and therefore influencing this image of America, were convicts. King James I had recommended deportation to America as a form of pardon in exchange for death sentences, but it was only in 1717 that an act of Parliament made transportation itself a new form of legal punishment. Intended as humanitarian, there is little doubt that this particular function assigned to the colonies involved the principle of fearful punishment, intended primarily to deter crime.[40]

It cannot be stressed enough that this assumption persisted in England until the American Revolution. In 1773 London police magistrate Sir John Fielding still argued that transporting convicts to America was "the wisest, because the most humane and effectual, punishment we have": it "immediately removes the evil, separates the individual from his abandoned connexions, and gives him a fresh opportunity of being an useful member of society." That it was indeed a frightening penalty may be seen from his observation that he had "heard several criminals declare that they had rather be hanged than transported a second time; and from the accounts they have given of their sufferings, he believed them."[41] In short, from the early eighteenth century, if not earlier, the American location itself was often seen in England as a place of penance and exile by virtue of its dreadful hardships and its remoteness—much as Australia was to become in the following century. The colonies probably owed some part of their negative image to the much older Black Legend of Spanish cruelty, familiar to many Englishmen since late sixteenth century, a view of America that blended notions of native barbarism and cultural degeneration of Europeans. When in 1709 one author in England was attacking immigrants from the Palatinate, he proposed sending them instead to faraway and ungodly places such as America:

> Let these good pious Palat'nates,
> And all such strange we know not-whats,
> In their wise interloping Freak,
> Go to the Devil's Arse a-peak,
> Or to the Plantations farther hasten,
> Not here their Standards fix nor fasten.[42]

By the mid–eighteenth century such terms as *America*, *Virginia*, and *Maryland*, now household words for Englishmen, had a familiar ring. The English literate public would now fairly often come across references to those "unhappily trapanned" to Maryland, "transported to the plantations," or "kept for Virginia" in prisons by court decision.[43] Departures from local prisons of convict groups destined for the colonies often became public events as curious crowds gathered in port cities to witness the processions of chained felons marching toward their ships. Nationwide collections provided another form of publicity. One author noted that in support of the philanthropic venture in Georgia, "collections were made all over England and large Sums raised, and the Parliament gave 10,000 l. which enabled the Trustees to entertain many poor People that offered, and to make Provision for their Transportation and Maintenance till they could provide for themselves."[44] The dumping ground image was also inadvertently popularized by promoters of colonization who, when lobbying for financial support, routinely listed convict transportation among the blessings of having foreign plantations.

In the Chesapeake region, the destination for the majority of deportees, the local gentry consistently voiced strong protests against the practice. Acts of Virginia (1722) and Maryland (1723) assemblies aimed at restricting the flow were repealed by the Privy Council, but the protracted conflict with England over this issue, begun in 1670, continued into the 1770s. In 1670 the Virginia assembly complained that "the Council and other gent. inhabitants" feared that "the peace of this colony is too much hazarded and endangered by the great numbers of felons and other desperate villaines sent hither from several prisons in England," and in 1752 members of the House of Burgesses were still protesting "the great propensity to Villainy" among the felons arriving in Virginia and demanded that London curb the influx. The American observers were worried about the very same problem that metropolitans attempted to eliminate by transportation: a subversion of social order and standards. One wrote that "it were to be wished that a Period were put even to the Transportation of Convicts from England and Ireland to Virginia and Maryland. Though some of those Felons do reform, yet they are so few, that their Malversation has a bad Effect upon the Morals of the lower class of inhabitants."[45]

But a deeper reason for such reactions—closely linked to the aspirations of the colonial elites to cultural legitimacy—was that the honor of the planter-gentlemen was at stake. They were well aware that accepting jailbirds seriously undermined their reputation in England. How else could one react to reading in English publications that the colonists were "the Sweepings of the streets of London and other Populous Places," that they were in the majority "necessarily rude and illiterate, irreligious and prophane," and that the principal reason for their presence in America was that it "eases England for that time of some useless Hands, which doubtless are a dead Weight upon every Country."[46] Almost all protests in the Chesapeake area came from the gentry, while the medium and small planters were more inclined to accept the supply of needed servants. No one, after all, was compelled to buy convicts as servants; for those numerous colonists of lesser status who were willing to do so, the problem of reputation was clearly secondary to the need for labor. By contrast, for the elite already lamenting the primitive and provincial environment and aspiring to a more genteel and improved one, convicts degraded colonial society and added to the embarrassment by feeding the derogatory British opinions of the colonists' plebeian and corrupt nature. Even tracts promoting the colonies in 1720s casually referred to "that Immorality charged on the inhabitants" and tried to explain it away by suggesting that there was "no just reason in it to distinguish them more than is too common in the streets of London and English sea-ports." It is no wonder that members of the planter gentry so often interpreted the practice of deportation in the language of honor, portraying it as a form of disrespect

The Curse of Provincialism

for their dignity and status. The *Virginia Gazette* asked rhetorically in 1751 "in what can Britain show a more Sovereign contempt for us than by emptying their jails into our settlements."[47]

The immensely popular novels of Defoe inadvertently helped to cultivate in the imagination of the English high society the stereotype of America as a land of exile for undesirables. In them he successfully propagated an image of the plantation colonies as havens of opportunity and moral reformation for lawbreakers. The heroine of his 1722 novel, Moll Flanders, a prostitute and a pickpocket, was transported together with her highwayman ex-husband to a Virginia plantation; ultimately they both became wealthy landowners. To the polite reader Virginia appeared as a refuge for the outcasts of society; consequently, even if some successfully achieved the rank of gentry by colonial standards, they remained upstarts by British criteria. To the nonelite reader the colony appeared—as was Defoe's intention—as a land of opportunity, even for those at the bottom of the social ladder. When in the grand finale of the book Moll returned to her former husband, she found him "as sincere a Penitent, and as thoroughly reform'd Man, as ever God's goodness brought back from a profligate, a Highway-Man, and a Robber." But there could be no true success without upward social advancement, so Moll took "special care" to buy him a whole arsenal of objects that symbolized high rank: "two good long Wigs, two silver hilted swords, three or four fine Fowling peices, a fine Saddle with Holsters, and Pistols very handsome, with a Scarlet Cloak . . . to make him appear as he really was, a very fine gentleman." When Defoe wrote that in America "many a Newgate-bird becomes a great man," he conveyed a message of hope for ambitious British commoners. But for the London elite engaged in a contest with the new gentry—of which Defoe himself became something of a symbol—such statements were just another admission of the parvenu nature of colonial elites. Such a view was inadvertently confirmed by Defoe when he had another character in the novel explain that when convicts arrived in Virginia, "we make no difference, the Planters buy them, and they work together in the Field till their Time is out; when 'tis expir'd . . . they have encouragement given them to Plant for themselves." And pointing to the notorious Newgate prison in London, she conceded that "'tis that cursed Place . . . that half Peoples this Colony."[48]

Thus, the image of America as a land of banishment not only had a very pronounced class dimension but also played an active role in the eighteenth-century struggles for the definition of gentility and virtue. While Defoe delighted in the fact that work and education could raise even someone released from London's prisons to wealth and rank, a refined member of the literary elite like Samuel Johnson could only smile at the "fine" quality of the highwayman turned Virginia planter and at Moll's confidence that wigs and cloaks make a gentleman. In fact, Johnson did more than smile. He consistently advanced the view of his class that the American colonists were not merely inferior but contemptible, and that their country epitomized primitiveness. Asked at a dinner at Lord Monboddo's what he thought about emigration to the colonies, he explained that "to a man of mere animal life, you can urge no argument against going to America, but that it will be some time before he will get the earth to produce. But a man of any intellectual enjoyment will not easily go and immerse himself and his posterity for ages in barbarism." Elsewhere, he claimed the colonists were simply "a race of convicts, and ought to be thankful for anything we allow them short of hanging." Reacting to church problems in Scotland, he wrote to William Drummond that not to advance Christianity "is a Crime of which I know not that the world yet has had an example, except in the practice of the planters of America, a race of mortals whom, I suppose, no other man wishes to resemble."[49] This view well summed up the position of polite society at the time. In Johnson's mind, the image of American colonies as a dumping ground was well aligned with generalizations about the low social rank and vulgar quality of their inhabitants.

Aggrandized Upstarts

In England in the 1720s Defoe was censured for his genteel aspirations. The colonial planter elite received much the same treatment even though it did not openly question the dominant definition of gentility and even zealously attempted to fulfill it. While for the Defoeans charges of being upstarts to gentility were a part of their struggle for influence and status in England, the same charges leveled at the colonials constituted only a segment of the larger syndrome of provincialism with which Americans had to grapple, a syndrome that also involved an awareness of rusticity and the disconcerting distance from the style-setting cultural centers of the metropolis.

At the core of the criticism directed at the colonists by the polite metropolitan society lay the belief that material riches—not backed by a long family lineage and traditions of education, refinement, and taste—were the Americans' sole and therefore invalid claim to gentry rank. Consequently, among the most common labels pinned on colonial gentry was that of ostentation, an attribute that combined a lack of moderation with bad taste. The colonial nouveau riche, eager to display his opulence, was regularly depicted as unable to meet the requirements of a true gentleman, who, as a popular courtesy books put it in 1723, was expected to be "neat without Gaudiness, Genteel without Affectation." Although "fine Feathers make fine Birds, yet surely gawdy Trappings can't make a fine Gentleman; for the Embellishment of Quality are Wit, Judgement and Behaviour; an Air that is noble without Haughtiness."[50] One of the best definitions of the colonial parvenu stereotype came from Hamilton, who considered himself a genteel Scotsman in the colonies rather than a colonist from Scotland. He censured the new colonial pretenders to refinement for what he considered their arrogance and lack of respect for true quality. In 1744, closely echoing the views of the colonists' many critics in Britain, he defined their provincialism as including three main elements: "narrow notions, ignorance of the world, and low extraction, which indeed is the case with most aggrandized upstarts in these infant countrys of America who never had an opportunity to see, or if they had, the capacity to observe the different ranks of men in polite nations or to know what it is that really constitutes the difference of degrees." Here, in a reflection of the tensions in Britain between old gentility and new wealth, was a clinical case of how the possession and control of the subtleties of legitimate high style presupposed or precluded membership in the upper "degrees" of society.[51]

The foundations of the reputation of slaveholding planters as simpletons who accumulated riches in America and assumed high-flown styles were laid mostly in the Caribbean colonies. As early as 1655 Henry Whistler's description of Barbados told the English reader that the "island is the dunghill whereon England doth cast forth its rubbish. Rogues and whores and such like people are those which are generally brought here." But instantaneous wealth made possible by profitable staple exports made these people from the streets of London into gentlefolk: "A bawd brought over puts on a demure compartment, a whore, if handsome, makes a wife for some rich planter."

According to another author, in the colonies all respectable ranks and professions were feigned to provide the impostors with status: "A broken Apothecary will make there a topping Physician, a Barber's Prentice a good Surgeon, a Bailiff's Follower a passable lawyer." But the strongest condemnation was reserved for ostentation, something one English writer in 1695 branded as the "Extravagant Excesses" of the members of the planter gentry. He described their lifestyle as extreme by any comparison, noting that "perhaps no People in the World have been more remarkable for a Luxuriant way of Living."52

Not only was the new wealth of the planters culturally suspect, but some British observers questioned its soundness in light of a financing system by which the exporter in America was credited and supplied with goods from Britain without the use of currency. The planter whose wealth was slaves and whose money was tobacco was seen at times as a strangely exotic pretender to gentility. A 1699 English tract mentioned an American "eminent planter" as a ridiculous case of "rich men without money." This colonist "had lived there for fifty years and never seen in the whole Term, Ten Pounds in Silver, and yet was Rated at a Thousand Pounds." But what to the same author seemed even more preposterous was the use made of this wealth. Colonial upstarts betrayed their hopelessly plebeian taste by ostentatiously spending their fortunes to impress the world. They built "stately Edifices, some of which have cost the owners two or three thousand Pounds in the raising, which, I think, plainly proves two old Adages true, viz. that a fool and his money are soon parted; and set a Beggar on Horse-back and he will ride to the Devil, for the fathers of those men were Tinkers and Peddlers." The conclusion was obvious: artless members of the "gentry" in the American provinces were more commercial-minded than genteel; they were men who "regard nothing but Money and value not how they get it; there being no other Felicity to be enjoy'd but purely Riches."53

By the early eighteenth century, such themes were established in English high culture and found diverse expressions in belles lettres. Thomas Southerne's play *Oronooko* was particularly popular with the London public and remained in the repertoire for a considerable time after it was first staged in Theatre-Royal in London in 1694. In it the character of the wealthy Captain Driver, a colonial trader, was depicted as a typically provincial simpleton who had made a fortune in business but could not disguise his plebeian

The Curse of Provincialism

origins, an "Upstart to Prosperity, one that is but just come acquainted with Cleanliness." Colonial planters in the play, who also "made their fortunes this way," praised the captain as a person "fit to be employed in Publick Affairs" because the colonies, as it was explained, could only thrive with such people.[54]

A truly comprehensive spectrum of the upstart qualities ascribed by the London literary elite to American planters was to be found in Aphra Behn's *The Widdow Ranter*, a play entirely set in Virginia, with Bacon's Rebellion as the main historical backdrop. Although its purpose was satirical (in itself a form of impressing certain images on British imagination), this play is notable for its comprehensive list of characteristics routinely assigned to colonial gentry in contemporary metropolitan writing. The vignettes of various members of the colonial gentry portray their practice of buying into wealth by marriage, their illiteracy, low social origins, pretensions to refinement, excessive drinking, and egregious lack of proper manners. The widow-heroine is depicted as presently belonging to "the country gentry," but we are told that her husband—who had died leaving her with a fortune that now made her an attractive candidate for marriage—bought her from a ship as a servant. This was to explain why she "retains some of her primitive quality still." It is noteworthy that the widow is portrayed as typical of the colony's upper class, for all the gentry was nouveau riche, descended from the lowest stratum of society, with criminal records rather than coats of arms as its heritage. London theatergoers learned that Virginia was "ruled by a Council, some of which have been perhaps transported Criminals, who having acquired great Estates, are now become your Honour, the Right Worshipful, and possess all Places of Authority." One character, Mrs. Flirt, claimed her father was a "barronet," but we soon learn he really was a "Taylor" who was broke "and so came thither to hide his head." Another figure, Parson Dunce, was now "a fine Gentleman, and makes the prettiest sonnets," but "they say he was a Farrier in England . . . and counterfeited a Deputation from the Bishop." Mr. Timorous, the local judge, who was illiterate and had to have lawbooks read to him, "was but a broken Excise-man who spent the King's money to buy his Wife fine Petticoats." Not surprisingly, for these gentlemen honor had been replaced by drinking punch and smoking tobacco, the two main activities that served locally as elements of "good breeding." The colonial court's only genuine concern was the size of the punch bowls; needless to say, the judges—in concert with the popular image of colonials—were continuously inebriated. At the same time the play's Virginia elite, driven by a greed for wealth and power, was untiring in its aspirations to gentility. Obsessed with signs of rank, its members constantly paraded their titles and were inordinately sensitive to anything "affronting their Dignity," an allusion that could not have been lost on the audience, well aware that commoners could not claim dignity and honor.[55] This text is significant for my argument because it nearly exhausts the catalog of negatives that London attributed in the following seven decades to wealthy colonial planters.

By the mid–eighteenth century these arriviste labels retained their essential substance—implying illegitimate cultural ambitions—but grew more subtly patronizing, more refined and ironical in their condescension, pointing more often to the lack of taste than the lack of birth and to the lack of virtue than to mere primitiveness. Perhaps one of the sharpest commentaries at the time came from James Reid, Edinburgh-educated visitor to tidewater Virginia and author of a rather bitter satire on the planter gentry of King William County in 1769. He applied what was explicitly an outsider's perspective to his firsthand observations of local society; as a result, his text was nearly obsessed with the parvenu character of the colony's ruling class. In Virginia, he claimed, "one may be a gentleman without having any Virtue at all." If one has "Money, Negroes and Land enough he is a compleat Gentleman. . . . Learning and good sense; religion and refined Morals; charity and benevolence have nothing to do in the composition." He referred to the still culturally new but economically established gentry, whose status could now pass from father to son, "the son being made a Gentleman by the Negroes and land given him by his father, who perhaps sprung from a race of Ignoramuses, and who still continues one himself." The effect was a breathtaking arrogance of both old and young. "This son, full of his own merit, and elevated with the figure he cuts in the world, and with his own importance, immediately assumes the swaggering air and looks big." There was no requirement of real honor among the local gentry, for "there are many men here who have crackt their honour times innumerable, and yet are accounted honourable." To qualify as genteel in the colony it was enough for a young man to have dogs and horses, to learn to "dance a minuet," to procure "a competent skill in racing and cock-fighting," and to play cards. "With these accomplishments . . . he becomes a gentleman of finished education, of consummate politeness, that is, impudence and arrogance."[56] Another contemporary visitor to Virginia found the display of wealth and living above one's means the most striking feature of local culture; he listed among the general attributes of the colony's gentry "extravagance, ostentation, and a disregard of oeconomy." External signs of refinement were of such importance that they even outweighed rational economic calculation; "it is not extraordinary . . . that the Virginians out-run their incomes; and that having involved themselves in difficulties, they are frequently tempted to raise money by bills of exchange, which they know will be returned protested, with 10 per cent interest."[57]

The parvenu character of the American gentleman was, of course, not a label assigned exclusively to those in the plantation region. Edmund Burke, in his relatively objective 1759 *Account of European Settlement in America*, saw an early and particularly outrageous example of such unseemly social rise in the person of William Phips, the first royal governor of Massachusetts. Phips, rightfully hailed as a very American prototype of the self-made man and an example of a rise from rags to riches, was for Burke a classic case of an usurper of gentility, a "man of the lowest birth and yet meaner education, who having raised a sudden fortune by lucky accident, was knighted and afterwards made governor of this province."[58] Oldmixon, too, portrayed Phips as a bumbling and unmannered provincial and ridiculed colonial authors who "have a Conceit, that the Country is much honoured by the Character of that Knight." It is not surprising that as late as 1786 the patriotic American authors of *The Anarchiad* blasted both "the envious Burke," with armorial "stars, ribbands, mantles, crowding on his brain," and European intellectuals, such as Raynal and Mably, for the "inflated pride" which in their writings made the "huge Mammoth" of America "dwindle to a mouse's size." As for Burke, in his treatment of the plantation elite he was a little more lenient than he was toward Phips; he acknowledged that a gentility of sorts had taken root among its members but saw it as still contaminated by parvenu style. Writing of the Virginians, he found "many of them genteel though somewhat vain and ostentatious people."[59]

It is important to note that those elements of the planter gentry stereotype which implied vulgarity and ostentation remained alive and well in English writing at the end of the colonial period, so that the Revolutionary generation of leaders still faced such views as a cultural obstacle to being listened to in Britain. When Edward Kimber wrote his novel *History of the Life and Adventures of Mr. Anderson* (1782), the figure of Barlow, a wealthy American planter, was a well-conventionalized stock character, representing only the typical ingredients of the popular image expected by readers. The colonist, "lord of many thousand acres and of several hundred slaves" was "haughty in his riches," addicted to "hard drinking," routinely practiced "defraud in traffic," and whipped servants brutally with "a cowskin." Despite his wealth, suitable for any gentleman, Barlow was not only arrogant but possessed a simple, uneducated mind; he "has little notion of the necessity of knowledge himself, as he could but just write his name mechanically." Kimber's contemporary, philanthropist and clergyman James Ramsay, who had spent some time in the sugar islands, offered in 1784 a very similar portrait of the West Indian slaveholder: "An English planter, if out of debt, must run away to England, which he calls his home, where generally lost to every useful purpose in life, he vies with the nobility in extravagance, and expence, while his attorney, and manager, are obliged to overwork, and pinch, his poor slaves, to keep up, or increase the usual remittances."[60]

Considering the highly cosmopolitan nature of gentility, unfavorable pronouncements by prominent aristocratic European authors about American endeavors to achieve it carried considerable weight among British upper classes, especially in the decades immediately before and after the Revolution. For instance, in 1794 Talleyrand found American materialism and lack of refinement appalling; a few years later the duc de La Rochefoucauld-Liancourt linked material greed to what he saw as the harshness of the American character. The memoirs of Chastellux, which had several editions in England, conveyed the same message, but with less open contempt for the upstart and a politer form of condescension toward provincials. Like many British authors, whenever he encountered good taste and refinement he justified their presence by pointing to some current European influence in the locality. Writing of Charleston, South Carolina, he conceded that "the manners there are polished and easy" and that "the inhabitants love pleasure, the arts, and society," but he attributed it to the fact that the city was a seaport "where foreigners have abounded, as at Marseilles and Amsterdam." His observations of gentry lifestyles would have satisfied Shaftesbury's criteria of high taste. He routinely noted that the charm of colonial ladies and gentlemen was rustic and provincial. On visiting Offley House, the Nelson family

The Curse of Provincialism

plantation in Hanover County, Virginia, he acknowledged the great hospitality but noted that the house was "neither convenient nor spacious," that everyone was crowded in the "parlour" all day, and that the lighter amusements were lacking, for " music, drawing, reading aloud, and fancy work by the ladies are resources unknown in America." When young Miss Taliaferro sang a few Italian airs, he observed that "her charming voice and the artless simplicity of her singing were her substitute for cultivated taste," although he did find some allure in "that shy, natural taste." Her mother was surprisingly "lively, active, and intelligent," but in this she bore "little resemblance to her countrywomen." On visiting the plantation of Mary Bolling, widow of Robert Bolling, he listened to her daughter play some music and concluded that she "touched her guitar and sang like a person unskilled in music, but with a charming voice." He did find some "spacious and well-ornamented" houses, but he detected an air of provinciality about them, discernible in a certain parvenu ostentatiousness, an excessive urge to acquire "furniture, linen, and silver plate." He was truly impressed by the good taste of Jefferson's first version of Monticello but saw it as an exception on the American scene. Because the house was "constructed in Italian style," he thought it "quite tasteful, although not however without some faults," and noted that it resembled "none of the others seen in this country." He could thus declare that "Mr. Jefferson is the first American who has consulted the Fine Arts to know how he should shelter himself from the weather."[61]

Reactions to Provincialism

The planters primarily responded to metropolitan castigation with an increased determination to attain at least some of the traits of genteel style and virtue. Nevertheless, colonial authors—especially from the early eighteenth century—repeatedly attempted to repudiate the negative images proliferating in Britain. The language of Hugh Jones's 1724 description of Virginia leaves little doubt that he was responding to such views; he complained about the English having "despicable Notions of Virginia" as crude and rustic and maintained that "few People in England (even of those concerned in publick Affairs of this kind) have correct Notions of the true state of Plantations." His denial took the form of an idealized picture of the colonists, whose lifestyle and culture "are much the same as about London, which they esteem their Home," who "talk good English without Idiom or Tone, and can discourse handsomely upon most common Subjects," and who "wear the best of Cloaths according to their Station" and show "good Manners and Address." As to the elite, "they live in the same neat manner, dress after the same modes, and behave themselves exactly as the gentry in London." To vindicate the "better sort," Jones emphasized his contempt for commoners by blaming them for the derogatory stereotype of all colonists: "The Servants and inferior Sort of People, who have either been sent over to Virginia, or have transported themselves thither, have been and are the poorest, idlest, and worst of Mankind, the Refuse of Great Britain and Ireland, and the Outcast of the People."[62]

Ebenezer Cooke, writing at the same time, also pointed to the gap between Virginia gentlemen and commoners. In his poem on Bacon's Rebellion, Bacon is portrayed as the leader of "headstrong Rabble," "a Man respected by the Mob," "elected by the Rabble to serve as Burgess, and leading "a factious, stubborn Crew, as e'er o'er the Seas for Refuge flew, of Servants, Slaves, and Overseers." Governor Berkeley's group, in contrast, stood for "Persons of the best Condition."[63] Robert Beverley acknowledged the impact of negative opinions of Virginia, complaining that what "makes this Country most unfortunate, is, that it must submit to receive its Character from the Mouths of not only of unfit, but very unequal Judges; For all its Reproaches happen in this manner." The colony was "abus'd" in such a way because the charges against it came mostly from Englishmen who were merely passing through and so could not learn its true character. John Lawson, surveyor general of North Carolina, presented its elite to the English reader in a similarly validating tone: "The Gentlemen seated in the County are very courteous, live very nobly in their Houses and give very genteel Entertainment to all Strangers and others that come to visit them." All these reactions countered criticism by accentuating the existence in the colonies of a true gentry, as defined by metropolitan yardsticks. It is evident that Britain's approval was critically important. Jack P. Greene has drawn attention to the colonists' acute sensitivity to slighting, wholesale labels pinned on them. Using the case of Barbados, he pointed to the immense colonial significance of metropolitan approval; it was perhaps "no less important than sugar, slavery, or the island's extensive wealth and population." It is also clear that much of the British literature promoting colonization—although motivated by disparate goals—was written to combat the flood of negatives about America in British publications.[64]

This criticism hurt. At times, reactions reached a boiling point and ended in bitter exchanges, as in the case of Robert Carter's passionate outburst in 1720 at William Dawkins, his merchant partner in England, who had alluded to Carter's provincial writing style. The Virginian was one of the most prominent planters in the colony, sometime member of the House of Burgesses and Council of State, commander-in-chief of militia in Lancaster and Northumberland counties, and rector of the College of William and Mary. Responding to Dawkins, who was overseeing the studies of two of Carter's children in England, Carter attacked the merchant as "a gentleman of such a tender, touchy, elevated nature that cannot endure a plain style" and informed him that he had given orders "to remove them to another person, who will treat me and them with more civility." The cause of this eruption was Dawkins's remark on the colonist's use of the ungenteel word *muckworm*. Deeply stung by such condescension, Carter accused the Londoner of "looking at me as one of your dependents and inferiors." Lecturing Dawkins on the proper meanings of the word in question ("if you want the skill to measure the force of words you should keep a dictionary"), Carter suggested that being more down to earth "would not puff us up with so much vanity and insolence, nor make us so uneasy with plain dealing." He left no doubt that he felt fully deserving of the respect due a gentleman, and that he resented any hint that he had displayed provincialism. "Where was your prudence, or rather manners, to use me with the language that was hardly fit for your footman, if you keep one? You might remember I was your Master's equal and all along have lived in as good a fashion as he did," which "gives me a title to your deference." In another letter, written the same day to Thomas Evans, he blasted Dawkins again for being "so overgrown with conceit of his greatness that I cannot bear it." Ambitious and educated provincials became very self-conscious about language because it was an important tool enabling them to participate in metropolitan culture; even nuances were important since they involved control over the symbols of refinement.[65]

Charges of rusticity were painful not only because colonials felt there was some substance to them, but because this awareness negated their efforts at refinement by English standards. The remarkably enduring power of such standards was acknowledged as late as 1766 by Benjamin Franklin, who publicly confirmed that for the colonists of British America, England remained the principal source of cultural authority and prestige. The colonists, he said, "had not only a respect, but an affection, for Great Britain, for its laws, its customs, and manners, and even a fondness for its fashions, that greatly increased commerce. Natives of Britain were always treated with particular regard; to be an Old England-man, was, of itself, a character of some respect, and gave a kind of rank among us."[66]

Throughout the eighteenth century the colonial elites were acutely aware of the rusticity around them and of its potentially negative impact on their honor and self-identity. While in England the old opposition between rusticity and gentility was rapidly being replaced by an opposition between the genteel and the commercial ethoses, in the rural environment of plantation America it lingered on longer. Images like that of rustic Maryland planters eating in wooden dishes "Homine and Syder-pap, which scarce a hungry dog would lap," popularized in England by Ebenezer Cooke, were to remain a staple of unfavorable comparisons between the colonies and metropolis.[67] Eliza Lucas Pinckney, a cosmopolitan woman with an English education, was untiring in her efforts to keep up her genteel spirits and intellect by correspondence and various creative projects around her South Carolina estate, but her letters show a pervasive sense of provincialism. In 1742, on returning to her plantation after a busy and enjoyable time in Charleston, she praised country life because it "used so agreeably to sooth my (for some time past) pensive humour, and made me indifferent to every thing the gay world could boast," but she feared that such a "love of solitude" would cause her to be excluded from genteel circles where the standard was that "every body that is always grave is religiously mad." There was a distinct note of resignation as she wrote of her life on the plantation as "solatary retirement." Twenty years later her yearning for the genteel life of England was no less intense. Writing to her friend the poet George Keate, she remarked that he and his friends "that live in the great world in the midst of Scenes of entertainment and pleasure abroad, of improving studies and polite amusement at home, must be very good to think of your friends in this remote Corner of the Globe." She mused how she, "an old woman in the Wilds of America," would have liked to "take you off an hour some times from attending Matine[e] and the other gay scenes you frequent," only to conclude sadly: "How different is the life we live here." William Byrd was equally melancholy in 1736, noting that he felt so isolated from the world on his Virginia plantation that when ships arrived, he would "tear open the letters they bring us from our freinds, as eagerly as a greedy heir tears open a rich fathers will."[68]

The reverse side of the coin has often presented an idealized picture of provincial life. One way of at least partially alleviating the burden of rusticity was to describe plantation existence with pastoral rhetoric, turning the provincial into the bucolic and the distance from the refinement of Europe into an unspoiled environment where noble virtue could flourish. Facilitated by the gentry's usually good knowledge of the classics, the notion of the pastoral simplicity of landed life as a noble virtue—perhaps best known from Virgil's *Georgics*—was being applied to plantation reality long before it became part of the Revolutionary controversy over vain courtly (British) elegance versus virtuous republican (American) simplicity. The landed ideal, at least in its Horatian model, assumed both enjoying life's pleasures and striving for moderation—without the corruption of the cities and courts. Since only virtue made such moderation possible, provincial simplicity could be portrayed as a validation of gentility.

Such a pastoral message certainly was meant when Landon Carter named his residence Sabine Hall, after Horace's own country retreat near Rome. Landon's father, first-generation great Virginian planter King Carter, had already seen himself as an independent country gentleman, removed from the immorality of town and court; he spoke with derision of Sir John Randolph, agent for the colony in England, as a "parasite" and "a servile courtier." He liked to stress the desirable simplicity of the landed ideal and praised its "ornaments" such as "humility, prudence, affability, piety, charity."[69] Hamilton, too, contrasted the vanity of courts with a noble simplicity sanctioned by the ancients; ostentation and pageantry were there only to "strike an awe and Reverence into the vulgar," while the wise should listen to virtues "preached from the mouth of a plain unornamented Solomon, Solon or Lycurgus."[70] Robert Beverley, one of the wealthiest planters in early eighteenth-century Virginia, was among the first to attempt to redefine rusticity from a provincial weakness into an American virtue. He did so by assuming the idyllic, original simplicity of the Indians in Virginia, an example of plain, pastoral harmony with nature, in contrast to European formality and corruption. In the preface of his book, he asked the reader "not to Criticize too unmercifully upon my Stile," for "I am an Indian, and don't pretend to be exact in my language; But I hope the Plainness of my Dress, will give him the kinder Impressions of my Honesty, which is what I pretend to. Truth . . . depends upon its own intrinsick Value, and, like Beauty, is rather conceal'd, than set off, by Ornaments."[71]

The fact that espousing pastoralism was more of a necessity than a choice did not diminish its legitimizing value. Byrd, writing to a friend in England, was well aware that "we that are banished from these polite pleasures are forced to take up with rural entertainments. A library, a garden, a grove, and a purling stream are the innocent scenes that divert our leisure."[72] In this role, pastoralism carried a wide appeal across all British plantation colonies. For instance, the mid-eighteenth-century Barbados gentry, so often the butt of English ridicule as provincial, began to present that island as a rural but peaceful and genteel Arcadia, as opposed to what seemed an increasingly corrupt metropolis. James Grainger, a slaveholder and physician in St. Christopher (St. Kitts) in the British West Indies, portrayed the plantation as a peaceful little kingdom, complete with happy slaves:

> While flame the chimneys, while thy coppers foam,
> How blithe, how jocund, the plantation smiles!
> By day, by night, resounds the choral song
> Of glad barbarity; serene, the sun
> Shines not intensely hot; the trade-wind blows.

But, like Byrd, he was candid about his awareness of provinciality:

> Yet, 'mid this blest ebriety, some tears
> For friends I left in Albion's distant isle.
> How would your converse polish my rude lays,
> With what new, noble images adorn?[73]

If pastoralism was a stylistic reaction to the cultural distance from Britain, a more practical one was to create little islands of gentility in the wilderness by escaping into the closed circles of elite membership in clubs and associations. An early form involved business meetings among planters. In 1728 Colonel Henry Darnall, an advocate of "settling a correspondency" between the Chesapeake planters and the English merchants to better organize the tobacco trade, acknowledged that a permanent network of such meetings was well established in Maryland. "I know not how it is in Virginia, but in Maryland I am told there are settled clubs in every county, where they talk over Affairs. With those clubs, I think it would be our mutual Interest to communicate Councils."[74] This sort of activity took on a more sophisticated form in 1745 when Hamilton founded the Tuesday Club in Annapolis. When he first arrived in town in the winter of 1738 from cosmopolitan Edinburgh, he was appalled at its provinciality, calling it a "barbarous and desolate corner of the world." The only cultural attractions were horse racing, dancing parties, and drinking at taverns. It had no universities, libraries, theaters, or literary life. Cooke had earlier called it "a City situate on a Plain, where scarce a House will keep out Rain," and Andrew Burnaby in 1759 noted that "none of the streets are paved, and a few public buildings here are not worth mentioning."[75] The club functioned as an antidote, providing an oasis of intellectual life, literary culture, and sophisticated entertainment in the form of mock trials, witty speeches, musical performances, verses, jokes, and "delicate puns." It operated successfully for eleven years, attracting such prominent gentlemen of the Chesapeake area as author Thomas Bacon, Judge John Beale Bordley, and Jonas Green, publisher of the *Maryland Gazette*. It was this role that inspired the founding of other similar societies, such as the South Carolinian Library Society, St. Andrew's Society, and St. Cecelia Society for fine music.[76]

Another refuge into closed, elite membership was available from the 1730s in the Masonic lodges. Participation in this English fraternity was an immense attraction because of the valuable cultural link it provided with the metropolis; American lodges were offsprings of the British ones (most worked under English constitutions) and remained linked to them until they became Americanized by the Revolution.[77] For the provincial gentry Masonry provided membership in a great, intellectually unified body that transcended frontiers. Its universal dimension enabled the colonists to see themselves as both a part of the British intellectual scene and a branch of the British elite. Above all, it made possible a formalized participation in a hierarchical order of members who perceived themselves as an aristocracy of merit. For Masons such as Dr. Hamilton, Washington, Madison, Franklin, and other colonial gentlemen, the lodge was essentially an elite club, a far cry from the shadowy and secretive organization that emerges from contemporary attacks upon it by church and political authorities.[78] What especially appealed to their ambitions was the aristocratic ingredient in the movement. The noble origin of its top officials was one of the distinguishing attributes of British Freemasonry since the founding of the Grand Lodge in 1717. In addition, its hierarchy of degrees and rites, its aspirations to perfection, its emphasis on the "ancient" origins of the organization, and its principles of participation can all be shown to have correlations to the aristocratic ethos. The British membership, according to the *Constitutions of Free-Masons*, reprinted in Philadelphia in 1734, consisted of "several Noblemen and Gentlemen of the best Rank, with Clergymen and learned Scholars," and their duties included the practice of such genteel virtues as "Honour and Honesty." Manifestly elitist assumptions defined membership and duties; only "good and true Men, free-born, and of mature and discreet Age, no Bondsmen, no Women, no immoral or scandalous Men, but of good Report" could belong, and members were obliged to "give Honour to whom it is due, and avoid ill Manners." Exclusiveness was to be strictly enforced; a member was told that "you may not be imposed upon by an ignorant false Pretender, whom you are to reject with Contempt and Derision." Stressing "the immemorial Usages of the fraternity" provided the coveted sanction of ancient lineage. The text of an official song of the order suggests why colonial gentlemen could see Masonic meetings as rites confirming the cultural validity of their rank:

> We make it plainly to appear,
> By our Behaviour every where
> That where you meet a Mason, there
> You meet a Gentleman.[79]

But few genteel authors in England supported either the protests or the glowing descriptions of refined colonial society. Oldmixon's ironical comments on Hugh Jones may serve as an example of the tenaciousness of metropolitan disapproval. In Jones's cheerful portrayal of Williamsburg, Oldmixon saw provinciality, observing that "not far from hence is a large Area for a Marketplace; whether there is a Market or not, Mr. Jones does not tell us; but near it is a good Bowling Green and a Playhouse. I am very doubt-

The Curse of Provincialism

ful of the Excellence of the Performance on the Virginian Stage, Notwithstanding the Genius for Poetry, which Mr. Jones has given us a Specimen of in his own History." Another account referred to the town as "far from being a place of any consequence. . . . There are few public edifices which deserve to be taken notice of . . . and they are far from being magnificent." It pointed to the lack of any meaningful social life; most of the time "the town is in a manner deserted," and only at times of general court sessions or assemblies was it "crowded with the gentry of the country."[80] For the colonists to break through the glass wall guarding the metropolitan stronghold of gentility was a formidable and usually insurmountable task.

Slavery: English Censure, American Advantage

A chapter in the history of the confrontations between colonial and metropolitan elites which demands separate attention involved slavery. Its most interesting aspect is that in the legitimating process, this institution played diametrically different cultural roles for each of the two sides. In Britain, with the rise of humanitarianism and middle-class sensitivity, it came to be used as one of the more forceful arguments against the legitimacy of the slaveholding colonial gentry. But in the colonies it not only vastly enhanced the planters' claims to landed ethos but also, more fundamentally, facilitated a lifestyle that reinforced such assertions. This reality was reflected in James Reid's sarcastic remark in 1769 that in Virginia owning slaves had grown to be a prime qualification—both material and symbolic—for being considered a gentleman, resulting in the exclusion of those like himself, who "cannot appear in polite company for want of Negroes."[81]

The association of planter elites with what was believed to be the inherently corrupting effect of slavery began to grow in prominence in Britain in the late seventeenth century, then coming mostly from religious quarters. The rise after 1700 of humanitarian and philanthropic movements that inspired compassion for the underprivileged and the unfortunate drew increasing attention to the depravity of virtue among slaveholders. This viewpoint led to a protracted campaign against slave trade and eventually to the delegalizing of slavery in England in 1772. The antislavery sentiment intensified considerably in the mid–eighteenth century; slavery, by then widely portrayed as cruel and detestable, came to be perceived as a peculiar specialty of the American planter. The *Gentleman's Magazine*, beginning in the 1730s and peaking in the last two decades of the century, published a substantial number of texts containing strong objections against this colonial practice.[82] The British reading public sensed that much of the wealth of the plantation gentry was directly tied to slave labor. This association generated repeated attacks by moralists linking avarice and luxury with the inhumanity of the planters' treatment of slaves. In this context colonial slavery gradually came to be viewed not only as objectionable but as a symbolic amalgamate of various vices routinely fused with the image of the planters as nouveaux riches.

Early opinions of this sort emerged in the late seventeenth century when slavery was only becoming a major labor system on the American mainland but was well established in the West Indies. One prominent voice was that of Morgan Godwyn, briefly a minister in Virginia, who on his return to England became a passionate antislavery publicist. In a 1685 sermon dedicated to King James II, he contended that he expected a hostile reaction from colonial planters (the "Rage and Malice of those incensed MAMMONISTS from abroad") but felt it a moral duty to condemn them for living on "vast estates" maintained by the "unmerciful labour" of the slaves, for they "come not thither to promote Religion nor save Souls but to get Money and Estates." In his view this greed overcame even their own cultural roots, for they "permit Polygamy to their slaves and also put them upon a necessity of labouring upon Sundays to prevent their starving all the week after," while refusing to baptize "those poor captive Slaves, out of whose Labours they live, and do thrive into vast Estates."[83] Four years later a former surgeon to the duke of Monmouth, Henry Pitman, who was exiled into servitude to Barbados, published a sensational relation of his experiences. His censure of the slaveholding planters for their heartless treatment of servants and slaves struck a note similar to Godwyn's. He depicted his master, Robert Bishop, as typically ruthless, a man who was never "moved to Pity" and "could not content himself with the bare execution of his Cane on my Head, Arms and Back, although he had played so long thereon like a furious Fencer, until he had split him in pieces."[84]

Their contemporary, Thomas Tryon, even more explicitly linked the brutality of slaveholders with new wealth. This affluence, he pointed out, flowed not from honest work but from exploiting the forced labor of Africans, a practice indulged in because "a false Conceit of Interest has blinded their Eyes and stopt their Ears, and rendered their Hearts harder than Rocks of Adament, more remorseless than hungry Bears or Tygers." An arrogant ambition to maximize profits without regard for morals and the humanity of other people filled the planters with "Devilishness, Cruelty, and Oppression." In the words of Tryon's slave narrator, they were "swaggering Christians, who sport themselves in all manners of superfluity and wantonness, and grow with our Blood and Sweat, gormandizing with the fruits procured by our Slavery and sore Labour." Of particular interest is the author's suggestion that the very practice of slavery by colonial gentry invalidated its claims to gentility. How could the planters, he asked rhetorically, "make it a genteel quality and honourable to break and violate that great command of the Creator . . . that Man should get his Bread by the Sweat of his Brows, which yet amongst the more Noble Christians, as you call your selves, is counted a poor, low, base and shameful thing." The reply of Tryon's planter was a model of upstart mentality: without slave labor, "how should we maintain our Grandure, and our Pomp, and raise great Estates for ourselves and children." Tryon was both condemning the immorality of slavery from a Christian position and, much like Defoe, criticizing from a practical, middle-class viewpoint the uselessness of English landed life and its central axiom that members of the gentry must not labor with their own hands but should live off estates. A landowner in his treatise proclaimed, "I am a Gentleman born and bred, who shall hinder me from taking my Pleasure in Carrouzing, pampering my Carcas, diverting my self in the manner of Uncleanliness and Idleness."[85] It was in such a context that the colonial slaveholder was emerging as a convenient symbol combining both evils, a fact that may partly explain why he became the object of so many attacks in England.

Scholarly, academic treatises also made their contribution to the shaping of disapproving English perceptions of the colonial slaveholder. Sloane's respected study of the West Indian colonies reported on the extreme harshness with which the planters treated slaves, such as "burning them, by nailing them down on the ground with crooked Sticks on every Limb and then applying Fire by degrees from the Feet and Hands, burning them gradually up to the Head." He noted with a scientist's meticulousness that for smaller offenses, the slaves "are usually whip't . . . till they be bloody, and several of the Switches broken. . . . After they are whip't till they are Raw, some put on their Skins Pepper and Salt to make them Smart; at other times the Masters will drop melted Wax on their Skins, and use several very exquisite Torments." Geographical descriptions and travel narratives repeatedly included similar themes. Writing in 1729, an English author describing himself as a merchant depicted planters as such "haughty and cruel men" that "no prayers or Tears can touch their harden'd Hearts, relentless as Rocks they know no Pity." The slaveholders, "led by Avarice and Luxury, commit the blackest Crimes without a Blush." This degeneration of planters' morals by slavery was so deep that eventually it defied even the power of greed itself, since "so far had the spirit of Rage and Cruelty the ascendant, that tho' the Fellow [a slave who committed an offense] was better worth than 50 l. per an. to him . . . yet the most earnest Requests and Intreatys of the Planter's Wife and other Friends present were all little enough to dissuade him [the master] from killing him." A similar impression was advanced in Leslie's factual and detailed description of Jamaica in 1740. It dwelt extensively on the lifestyle of the local gentry, including its elegant dress and polished diversions, which the author deemed comparable to those of European polite society. Then, as a stark contrast to this refinement, he observed that "no country excels them in a barbarous Treatment of Slaves, or in the cruel Methods they put them to Death." For instance, "a rebellious Negro, or he that twice strikes a white Man, is condemned to the Flames; he is carried to the Place of Execution, and chain'd flat on his Belly, his Arms and Legs extended, then Fire is set to his Feet, and so he is burnt gradually up; others they starve to death with a Loaf hanging before their Mouths." In case the readers doubted the veracity of his account, the author assured them he had personally witnessed such scenes: "I have seen the unfortunate Wretches gnaw the Flesh off their own Shoulders and expire in all of the frightful Agonies of one under the most horrid Tortures."[86] In an age of a growing emphasis on compassion and even sentimentality, such descriptions struck new chords of sensitivity and reinforced the stereotype of the slaveholding planter with a new dimension of emotionality.

A number of stories involving slavery cut across literary and popular culture, reaching wide audiences either as legends and tales or transformed into more sophisticated literary shapes. One account that gained huge popularity and was retold many times over the span of a century by various writers was that of Inkle, a young Englishman, and Yarico, an Indian woman who became enamored of him and saved him from dire straits, only to be rewarded by being sold into slavery in Barbados by the heartless European. It became a subject of literary works from those of Jean Mocquet in his *Voyages* (1616), through Richard Ligon in his history of Barbados ((1657), Richard Steele in one of his *Spectator* essays (1711), Oldmixon in his history of the American colonies (1741), and a number of eighteenth-century poets. All versions of this story accentuated the corrupt and greedy nature of plantation colonists and pointed to slavery as its root source. The legend of Oronooko played an analogous role, except that here the noble hero was an African. Aphra Behn's 1678 novel, which popularized this story in Britain, had numerous editions and a number of dramatized versions—from the one by Southerne to those of John Hawkesworth, Francis Gentleman, and J. Ferriar—staged throughout the eighteenth century. Oronooko, a noble African prince enslaved by British colonists, chose to kill his lover Imoinda rather than see her dishonored and was himself cruelly executed for stirring up a slave rebellion in pursuit of liberty. The various renderings of such popular stories display a characteristic development which took place during the eighteenth century. Behn and Southerne, writing from a genteel perspective at the turn of century, put more stress on the vulgarity of slavery than on the institution itself. Only later in the century, as the moral messages of such accounts were considerably reinforced by a new emphasis on their sentimental aspects, did the story come to express antislavery and humanitarian viewpoints more specifically. In 1784 the history of Quashi, related by James Ramsay in his essay on slavery, appealed mainly to such emotions. Quashi, a slave of noble spirit, became a trusted friend of his owner but upon some minor suspicion was ordered to be whipped, for the first time in his life. A struggle ensued, and Quashi, holding a knife to his master's neck, proclaimed that such an accusation by someone whom he had "loved as himself" was "a mortal wound to his honour." He then cut his own throat in the ultimate demonstration that he, and not the master, represented the true genteel ethos. But whatever the changes in narrative styles and emphasis, all these stories had a common theme: the depicted characteristics of wealthy American slaveholders—greed, coarseness of manners, and immorality—were antithetical to gentility and virtue.[87]

Such episodes enabled the old gentry in England to exclude colonial planter elites from the polite sphere, and thus to underscore their own allegedly much more humane and charitable dispositions. Few stories make this point as well as that popularized in Thomas Bluett's 1734 book *Job, the Son of Solomon the High Priest of Boonda in Africa*. Job, according to the author, was kidnapped by slave traders from his native "kingdom of Senega" and sold to Maryland, where some of the local slave owners became aware that he was not a commoner and allowed him to write a letter in Arabic to his father. He was then transported to England, thanks to the interest taken in him by General James Oglethorpe, where he was received by the "gentry . . . who were mightily pleased with his company" and who promptly decided to purchase his freedom. Before he was sent back to Africa, he was introduced to the king, who "was pleased to present him with a Gold Watch." The story was followed by a lengthy reflection on the English gentry's benevolence and nobility of character for "having acted so good and generous a Part to a distressed Stranger." There was quite a bit of self-congratulation on "the Pleasure that results from the Consciousness of a generous Respect for our common Humanity," as well as on hospitality, which "is one very honourable part of the character of the English."[88] Of course, the distressed stranger was a prince, not a commoner, and therefore was nominally equal in his noble rank to the hosts, a fact that made such magnanimity conform more easily with English notions of honor.

The development, from the mid–eighteenth century, in attitudes toward the colonists that increasingly stressed sentiments and the need for the abolition of slavery was also visible in Edward Kimber's account of his 1745-46 trip across the mainland American plantation colonies. Here too, slavery was linked with the new wealth and moral corruption of the planter gentry. In Virginia he saw much more substantial wealth than in other parts of British America. As soon as he entered the colony, he was struck by "more considerable marks of Opulence," as the Virginians began "to regale" him "with excellent Wines, good Brandies and Rum." Although impressed by the affluence and hospitality of the gentry, he was outraged at the iniquity of the slave system on which all this prosperity rested. His examples included the slave-owners' cynical inducing of the Africans to procreate, "setting them as Stallions to a whole neighbourhood," and the slave market; "'Tis really shocking to be present at a Mart of this sort, where the Buyers handle them as Butchers do Beasts in Smithfield, to see if they are proof in Cod, Flank, and Shoulders." Such total mastery over other human beings, in his view, inevitably resulted in a slide down from polite standards of civil conduct. He recounted "an Instance of a late Sea Officer . . . that for a mere Peccadillo order'd his Slave to be ty'd up and for an whole Hour diverted himself with the Wretch's groans." When the author arrived on the scene, "the Brute was beginning a new Scene of Barbarity, and he belabour'd the Creature so long with a large Cane, his Overseer being tir'd with the Cowskin." Kimber's emotional admonition of slavery was one of the strongest in contemporary British writing: "Thou worst and greatest of Evils! I view thy sable livery under the torture of the Whip, inflicted by the hands, the remorseless Hands of the American Planter."[89] His text was published in the prestigious *London Magazine*, a journal that reached many opinion-shaping readers and members of the metropolitan intellectual elite.

The theme of corruption of morals and manners by slavery became a standard one on the British intellectual scene in the 1760s and 1770s. Antislavery crusader John Woolman was outraged at the corruption to which the children of slaveholders were exposed early in life. He pointed out that "if Children have also the Opportunity of lording over their Fellow Creatures, and being Masters of Men in their Childhood, how can we hope otherwise than that their tender Minds will be possessed with Thoughts too high for them." Reid observed in 1769 that in Virginia the outcome of slavery was that planters were "brought up in ignorance, nourished in pride, encouraged in luxury, taught inhumanity and self conceit." Chastellux pointed out that although the slaves in Virginia were not treated as harshly as "in the sugar colonies," they were "ill lodged, ill clothed, and often overwhelmed with work," and that the planters' "tyranny which they exercise over those who may at least be described as of their own species" produced many "ill effects." For instance, among southern gentlewomen, whom the Frenchman did not deem very urbane, "the convenience of being served by slaves still further increases their natural indolence." In Richard Cumberland's play *The West Indian*, performed in Drury Lane in 1771, one of the main characters, Belcour, an English colonial planter, was a walking stereotype of his class, "haughty, vehement, and unforgiving." His arrogance and impatience with those below him were explained as a result of his life as a slaveholder. His impertinence was revealed in the play as soon as he stepped off the ship upon arrival in England. Angry with the formalities, "accustomed to the land of slaves and out of patience with the whole tribe of custom-house extortioners, boatmen, tidewaiters, and water-bailiffs," he proceeded to beat them with his rattan cane, much as he would treat his plantation dependents. This stereotype was not merely a myth. Philip Greven, in his study of child rearing in colonial America, observed that among the southern gentry, whose nurses, servants, and slaves tended to most of the daily care of children, the latter "too often seemed undisciplined, too free in their behavior, spoiled in their clothes and diet, vain, arrogant, and unchecked."[90]

A synthesis of the now well-established view of the colonial slaveholding gentry can be found in Burnaby's 1759 description of the Virginia elite. Having acknowledged the evils of slavery, he attributed their origin to the planters' low cultural qualifications. "Their ignorance of mankind and of learning," he believed, "exposes them to many errors and prejudices, especially in regard to Indians and Negroes, whom they scarcely consider as of the human species." An older element of the stereotype, the wealthy planter's ungenteel origins, was now blended with the newly spreading belief that he was being corrupted by the economically and socially destructive practice of slavery, his "insurmountable cause of weakness." The depravity of slavery warped the character of planters, bringing out the worst attributes of character: "authority over their slaves renders them vain and imperious, and intire strangers to that elegance of sentiment, which is so peculiarly characteristic of refined and polished nations." This opinion exemplified the emerging divergence between colonial and metropolitan perceptions of plantation slavery as a pattern in American culture. What the Virginians by then regarded as a source of prized liberty and patriarchal independence—incidentally, two central and time-honored components of the old landed ethos—a visitor from England saw as essentially antithetical to gentility.[91]

Although there is little doubt that this ostracism deeply frustrated the American planter, it should not mislead us into assuming that a lack of cultural acceptance undermined his pursuit of the genteel model. On the contrary, slavery not only created the indispensable economic and material base for a landed lifestyle but also—by means of the paternalistic formula—made possible its validation within the provincial cultural marketplace. Thus, slavery—although a source of much metropolitan contempt—contributed hugely to the attractiveness, success, and durability of the gentry model in plantation America. Even English observers acknowledged that the objective conditions of the plantation resembled the old landed model. "The Masters,

The Curse of Provincialism 119

Merchants, and Planters, live each like little Sovereigns in their Plantations," noted Oldmixon; "they have Servants of their Household, and those of the Field; their Tables are spread every Day with Variety of nice Dishes, and their Attendants are more numerous than many of the Nobility in England; their Equipages are rich, their Liveries fine, their Coaches and Horses answerable; their Chairs, Chaises, and all the Conveniences for travelling, magnificent." Kimber marveled that in the Chesapeake "prodigious Numbers of Planters are immensely rich, and I think of one of them at this time, numbers upon his Lands near 1000 Wretches that tremble with submissive Awe at his Nod, besides white servants." Another contemporary English author claimed that in Jamaica "the Gentlemen very much resemble those of England who lead Country Lives and have all within themselves, as we call it, only in one respect they may rather be deemed as Princes from that absolute Dominion they have over their Slaves, extending to everything but taking away their Lives, nor would that be very difficult." Fithian noted of Virginians that possessing slaves "blows up the owners to an imagination . . . that they are exalted . . . above other Men in worth & precedency."[92] Wealth, independence, control over slave laborers, and perceived civilizational superiority over non-Europeans became ingredients of a colonial mentality of mastery which eagerly, and with much success, sought legitimation through gentility.

This mentality was substantially reinforced by the concept of civilizational hierarchy. In the absence of old gentry and nobility, colonial elites apparently made more use than their metropolitan counterparts of antimodels in the process of self-definition. In Britain the plebeian served as such an antimodel of gentility; Defoe maintained that people of "mean rank" merited contempt and referred to them as "the despicable Throng of the Plaebeii." On the plantation the existence of slaves provided an opportunity to reconstruct such opposites by local means. The categorization of slaves as culturally inferior—just as it had in the case of Indians—became one of the more effective strategies for the new gentry to define its own place at the top. The fact that its power over slaves was greater and more immediate allowed an easy replication of attitudes toward the poor in Britain. For Hugh Jones the slaves were "naturally of a barbarous and cruel Temper, yet they are kept under by severe Discipline upon Occasion, and by good Laws." Contemporary science provided an additional sanction for the newly popular theory of the evolution of cultures: it hierarchized them in an order of civilizational development, with Europeans at the highest rung of the ladder. One of the most penetrating observations on the colonial relationship between slavery and genteel rank was made by Chastellux. He identified slavery's main role as that of providing for the Europeans both a unity of interest and an elevated status. He noted that even "in the midst of the woods and rustic tasks, a Virginian never resembles a European peasant; he is always a free man, who has a share in the government, and a command of a few Negroes," with the result that "he unites in himself two distinct qualities of a citizen and master." But more significant was the French aristocrat's reflection that "dignity increases as a man considers his relationship to the classes beneath him. It is the plebeian who makes the dignity of the noble, the slave that of the free man, and the Negro of the white."[93] It was by providing these three usable sources of dignity that slavery contributed so immensely to the affirmation of the gentry's authority within the colonial setting.

A particularly serviceable ideology used by the great eighteenth-century slaveholders to interpret and validate relationships between them and their subordinates was patriarchalism, which was conveniently able to integrate various legitimizing strategies. Based on the old landed ethos, with its landlord-tenant obligations, patriarchalism was rapidly becoming obsolete in the growing capitalist economy of early modern Europe, but it experienced a partial revival—made possible by slavery—on the great plantation. For instance, one of the components of this ideology was the principle of mutual obligation: the responsibility of a landed gentleman to care for his dependents and the duty of inferiors to labor and remain loyal to their betters. On the plantation similar links of dependence were reconstructed and extended from the owner down to everyone who lived in this microcosm. They allowed the great planters to validate their genteel aspirations by claiming that their close and steady interest in the lives, work, and health of all the members of this little universe was a fulfillment of patriarchal obligation.

Byrd's manifestly patriarchal vision of his own role as master and pivot of his Virginia estate has already been used to illustrate the conservative nature of the genteel ideal; here it demonstrates the way slavery specifically served the legitimizing pattern of patriarchalism. A good example of how the idea functioned across the British plantation colonies is provided in Grainger's poem portraying life on a sugar cane plantation, an attempt to harmonize an idealized image of landed gentility with plantation realities.

The plantation—much as in Byrd's vision—was depicted in terms of the Renaissance landed ideal, pastoral and serene in comparison with the chaos of cities and providing everyone with a secure livelihood. In an expansion of the European genteel-vulgar dichotomy, the assumption of the slaves' cultural inferiority provided Grainger with a moral argument to claim that the planters were actually saving them from themselves and from the chaos and barbarity of Africa. As part of the gentleman's obligation toward inferiors, slaves were taken care of and provided with necessities, medical attention, and guidance, while in return they owed him their work and duty. "Ye Negroes, then! your pleasing task pursue," appealed the author. "And by your toil, deserve your Master's care." The poem depicts slaves in two different roles: that of an inferior laboring class (like commoners in England) and that of an inferior, barbarian culture (a peculiarly colonial feature). Both enabled the planter to present himself as a true gentleman: benevolent and respectful of the golden rule of moderation ("extremes are dangerous"). For instance, to help adjust the new slaves to the climate and place, Grainger suggested that it was proper to begin with a mild and gradual regimen:

> Let gentle work
> Or rather playful exercise, amuse
> The novel gang: and far be angry words;
> Far ponderous chains; and far disheartening blows."

The owners were entreated to allow some recreation; for instance, "On festival days; or when their work is done; Permit thy slaves to lead the choral dance." The planter was to be magnanimous toward his dependents:

> Yet, planter, let humanity prevail . . .
> Ah, pity then these uninstructed swains,
> And still let mercy soften the decrees
> of rigid justice, with her lenient hand."

But in a manner quintessential for the colonial version of gentility, in the midst of all this landed patriarchalism there lurked a barely hidden world of commercial values. The poem is dense with detailed recommendations on how to invest in a slave: "those from Congo's wide-extended plains . . . ill bear the toilsome field, but boast a docile mind"; how to avoid expensive health problems: "pronest they to worms, who from Mundingo sail"; reduce investment risk: "But planter; from what coast soever they sail, buy not the old: they ever sullen prove; with heart-felt anguish, they lament their home, they will not, cannot work"; and ensure productivity: "let health and youth their every sinews firm; clear roll their ample eye; their tongue be red." Indeed, the planter's supposedly genteel virtue of magnanimity appears to be more a profitable venture than a broad moral principle, much as in the case of Defoe's Colonel Jacque, who determined that benevolence was beneficial to profits, for slaves on his Virginia plantation would work more "faithfully and cheerfully" if treated with "gentler methods."[94] Although the commercial roots of the planter gentry unmistakably show through Grainger's pastoral images, for him they did not invalidate colonial claims to authentic gentility, as they would for a member of the old metropolitan elite.

When the legitimizing potential of patriarchalism is specifically considered within provincial reality, some of the arguments made against it as a valid cultural pattern in the plantation colonies seem less sustainable. For instance, it has been argued that the idea of reciprocal obligations could not have consistently functioned under the slave system since fulfillment of the "obligations" to the master could only be elicited by coercion. While this role of coercion is obvious to us, the fact that slaves had radically different motivations than the masters was not necessarily so evident to the slaveholders, who saw the obligations of inferiors to their betters as part of a culturally, if not divinely, sanctioned order. Another argument has been that since slaves were not only bond laborers, like European serfs earlier, but also property and capital assets, their status offered none of the protection that was part of the patriarchal tradition of reciprocal obligation. Yet it may be argued—as Grainger's example certainly implies—that the feudal protection was at least to some degree replaced by the protection of property, especially since planters compounded the old landed model with business attitudes. In any case, the moral power of the obligations of the European serf or villain should not be exaggerated: they were hardly motivated in their duties to the manorial lord in ways other than through economic and physical coercion, sanctioned and embellished by the forces of cultural tradition. In any case even late eighteenth-century diaries and correspondence of major American slaveholders show relatively few signs that they were seriously haunted by doubts about the inconsistency of new republican ideas with either social hierarchy or slavery. Rare cases like that of Richard Randolph, who in his will of 1796 (but not in his lifetime) ordered the freeing of his slaves because he felt that holding them in bondage was "contradictory to the declaration of rights," was an exception rather than the rule.[95]

Eugene Genovese's work has widely popularized the idea that slaveholders, as a master class, represented a paternalist, "aristocratic" ideology, anti-bourgeois in character, with a code of honor that rejected profit as a goal of life and a basis of human relations. But even he analyzed this ideology in relation to its inevitable future defeat by the forces of free-market commercialism and called it "the plantation myth," adding to other historiographical labels suggesting its artificial and temporary character. James Oakes accepted this view of paternalism and, by arguing that it was already giving way to liberalism throughout the colonial and antebellum periods, emphasized its supposed fragility. Both of these approaches have focused almost exclusively on American, southern culture, almost as if the paternalist ethos was a peculiarly colonial device to justify American slavery, and not part of much older, more complex, and well-established European model of landed gentility.[96]

The great planters were not particularly bothered by what we today see as a flawed application of the patriarchal ideal. On the contrary, they widely expected the slaves to do their duty and thought them irresponsible if they did not. Landon Carter explicitly embraced a concept of mutual obligations that bound everyone living on his Virginia plantation. He believed his supremacy as a master and father, an "authority founded in natural justice," linked him with all of his dependents, including his family members—whose failure to respect these obligations provoked his constant complaints—as well as his overseers and slaves. He realized he was severe in "correcting" his slaves, but he saw it as his duty to provide paternalistic supervision, just as attending to the slaves' health fulfilled another duty toward his subordinates. He sincerely considered himself a benevolent gentleman. In a note in his diary about Jack Lubbar, an old slave he especially valued, he described the relationship between them as "a Slave gratefully endeavouring to serve a very kind Master." For Carter, it was a case of mutual obligations fulfilled. Jack "gratefully discharged his duty," and when he was too old to work, he was allowed to retire on one of Carter's plantations and live "under my constant kindness." When "the poor old creature took to his bed," Carter tried all available medications to help him, invoked "God's good will," and concluded that whatever happened, "I hope I do my duty, more I know I cannot do."[97] Patriarchal ideology was thus applied to satisfy a specific need in time and place; to authenticate Carter as a gentleman, it did not have to fully replicate the earlier European model.

Upon examining the syndrome of provincialism, and especially the causes of the metropolitans lashing out against the colonials, it appears that they lay not so much with the American elites as in England. First, the hard truth was that for the British ruling classes the relevance of colonial America was defined mainly in utilitarian, instrumental terms: it was a remote outpost of the empire, populated by a humbler sort of Englishmen and existing essentially for the benefit of the metropolis. The planter deserved respectability insofar as he made himself useful by "cultivating of the Growths of the Place, and exporting them to England, from whence he yearly draws so many Manufactures, as maintain several Families in the Kingdom." Second, charges against the American nouveau riche were to a large degree a function of change in Britain—an attempt by the old elites to maintain the cultural demarcation lines of their own authority. When Edmund Burke reflected in the 1780s on the role of the noble ethos, what he saw was the decline of a great civilization based on gentility. It was being replaced by one that was vulgarly materialistic. "The age of chivalry is gone. That of sophisters, economists, and calculators, has succeeded; and the glory of Europe is extinguished forever." For him, gentility was related to the "beautiful," that is, to pleasing harmony and polish, but it was contradictory to plebeian "robustness and strength."[98] This was clearly a defense of a waning world, fading under the pressure of dynamic capitalism and social mobility. It was against such a backdrop that the polite aspirations of the eighteenth-century American gentleman amid frontier conditions, climatic hardships, Indian wars, aggressive business dealings, and the daily violence of slavery were being labeled the antithesis of the fragile and endangered British gentility.

On the other side of the Atlantic, however, American elites (and not just in the plantation region) became mature by the mid–eighteenth century and were not only conscious of their own honor but very touchy about comments that cast doubt on their dignity. They acknowledged colonial rusticity but saw America as an extension of the mother country and themselves as deserving members of the British gentry. That they bitterly resented the patronizing treatment received from London was acknowledged in Franklin's comment in 1766 that British Americans "consider themselves as a part of the British Empire, and as having one common interest with it; they may be looked upon here as foreigners, but they do not consider themselves as such." The same sensitivity was poignantly exhibited by Benjamin Rush during his 1768 visit to the House of Commons in London, where he stood in the same spot where William Pitt had delivered his celebrated speech against the Stamp Act. Rush noted that he heard the words "Americans are the sons not the bastards of Englishmen" ring in his mind and was so overcome with emotion that he "was ready to kiss the very walls that had re-echoed to his voice upon that glorious occasion, and to ask them to repeat again the enchanting sounds."[99]

The syndrome of provincialism was perhaps the most enduring pattern in the colonial-metropolitan relations; its unbroken chain of continuous presence extended from the founding of the colonies to the Revolution. Yet its complex effects on the shaping of colonial elites have not been fully understood. What has usually been stressed is its role in rendering the genteel ambitions of provincials pointless, fragile, and unrealistic. Disapproving metropolitan opinions were both extremely important and vexing for the aspiring colonists, because the norms of legitimacy were ultimately defined in London. But the main effect of the provincial syndrome on the culture of the plantation gentry lay in providing a powerful and sustained stimulus to adopt the tenets of the traditional landed ethos as a system of ideas that reflected and validated their American experience. There is little evidence that metropolitan contempt deterred the colonial gentry in this quest. On the contrary, the unwavering continuity of this pursuit throughout the eighteenth century must indicate that the gentry saw it as the principal assurance that such contempt would someday be refuted. We have often been told that this never occurred, and that history forced the colonial gentry in the 1770s to abandon this Old World ethos for a new republican one. But it was precisely then that such a refutation did arrive. Thanks to the firm hold that the genteel ethos had acquired over their culture, Revolutionary gentlemen-planters such as Washington, Jefferson, Madison, Bland, and Mason found themselves sufficiently equipped with its constituent values of independence, liberty, and equality to stand up confidently and defend those values as rightfully their own. The ensuing separation from the metropolis was not only political and constitutional in its roots; it should also be seen as a successful cultural attempt to overcome the long-lived, humiliating burden of provincialism. It removed the urgency of respecting the English adjudicators of culture and at the same time validated the American gentry's own independent worth as an elite. This, however, was accomplished without a rejection of the old ethos, because the members of the American gentry now saw themselves as its legitimate carriers and looked upon the former arbiters in England as its transgressors.

CHAPTER 4

Beautiful Order and Politeness

> "The good Taste, the Decorum, the je ne Sçay quoi, inexpressible something must all concur to make up that elegant Coincidence and Agreement, from whence the beautiful Order and politeness result, which charm us in all the perfect Works of Art."
>
> Baltasar Gratian, *The Compleat Gentleman*, 1730

From Taste to Rank

It can be argued that of the several avenues available to the colonials in their pursuit of gentility, stylizing life and commanding objects of approved taste were the most successful. In this arena their quest had seen the most earnest and enduring efforts. Other avenues, such as intellectual improvement, literary and artistic creativity, or political and legal endeavors have been extensively studied, but the specific role of taste as a component of the eighteenth-century legitimizing process has not received much attention, probably because of the fairly widespread assumption that its ultimate success was frail and limited due to provincialism and the imitative nature of colonial styles. But the American successes of the genteel model should properly be discussed in terms of its selective and fragmentary applications in the colonies, invariably the result of a cultural improvisation between the locally available means and the goals set by the legitimizing paradigm. Such limited applications of style did not necessarily reduce or annul its validating effect because the colonial gentry was an elite in itself, while in England demands for more thorough gentility were prompted and enforced by the presence of the old noble classes, as Byrd discovered during his stay in London.

This is not, therefore, a survey of the colonial history of taste, art forms, or material culture but an examination of how certain select American applications of European genteel style and taste acquired meaning as effective legitimizers in the provincial context. The guiding assumption is that colonials sought gentility not only for the sake of refinement, beauty, or harmony in some abstract, Kantian sense but because identification with approved taste was a major mode of culturally constructing their rank as gentry, perhaps even to a greater extent than it was in England, where such taste complemented titled ranks. The evolution of eighteenth-century colonial taste clearly shows generational differences. The first-generation members of the gentry were the most eager to stylize behavior and to acquire objects of taste, while those of the second generation, and even more typically those of the third, already born into a more polished environment and taking it for granted, showed less pedantry and passion for such endeavors.

By what process did lifestyle and command over objects of taste authenticate gentry rank? "Taste classifies," observed Bourdieu, "and it classifies the classifier." People thus categorized "distinguish themselves by the distinctions they make, between the beautiful and the ugly, the distinguished and the vulgar, in which their position in the objective classifications is expressed or betrayed."[1] Objects of taste, once they had become validated by culture, were themselves possessed of the power to signal the quality of persons appropriating them. Controlling such objects implied contempt for contingencies and a claim to superiority over those who remained dominated by ordinary necessities. "Good company can only mean persons of noble sentiments, refined manners, and enlightened understandings," declared a courtesy book published in America as late as 1790, because "these qualities are not to be expected, where the scantiness of fortune has absolutely excluded the means of education; for the human mind becomes everything by culture. It is therefore found, that in the lower ranks of society, where poverty has denied time and abilities for that happy employ, the worst habits and most depraved morals prevail."[2] But wealth itself was not a sufficient gauge in the legitimizing process; one needed to know how to properly consume it. A gentleman's letter to the *Royal Magazine* in 1762 pointed out that "not the mere possession, but the due application of wealth merits praise." Baltasar Gratian, much respected in Britain as a theoretician of genteel style, referred to this cultural symbolism of external style when he wrote that "the Manner is that which is always most obvious and visible; 'tis the Outside, the Mark, the Sign, and the Specification, as it were, of the Thing: By that external we come to the knowledge of the internal. . . . A Man, likewise, whom we never saw in our Lives, makes himself known to us in some Measure by his Air and his Figure."[3] Significantly, this refinement of taste and lifestyle was not abstract but was closely linked to the larger ethos of the gentry as a group. For instance, the elegance of a person was not merely physical but involved propriety as part of a larger world order. In the words of one author, if "we should see a Woman richly habited, and of Gentile Aspect, washing Dishes in a Brook by the Way side, tho' you know nothing of her, yet would you be offended at the sight, as it represented several persons ill put together; the Woman seemed outwardly to be one of Fortune and Birth, but the Action she was employed in, was fit only for a Scullion-Wench."[4]

Aesthetic needs emerged as a result of a combination of new economic resources and accepted models of consuming. Both were closely associated with concepts of hierarchy. For instance, in 1741 an English author classified American colonists according to their eating customs: "The Bread which the better Sort of People use is generally made of Wheat; the poorer eat Pone made of Oppone, or Indian meal. . . . Their Drink is according to their Circumstances; the Gentlemen brew small beer with English Malt; strong Beer they have from England, as also French Wine and Brandy. . . . The Poor brew their Beer with Melasses and Bran, or Indian corn dried in a stove." Similarly, "Indian Corn . . . is generally used here among the lower Sort of People, and perhaps will always be so."[5] Hamilton encountered tavern keepers in 1744 who "had no cloth upon the table, and their mess was in a dirty, deep, wooden dish, which they evacuated with their hands." They not only could not afford the amenities that the doctor thought indispensable "for the luxury and elegance of life" but most likely did not think they needed them. On the other hand, when the Maryland doctor encountered some Quakers who could afford elegant lifestyles but rejected them, he pronounced them ungentle for their "aversion at these innocent amusements, for the most part so agreeable and entertaining to the young and gay, and . . . conducive to the improvement of politeness."[6]

It is vital to recognize this role of economic factors in the rise of colonial demand for high style, for it is through the economy that people most dramatically experience and define their lives. It is the economy that structures experience more than other so-called objective givens of social status such as age, gender, or race. The pursuit of style could only gain a substantial social dimension when in the early decades of the eighteenth century the concentration of wealth in the mainland plantation colonies reached a certain critical mass, and when the distance from necessity rapidly increased. The rising new elite now had the freedom to need refined objects and lifestyles and could embark on what amounted to an aesthetic revolution, a struggle to create cultivated typicality, a sweeping effort at a genteel stylization of their lives. Before this economic threshold was crossed, form usually remained subordinate to function, but afterwards, taste and style became priorities. All sorts of aesthetic forms, from the style of close stools and dessert wineglasses to the rituals of entering church—"it is not the Custom for Gentlemen to go into Church till Service is beginning, when they enter in a Body, in the same manner as they come out"—began to carry newly potent messages of quality, rank, and order.[7] The genteel aesthetic idiom became a value in itself and a mobilizing directive of behavior because its legitimizing power was now combined with its easier accessibility. This enabled it to play a variety of roles, such as integrating the new elites, setting them off from the nonelite, creating order and hierarchy among a fluid populace, and validating authority and power. This is not to say that personal cultivation was not pursued—on the contrary, it was keenly sought after by ambitious gentlemen from Byrd to Washington—but only to point out that sensitivity to propriety of appearance was becoming very acute, often eclipsing receptiveness to the less culturally useful high art, literature, and theoretical reflection.

By the mid–eighteenth century, the English language, which as a prereflexive form of knowledge can be used as a good indicator of cultural dispositions, reflected such established classification of ranks by taste. On a visit to the colony of Antigua in 1764, Lord Adam Gordon, then colonel of the British Sixty-sixth Regiment of Foot stationed in the West Indies, described the local planter gentry with a commonly employed aesthetic category when he noted in his journal that "almost all people of fashion live on their Estates in the Country." "People of fashion" denoted those who possessed genteel taste, but it simultaneously implied that they had the means to live in a style expressing such taste, which is why he used the phrase interchangeably with "gentlemen of property."[8] Such classifications did not refer simply to outward clothing styles but to broader inner qualities deemed exclusive to the noble classes; genteel elites widely considered simple commoners as conspicuously lacking any higher aesthetic sense. "The mobile," explained Hamilton, "which is by far the Greatest part of mankind, not being in any degree furnished, with the refined and double refin'd faculties of Philosophers . . . cannot possibly perceive any beauty or deformity in nature, but what strikes the outward organs of Sense."[9]

For the earliest American elites, one of the foremost problems of self-identity was the fact that society was much more homogeneous in the colonies than in Europe, with a cultural hierarchy that was not very visibly polarized. In the plantation region even such traditional British social distinctions as *husbandman* or *yeoman* soon disappeared from the language to give way to *planter*, a term applied to free colonists regardless of their wealth or amount of land. In the minds of the early ruling elites, this cultural and stylistic homogeneity profoundly threatened good social order and even the ability to govern. Lord Baltimore in 1671 urged the Maryland council to "take seriously into your Consideration to finde and speedily to propose unto us some Convenient way . . . for the making of some visible distinction and Distinctions between our Leivetennant Generall, our Chancellor, Principal Secretary, Generall Officers, Councellors, Judges & Justices, and the Best of the People of our said Province, Either by wearing of habbits, Medals, or otherwise."[10] While it was probably not very likely, considering the usual hardships of life on the Chesapeake, that the better sort of Marylanders would agree to wear gowns and badges, this project indicated a peculiarly colonial aspect of early elite style. Unlike in highly hierarchized Europe, style was assigned a role not so much aesthetic as practical: to create visible demarcation lines in a society otherwise little differentiated. Not too many decades after Baltimore's suggestion, the blurring of stylistic lines seemed so much a threat in France that it was suggested to the king that he decree an obligatory wearing of blue ribbons for aristocrats, red ribbons for lesser nobility, uniforms for the military, and livery for servants.[11]

Perhaps one of the best examples of the link between the early development of the Virginia gentry and the accompanying emergence of the need for items of approved high taste was William Fitzhugh's untiring passion for importing from England large amounts of silverware for his household. As his plantation prospered, he invested massive amounts of money in these articles of genteel lifestyle; when he died, the inventory of his estate listed "122 pieces of Plate." His letters abound with orders for silver candlesticks, salt-cellars, snuffboxes, plates, ladles, knives, and spoons. For instance, on July

21, 1698, he urged his English merchant George Mason to send as soon as possible "two large Silver Dishes containing about 80 or 90 ounces each dish. A Dozen of Silver plates. Two silver bread plates, A pair of Silver Candlesticks large & fair. A pair of Silver snuffers & Stand." Not only were they intended to be displayed to visitors, but their legitimizing value was to be enhanced by a symbol of pedigree; in the letter he mentioned his intention to have them engraved with his coat of arms. At the same time, his scrupulous attention to the weight of the silver indicates that he saw these purchases as both a cultural and an economic investment. In this, he represented a typical case of duality in the emerging ethos of the colonial gentleman: investing in refined objects while preserving the practical, commercial mind-set that elevated him to economic success in the first place. How else can one interpret his comment, made in a letter ordering a substantial number of silver pieces, that he wished "no letters engraved upon them nor Coat of Arms, having a servant of my own singular good Engrave[r], & so can save that money." An identical attitude combining a desire for elegant taste and pregenteel practicality was apparent in William Byrd I's order, made in 1690 to the firm of Perry and Lane, for "One Bed Bedstead Curtains, with all manners of furniture, Chairs, table, Looking Glass for a Chamber to be Handsome & Neat but cheap."[12]

But for his son William Byrd II, born into his father's Virginia wealth and no longer committed to the canon of business values, objects of taste—while still retaining their immense validating significance—became more of an aim in themselves, a part of expected refinement. Byrd II regarded his collection of elegant silver plate as one of the most prized possessions in his house. When word of a French threat arrived at Westover, his first two moves were to request "guns and ammunition from Appomattox" and to send "the plate and several things of value to Captain Drury Stith's, the place being more secure than this." Early Virginia gentry expended much effort on protecting items of taste and on ensuring that their style conformed to current vogue. One of the earliest examples of such taste consciousness was Colonel Richard Lee, who in 1655 carried with him to England a whole trunk of silverware in order to have it redesigned to comply with new fashion, a project that got him into much trouble with customs officials when he tried to take his collection back to America.[13]

At this early stage, possessing items of taste was of primary importance, but in the early decades of the eighteenth century when the mainland planter gentry grew more established, the cultural stress shifted to lifestyle and the manner of consuming. As in contemporary England, the concern now became to claim exclusive rights to possess and to judge taste, for only through such exclusion could demarcation lines be drawn. Stylistic claims inappropriate to one's rank not only undermined a certain order but also detracted from the specific honor due a given rank. An English country gentleman signing himself as Marmaduke Armstrong complained to the *Royal Magazine* in 1762 that in a poor cemetery "in the wilds of Kent" he had come across tombstones of local residents stylized and inscribed to suggest a "variety of monumental descriptions of their gentry," even though they actually commemorated mere commoners such as "a grocer of the parish." He concluded that "yeoman would be at once a far more suitable and respectable appellation."[14] In England such nuances were a question of maintaining the already existing social lines, but in America it was drawing such lines across the relatively homogeneous fabric of provincial culture that was paramount, especially for the first-generation elites.

Even in England the frontiers of taste were becoming an object of heated confrontations, occasioned by the growing volume and availability of manufactured products that duplicated elite styles, a process which intersected with social mobility. One author complained that undertakers who had begun to reuse such equipment as "cloaks, hangings, coach coverings" were undermining order, because "Persons of ordinary Rank may for the value of fifty Pounds make as great a Figure as the Nobility and Gentry did formerly," so that the "Gayety and Splendour both of the Nobility and Gentry is hereby much eclipsed."[15] A parallel consumer revolution was taking place in colonial America. Cary Carson has recently shown how the newly available consumer goods simultaneously defined social differences and contributed to the democratization of society. It is significant, however, that the essential antagonism between these two functions heightened the gentry's emphasis on the exclusiveness of taste rather than reducing it. In addition, the rapidly growing gap in wealth between the great planters and the rest of society facilitated the elite's monopoly of taste, despite certain visible democratizing effects of the increasing supply of consumer goods. Of course, any competition for legitimate lifestyles, as Norbert Elias noted, routinely brought increased stigmatization by the upper class of those who trespassed against the common distinguishing code. English journals supply ample evidence for this. In a 1762 letter to the *Royal Magazine*, Jasper Tregagle lamented current sartorial disorder, arguing that for centuries apparel matched social position, as "none were allowed to wear scarlet, purple, or velvet, but persons of rank and substance, whereas since the abolition of these acts in the reign of James the First . . . a general confusion has ensued, the lowest of the people run into the fashionable modes of dress so that it is impossible to distinguish the servant from the master, the gentry from the commonalty." He saw this process as inseparable from the emergence of parvenu gentry: "In the district where I now sojourn there are no less than thirteen esquires, though not a man of them can produce imagines Majorum, but are the direct, immediate descendants of hewers of wood and feeders of swine . . . creatures of this cast rather deserve the utmost contempt than the least regard."[16] The old gentry also was censured—for transgressing its own code of taste. "A Man's Table ought to be proportionate to his Estate," lectured the *Gentleman's Magazine* in 1738, but some of the gentry, driven by "Vanity and the Desire of appearing Men of Taste," imitated the leisurely style of aristocracy, "people whom all inferior ranks imitate as far as they are able and commonly much farther. It is their fatal example that has seduced the Gentry." Crossing the line of taste downwards was equally stigmatized; the same journal castigated younger sons of gentry for "imitating the inferior class of Mankind" by dressing improperly in caps instead of hats and driving their carriages themselves. Another author criticized breaches of appropriate lifestyle by those who spent too much time in cities, where "a Man of Quality must blush to be found in the Company of Mechanicks, Footmen and Sharpers, at a Gaming Table; Gentlemen used to assert the Dignity of their Rank in other Assemblies: how came they then to debase their Quality, and herd with the vilest of Men."[17]

In this cultural context of sharpened awareness of distinctions, American gentlemen, both those few confident of their gentility and those numerous ones still struggling to authenticate it, practiced their own discrimination by style. Even the appropriation of minor objects of genteel taste by commoners elicited contentious reactions. When in 1744 Hamilton and the Reverend John Milne stopped during their travels at a "log cottage" of "one Stanespring" to obtain water and milk, the minister found the presence of pewter spoons and a teapot in the house not only "superfluous" and "unnecessary" but also indicating an unbefitting "inclination to finery in these poor people." On the other hand, a musket was "as usefull a piece of furniture as any in the cottage." The firearm, a strictly utilitarian tool, was suitable for a man of low rank; objects involving high taste encroached on the field of legitimacy reserved for the genteel. When Landon Carter visited one of his outlying plantations, he was much irritated to see the manager's wife "act the part of a fine Lady in all her towering apparell with at least two maids" and noted that he would have rather seen a "diligent industrious woman" instead.[18]

Social distinctions were often expressed in the language of aesthetic categories. Washington dismissed the inhabitants of the Shenandoah Valley as "an uncouth set of people." For Byrd II the simple lifestyle of the inhabitants of North Carolina constituted a defining opposite of his own refinement. What struck him most about the town of Edenton was that it was tastelessly built: "A citizen here is counted extravagant if he has ambition enough to aspire to a brick chimney." Hamilton routinely described commoners in aesthetic terms, such as "a fat, pursy man . . . lumpish and heavy," a "greasy thumb'd fellow," or a "house maid, a dirty piece of lumber."[19] Describing in his diary the elopement of a neighbor's daughter in 1732, Byrd could not hide his disgust with the "young gentlewoman" who committed a "humble marriage" with a man below her rank. Had she "run away with a gentleman or a pretty fellow, there might have been some excuse for her, though he were of inferior fortune: but to stoop to a dirty plebeian, without any kind of merit, is the lowest prostitution." Not only did he use the language of aesthetic features to depict social ranks, but its defining power ran so deeply that Byrd was willing to accept elegant looks—a genteel appearance, even without genteel substance—as having some "merit" that would justify the elopement. A similar categorization can be found in Oldmixon's description of Colonel Nathaniel Bacon, leader of the rebellion in Virginia, as "a Gentleman who had been liberally bred in England, having studied sometime at the Temple. He was young, bold, active, handsom and eloquent; his Merit advanced him to the Degree of a Counsellor, and his good Qualities got him the Love and Respect of the People." Aesthetic attributes such as elegant demeanor and polite speech were among the top qualities rating him a gentleman.[20]

In sum, from the 1730s, and especially from midcentury, as it struggled to institute ranks in a society culturally much more homogeneous than that of the mother country, the Chesapeake planter gentry increasingly used taste to classify people. In the early phases, possessing objects of style was sufficient. Once these became more widely attainable, claims to exclusive taste took center stage as colonists emphatically rejected the ugly and claimed a monopoly of elegance. It mattered little that the objects of such claims were sometimes as modest as a teapot, as long as they successfully served as aesthetic indicators of rank and refinement.

The Trouble with Taste: Having vs. Consuming

Even with adequate wealth to finance the genteel decorum, ambitious eighteenth-century planters faced more than just the impediments of rusticity and distance from London. The ability to consume genteel culture was not automatically proportionate to the ability to spend on such consumption. The newly rich usually have to learn how to spend their money. Refined lifestyle and taste were not something that could easily be cooked up from a prescription. To claim certain patterns of cultivation as naturally one's own called for time—a commodity the provincials did not have to spare— to acquire the nuances of manner and style that could not be contained in a simple definition but were instantly recognizable among the fully anointed. A shortcut to cultural capital was therefore necessary. The most common strategy to replicate among the new men the accumulation of objects of taste so characteristic of old genteel families has been to acquire articles that indicated objectified taste. Accordingly, much of the new colonial wealth was directed to the purchases of such sanctioned items: stylish residences, furnishings, clothes, and items required for hospitality and entertainment.[21] As drawn up by metropolitan legitimizers, however, the recipe for gentility emphasized not just possessing such objects but possessing them disinterestedly. The underlying assumption was that they were acquired as heritage, and so could be savored and appreciated without undue regard to obtaining or possessing them. The ability to properly appreciate taste and style was central to their legitimizing potential in England; it also made possible the rapid detection of those who confused having with being. According to one eighteenth-century English courtesy book, "It is not having, by which we can measure Riches, but by enjoying."[22] Without losing sight of this criterion, it may nevertheless be said that for the new American gentry, with its limited command of high culture, "having" often quite successfully satisfied the need for social edification and cultural improvement, priorities far more vital to them than specific nuances of high taste.

This is not to say that cultivation was not slow and trying. For members of the old classes, it came from a long contact with refined people, objects of art, and approved taste and, above all, from being part of a particular environment that fostered such practices. It was passed on to the following generations as a disposition, without much systemic awareness; this was why it seemed natural, and why its rules were usually noticed only when they were broken. Few first-generation great planters in the American colonies had such a luxury; their road to European-style cultivation required much more painstaking and demanding efforts to reach the level of a Washington or a Jefferson. Instead of dismissing these persistent and resolute efforts as either misdirected or imperfect, as has been done so often in the past, we ought to examine their part in the emergence of a distinctly American culture by the end of the eighteenth century.

Often not very apparent, but playing an immense role in the self-improvement of aspiring provincials, was the drive for perfection that was built into the very process of pursuing gentility. Fear of betraying a lack of propriety was a powerful motivator of new gentry both in America and in England. Even Defoe, himself a "new man," found attacking the parvenu an effective means of identifying himself with the truly polite universe. He portrayed the first-generation gentleman as "purse-proud, insolent, without manners, and too often without sence," someone who "discovers his mechanick quallifications on all occasions; the dialect of the Alley hangs like a brogue upon his tongue, and if he is not clown clad in his behaviour, 'tis generally supplied the usuall air of a sharper and a bite, and he can no more leav the ravening after money, Fas aut nefas, than an old thief can leav off pilfering, or an old whore leav off procuring."[23] Jonathan Swift warned the presumptuous upstart: "Those who are always undervaluing the Advantages of Birth, and celebrating Personal Merit, have principally an Eye to their own, which they are fully satisfy'd with, and which no Body will dispute with them about; whereas they cannot without Impudence and Folly, pretend to be Nobly born: Because this is a secret too easily discovered." He warned that there was no place to hide for such individuals, "for no Mens Parentage is so nicely inquir'd into, as that of assuming Upstarts; especially when they affect to make it better than it is, as they often do, or behave themselves with Insolence."[24] For the old elites, upstart insecurity was a constant source of amusement; as one author observed of a parvenu, "Were you to tell him of his former Employment, you would soon find the Pride of the Gentleman improved by the Rage of the Butcher."[25] Literature provided a myriad of similar admonitions. Henry Peacham noted that commoners who "weare the Cloath of a Noble Personage, or haue purchased an ill Coat at good rate," can have no honor; "pure Oyle cannot mingle with the water." Gratian advised that "there is a sort of People in the World, that are always to be treated with an Air of Superiority," namely, those who "are generally such, as Nature had wisely plac'd in a low Sphere, till the undistinguishing hand of blind Fortune lifted 'em up from their Dung-hill and Obscurity. God deliver us from this sort of Gentry." Richard Steele in the *Spectator*, which carried much authority with the colonial gentry, ridiculed the style of false gentlemen by referring to them as "Pretenders to Mirth" in whose company one is "usually pester'd with constrained, obscene, and painful Witticisms" delivered by those who have no "Talent of pleasing with Delicacy of Sentiments."[26] As late as 1789 an American edition of John Mason's treatise on self-knowledge warned readers that "for a Man to assume a Character, or aim at a Part that does not belong to him, is Affectation" and consequently "exposes Men to universal and just Contempt." It was crucial, argued the author, that "we are not to take example of conduct from those who have a very different Part assigned them from ours."[27]

For the colonists this was a serious matter. In their determined ambition they closely monitored and censored the propriety of style among themselves. Apprehensions about being discovered as an upstart by some coarseness of manners or vulgarity of taste were commonplace. Colonial journals advocated good breeding as a major guarantee against false politeness. Only "breeding . . . denotes a Person's Deportment or Behaviour in the external Offices and Decorums of Social Life." Upstarts could not possess it, "for thin Disguises or pretended private Virtue and Public Spirit are easily seen through, the Hypocrite detected and exposed." The telltale signs were usually excessive greed and intemperate enthusiasm, for "even Men of excellent Understanding and eminent Learning . . . aiming at nothing but Riches and Power are religious Hucksters and Learned Stockjobbers." Impostors were defined as "those guilty of an Immorality who put on a look foreign to their Mind, cheat you by their Aspect, and carry a Lye imprinted on their Countenance." Edward Cave's prestigious *Gentleman's Magazine*, subscribed to by prominent Virginians, declared that "false politeness, like false wit, has something glaring in it, which strikes the Injudicious with a kind of Pleasure and Admiration, but has no other effect on people of Sense than to provoke Ridicule and Contempt."[28] How closely late colonial writing—even in the nonplantation region—followed this theme is demonstrated by John Trumbull's 1773 satire in which one of the chief characters, the wealthy but rustic Dick Hairbrain, whose "airs provoke Th' obstrep'rous laugh and scornful joke," was made an object of such ridicule. Although Richard Bushman has suggested that this was a case of backlash in the Revolutionary decade against gentility as such, occasioned by its association with British corruption, Trumbull—himself coming from a genteel background—more likely was satirizing a false gentleman, as opposed to a legitimate one. This is indicated by his listing of the usual litany of accusations against the parvenu—low social origins and new wealth: "And ev'ry money'd Clown and Dunce Commences Gentleman at once, For now, by easy rules of trade, Mechanic Gentlemen are made"; rustic cultural background: "But bred in distant woods, the Clown Brings all his country-airs to town"; lack of genteel ease: "The odd address with awkward grace"; and lack of taste: "The suit right gay, tho' much belated, Whose fashion's superannuated."[29]

The pressure to conform to valid styles created two phenomena in colonial gentry culture: a constant attention to propriety, combined with a heavy dependence on distant, metropolitan arbiters for a definition of what was proper. When Byrd II was preparing for a visit of Governor Spotswood at Westover, he spared no effort to ensure that nothing marred the elegance of the reception. "The house and ground was made clean," he "caused all the rut to be cut away that lay at the woodpile and the pasture to be made clean," "all the wood was removed from the place where it used to lay to a better place," he "settled several things in my library," and he sent a servant "to kill some blue wing." He was obviously delighted that the visitor "was pleased with everything." It was the Virginians' incessant attention to signs of proper style that Fithian noted when he warned John Peck, about to arrive in the area, that "any young Gentleman travelling through the Colony . . . is presum'd to be acquainted with Dancing, Boxing, playing the Fiddle,

& Small-Sword, & Cards. Several of which you was only entering upon, when I left New Jersey . . . and if you stay here any time your Barrenness in these must be detected." Eliza Pinckney, despite her complaints about the rusticity of life on her remote South Carolina plantation, was not deterred but encouraged to respect polite forms at all times, She took pains to "dress for dinner" every day, even if there were no visitors.[30]

In 1758 Grace Growden Galloway, just married to Joseph Galloway, born in a wealthy Maryland family and now a member of the Pennsylvania assembly, described to her sister the "endless ceremonious farse" of visits, introductions, toasts, compliments, and kisses that she had to endure as a newlywed. "I had upwards of Seventy Men," she complained, "to do me the Honour of a kiss, which I would have given the world to be excused from—I give the more particular account of our customs that you may Judge of the Politeness of the people who I assure you, are vastly Ceremonious."[31] Landon Carter was annoyed at the pretentious imitation of foreign fashion and vocabulary among Virginians ("a Macaroni in dress must be a Macaroni in Pronunciation"), but he himself, rather than magnanimously rise above pedantic trifles, engaged in heated arguments over them. Unable to resist "the pleasure of correcting our errors," he was motivated by the belief that to preserve complete gentility he had to maintain a constant vigil for deviations from it.[32] Hamilton laughed at the Marylanders who memorized elegant and witty sayings from "Collections and publications of Conundrums, Composed for the entertainment of persons of quality." He warned that it was essential to possess proper grace even to present such wit, or else "if he be one whose genius does not enable him to enter so far into the Spirit of a Joke, as to tell it with a proper Emphasis and Grace, the Joke by this means" is on the teller. Such comments would not have been much appreciated by ambitious first-generation gentlemen such as young Byrd or Washington, whose commonplace books were intended to provide them with exactly such "magazines" of polite sayings and rules of propriety.[33]

The emphasis on propriety was visible not only in such obviously impressive forms as the architectural designs of great plantation residences but also in small literary forms; both of these meticulously followed the blueprints of British style. Indeed, proper form sometimes was more important than depicting specific American realities. For instance, a collection of poems written by William Dawson—who called himself "a Gentleman of

Beautiful Order and Politeness

Virginia"—and published in Williamsburg in 1736 helped set such patterns for the following period. They were full of anacreontics, allusions to Milton and Pope, and such classical characters as Philomela, Phoebus, Chloe, and Cupid. Similarly, poems published in the early decades of the *Maryland Gazette* were full of obligatory allusions to classics (Melpomene, seraphick love, etc.) and at the same time almost entirely devoid of references to colonial realities. Byrd's attempts at poetry conformed to the same rule in the choice of subjects and styles. It is quite irrelevant here that they were at times awkward; so were many poems published in genteel British magazines at the time. Their truly revealing feature is that they so keenly adhered to forms currently approved of in the English literary circles.[34]

For most of the eighteenth century, English high culture remained the exclusive consecrating agency of taste and style for the colonial gentry, and conversely, English authors judged provincial culture strictly by the degree to which it conformed to these norms. When Leslie praised the Jamaican planter gentry in 1740, his yardstick was the cultural distance from London. He noted that "they have frequent Balls, and lately got a Play-House, where they retain a Set of Extraordinary Good Actors. In short, they live as happily as if they were within the Verge of the British Court." For Oldmixon, certain Barbadian gentlemen deserved respect because "being generally bred at London, their Behaviour is genteel and polite; in which they have the advantage of most of our Country Gentlemen, who living great distances from London, frequent the World very little; and from conversing always with their Dogs, Horses, and rude Peasants, acquire an Air suitable to their Society."[35] In this context the only realistic way for the provincials to validate their claims to gentility was to try and reduce the cultural distance from the metropolis. No competing models of lifestyle—the otherwise successful Quaker alternative comes to mind as an example—could reproduce the authority of the British ruling class.

Preoccupation with the propriety of style led to an unusually high degree of dependence on current European criteria of high taste, which in practice meant relying either on imported publications or on contacts in Britain. George Washington's orders for supplies to be shipped from England to Mount Vernon by his merchant Robert Cary exhibit two conspicuous characteristics: first, an acute concern that all objects be as close to what was currently the approved high taste as possible and, second, an equally acute reliance on Cary to decide for Washington what was "in the newest taste." The Virginian already possessed the means to acquire objects of genteel style but was limited by the provincial syndrome in what had earlier been called the "due application of wealth." Among the articles listed in two invoices made in 1759 are descriptions of various household items, all with emphatic suggestions that they represent latest style:

> "1 Mahogany Close stool Case in the Newest taste wt. place for Chamber pot & ca."
> "1 Tester Bedstead 7½ feet pitch, with fashionable bleu or bleu and White Curtains to suit a Room lind w't Ireld. paper."
> "1 fine Bed Coverlid to match the Curtains. 4 Chair bottoms of the same; that is, as much Covering suited to the above furniture as will go over the seats of 4 Chairs (which I have by me) in order to make the whole furniture of this Room uniformly handsome and genteel."
> "1 Fashionable Sett of Desert Glasses, and Stands for Sweet Meats Jellys & ca. together with Wash Glasses and proper Stand for these also."
> "4 Fashionable China Branches, & Stands, for Candles."
> "2 Neat fire Screens."
> "2 pair of fashionable mix'd, or Marble Cold. Silk Hose."
> "1 piece of finest and most fashionable Stock Tape."
> "1 Suit of Cloaths of the finest Cloth, & fashionable colour made by the inclos'd measure."
> "Half a dozn. pair of Men's neatest Shoes and Pumps to be made by one Didsbury."[36]

What emanates from the language of this list is both an intense ambition to acquire items of recognized, current taste and a profound dependence on the arbiters of such taste in Britain. A cycle of such dependence was built into the ambition itself, for to achieve it, the power to make the ultimate selection had to be delegated to the agent. The pattern worked thus: the higher the provincial's wealth, the greater the need for symbolic statements of legitimate authority as gentleman; the more intense this pursuit, the greater the dependence on metropolitan authority of taste. This reliance on England, although indispensable for the legitimating mechanism, could also be very frustrating, as the Revolutionary tensions were soon to demonstrate.

In this culturally mandated compulsion to adhere closely to current taste, the colonial dependence on such taste apparently was much greater than that of similar aspirants to gentility in Britain, another hindrance to the development, at that stage, of an alternative American model of elite culture. Two episodes illustrate this elusive difference in the impact of high taste on the two sides of the Atlantic. In 1761 an anonymous letter to William Pulteney, earl of Bath, urged him to refurbish his residence in London because its style did not distinguish it sufficiently from middle-class buildings. "A zeal for the glory of the Nation and of the Town, also of your Lordship," wrote its author, "induces me to recommend to you to modernize your House in Piccadilly, at least externally, by facing it with Stone or Stucco, as Brick has an ignoble appearance, and is conceived by foreigners only fit for a Maison bourgeois." The letter referred to the same English architectural yardstick that George Washington was then applying to his residence on the bank of the Potomac. Mount Vernon, a converted farmhouse that he redesigned with the help of English building manuals, was being given a facelift. Washington hoped that roughing and grooving the wooden boards of the outside walls would make them resemble the more genteel-looking stone blocks. He admitted that his primary wish was to achieve a desirably elegant effect, and that he was much less concerned with the arcane rules of architecture and principles of design.[37] Both of these buildings were thus expected to conform to the current style of genteel residences. The difference was that even without the stucco facing on his house, Pulteney retained the prestige of his rank, while in Virginia the perception of Washington as a gentleman was much more dependent on the actuality of the taste displayed at Mount Vernon.

Pedantry and Politeness

Strong dependence on a distant authority of taste could only lead to a certain pedantry in colonial styles. It is precisely this rigidity of American genteel pursuits that has fueled so many disapproving analyses by historians who have seen it as a stubborn and misapplied determination to achieve a lost cause. This is a misleading appearance, again occasioned by applying standards of English high culture to provincial reality, where a degree of determined and meticulous effort was perhaps the only means to secure the goals of refinement and to defy rusticity.

It was true that according to metropolitan criteria, too enthusiastic a pursuit of proper taste violated the principles of ease and unaffected grace, presumed to indicate liberty from excessive servility to fashion or profession. The rule was:

> Ne'er sweat to shew in Learning you excel,
> Yet ne'er blush to own, that you can spell.
> In Dress ne'er quit the fashionable Road,
> Yet be not first in ev'ry mushroom Mode.[38]

A lack of such ease invoked the dreaded label of pedantry. In his 1745 book of poems, John Adams, an American clergyman and scholar, described the perfect gentleman as one "Whose Learning is pure without the base Alloy of rough ill-manners, or worse, Pedantry."[39] Richard Brathwaite, whose classical 1630 treatise on gentility was still read in eighteenth-century America, defined the gentleman as "a man of himselfe, without the addition of either Taylor, Millener, Seamster or Haberdasher," someone who did not allow any occupation or pursuit to excessively "enthrall him." Della Casa stressed that "a person of Breeding remits of Forms, when it is proper to be Free; whereas a Fop is the same formal stiff Creature wherever he comes." Another author asserted that even the greatest "Genius for Invention," as well as "the most rational Discourse, the most learned Book, the greatest Eloquence, the profoundest Erudition, all this I say, if the Ornaments of Politeness be wanting, will be only look'd upon as barbarous Pedantry." In a 1738 parody—probably written by Jonathan Swift—the author ridiculed the pedant upstart by demanding that "whatever Person would aspire to be completely witty, smart, humorous, and polite, must by hard Labour be able to retain in his Memory every single Sentence contained in this Work . . . as to be never at a Loss upon any Emergency."[40] The requirement of ease remained fairly constant throughout this period, although in the last decades of the eighteenth century more emphasis was put on grace. Chesterfield's letters, published 1774, stressed that gentility was not reducible to a canon of courtesy rules and social skills like dancing or fencing, which, if pursued alone, constituted only a pedantically proper external style. The essence of gentility was grace, which engendered a pleasing tranquillity of society. Nothing, he wrote, was "so difficult to attain, or so necessary to possess, as perfect good-breeding; which is equally inconsistent with a stiff formality, an impertinent forwardness, and an awkward bashfulness." And Hamilton, when he arrived in Maryland, cheerfully applied this same measure to his contemporaries, ridiculing the "Stupidly Solemn" and their "affected primness, preciseness and ceremony, the darlings of triffling fops."[41]

But in America, with the provincial cultural distance to overcome, minute attention to propriety was not only unavoidable but desirable. To meet this demand, the *Virginia Gazette* carried from its earliest years detailed descriptions of the current vogue. Readers in 1736, for instance, could learn that at a recent ball at St. James's in London, "the Nobility and Gentlemen were dres'd either in Flower'd Velvets of various Colours, or dark coloured Cloth laced with Gold and Silver; the Breeches were either the Colour of the Coat or black Velvet and all in general very rich Waistcoats, either of Gold Stuffs or rich Brocade, and some had the Sleeves of their Coats the same as their Waistcoats." They were also instructed that "Cloaths were much longer waisted than formerly, their coat Sleeves much longer and in general open, the Plaits on the sides were wadded to stick out, tye Wiggs were pretty generally wore with rising Foretops with both types behind, and tyed long and fuller . . . the Swords not so very short as formerly." Annapolis merchant Charles Cole was a contemporary example of how such news was put to practical use. He used to wear "a large full flaxen wig, sometimes too a laced hat, his favorite color was red, for he often wore a Scarlet Coat, edged round with gold galoon, and ornamented with gold buttons and button holes, but this was properly his military dress, he being Lieutenant General of the Independent foot Company of Annapolis." When out of uniform, he was equally conscious of style, wearing "a red or green velvet cap, a large blue wrapper, Girt about with a red military sash, a blue Silk Jacket with Silver mounting, and a genteel clouded cane." Cole's concern with "elegant taste" included his house where "he understood perfectly well how to set out a mantle piece or bofett, with plate, Glass, and China, in the neatest and most Showy order; how and in what place to dispose of flowers in the season, how to paper candlesticks and adorn glass Sconces, how to hang pictures, filigrans and pettipoints." When entertaining guests, he paid such attention to table settings that "it was delightful to behold in what elegant order and Symmetry the table furniture was disposed, how charmingly the cloth was plaited, and pinched with regular figures in many places, how the plates, knives, forks, dishes, Salts, boats, cruets &ct: were ranged in beautiful order."[42] An important part of the plantation decorum was the costumes worn by servants. An English novelist may have made fun of the colonial landowner who was so keen on emphasizing his English-like lifestyle in the American wilderness that his "vanity imposed a livery" upon his indentured servants, but the wealthiest planters were far from seeing such details as superfluous. Washington had his slaves at Mount Vernon carefully dressed in white coats and scarlet waistcoats trimmed with colors corresponding to the family coat of arms (fig. 4), while the servants of the John Tyler household were obliged to wear family blue.[43]

4. Portrait of the Washington family by Edward Savage (1798). (Courtesy, Winterthur Museum)

From the 1730s onward, attention to clothing styles worked well as a means of immediate social identification in the colonies, coming to play the same role as the symbolic medals advocated in 1671 by Lord Baltimore to combat social heterogeneity. Breaking the rules of stylistic appropriation was seen as a source of unwelcome confusion. A traveler in the Chesapeake noted that the Pamunkey Indians "commonly dress like the Virginians," which led him to have "sometimes mistaken them for the lower sort of that people." Another visitor was struck by the emphasis that members of the Virginian gentry put on drawing the lines of taste which divided them from their inferiors. The colony's "gentlemen," he noted, "look down with an air of Contempt upon the neighboring Patentee Colonies" as inhabited mostly by the vulgar sort. To the inhabitants of the Maryland Eastern Shore "they give, ironically, the Epithet of Buckskins, alluding to their Leather Breeches and the Jackets of some of the Common People, which is, all over Virginia, as great a Reproach as in England to call them Oaf or Clown or Lubberkin." *Buckskin* as an aesthetic code word for the low and the vulgar was commonplace in the area; a man inquiring of a gentleman if the woods of Maryland were safe to travel in was told that "the most dangerous wild beasts in those woods were shaped exactly like men, and went by the name of buckskins . . . something, as it were, betwixt a man and a beast."[44]

Adherence to propriety was a cardinal rule throughout the development of colonial high taste, but it was markedly more rigid in the early phases. At the end of the seventeenth century in Jamaica, silk stockings, periwigs, waistcoats, cravats, cuffs, and hats were still worn by the elite, despite the obvious discomfort they brought in the hot and humid climate. Sloane observed that members of the plantation gentry, unlike their servants and slaves, "continue here to Cloth themselves after the same manner as in England whereas all inhabitants between the Tropics go even almost naked," with the result that the elite suffered considerably more from the heat than their subordinates. Even in the Leeward Islands, where obtaining elegant clothes was more difficult, aspiring planters dressed, in the words of one, "beyond their abilities, or at least their qualities." Such sacrifice of comfort for proper style was not unusual in Europe among the lesser or new gentry, whose rank was not immediately obvious. An eighteenth-century description of Poland, where the gentry class was numerous but very stratified, noted that the petty gentry took extraordinary pains—even under the most dramatic of circumstances—not to be separated from the three symbols of their rank: hats, swords, and horses.[45]

By the mid–eighteenth century clothing styles in Britain's mainland and Caribbean colonies had evolved to allow for more comfort, but characteristically, this change drew negative comments from British observers, confirming once again that local gentry could little afford to deviate from propriety. One author noted disapprovingly in 1741 that climate forced Jamaican planters to abandon proper attire: "The common Dress here is none of the most becoming, the Heat makes many Clothes intolerable, and therefore Men generally wear only Thread Stockings, Linnen Drawers and Vest, a Handkerchief tied round their Head, and a Hat above." Only special occasions forced the gentry into polite apparel; "wigs are never used but on Sundays or in Court Time, and then Gentlemen appear very gay in Silk Coats, and Vests trimmed with Silver." Only the women kept up cosmopolitan standards: "The Ladies are as gay as any where in Europe, dress as richly, and appear with as good a Grace. Their Morning Habit is a loose Night-gown, carelessly wrapped about them; before Dinner, they get out of their Dishabille, and show themselves in all the Advantage of a becoming rich neat Dress."[46] The situation in the climatically comparable Chesapeake colonies was analogous. An English traveler in the area found it inappropriate, if not ridiculous, that the local gentlemen were hesitant to wear wigs and noted that "'tis an odd Sight that except some of the very elevated sort, few Persons wear Perukes, so that you would imagine they were all sick, or going to Bed."[47] But clothing, which due to American climate was prone to deviations from European rules, was an exception in the field of genteel stylizations; in most areas where it was feasible, the gentry scrupulously attended to approved forms.

Since this could only be achieved in the colonial context by painstaking attention to all activities aimed at improvement, it should not be seen as primarily a sign of cultural brittleness. William Byrd II, Landon Carter, Thomas Jefferson, and George Washington all had rigid daily schedules devoted to achieving some of their goals as cultivated gentlemen. Perhaps the best-known example of such a strict daily autodidactic routine was that practiced by Byrd. Of thirty entries in his diary for April 1721, a typical month, twenty-eight record rising early and reading fragments from classical or English authors, an unyielding pattern broken only twice by illness. There is little doubt that had Jonathan Swift or Edmund Burke read his diary, they would have pronounced him a pedant—for his methodic manner, his strict orientation toward hard facts, and a conspicuous shortage of sentiments and reflections, features so pronounced in the English diaries of Samuel Pepys and James Boswell. His literary works reflect a similar pattern; the more formal early ones are very studied, while his more witty and relaxed late texts went through numerous drafts before he made them public. As Kenneth Lockridge adroitly observed, Byrd's love letters, however strictly patterned on the current literary fashions and figures of speech, lacked "the gently mocking tone which, in the early eighteenth century, was expected."[48] Byrd and others like him who were not born into a long-established genteel cultural environment had to labor to achieve refinement in a provincial setting. It is the ambition that drove this effort—an ambition requiring a great deal of willpower and a rigid regime—that deserves our attention, rather than the colonial transgressions in relation to the European high model of gentility.

Years later, another first-generation gentleman, George Washington, was just as aware that only scrupulous attention to detail could guarantee the desired effect of conforming to rightful taste. His order of 1768 for a new carriage from Robert Cary in England speaks volumes about this peculiarly provincial style consciousness:

> I would willingly have the Chariot you may now send me made in the newest taste, handsome, genteel and light; yet not slight and consequently unserviceable. To be made of the best Seasoned Wood, and by a celebrated Workman. The last Importation which I have seen, besides the customary steel springs have others that play in a Brass barrel, and contribute at one and the same to the ease and Ornament of the Carriage; One of this kind therefore would be my choice; and Green being the colour little apt, as I apprehend to fade, and grateful to the Eye, I would give it the preference, unless any other colour more in vogue, and equally lasting is entitled to precedency, in that case I would be governd by fashion. A light gilding on the mouldings that is, round the Pannels and any other Ornaments that may not have a heavy and tawdry look (together with my Arms agreeable to the Impression here sent) might be added, by way of decoration. A lin-

ing of a handsome, lively cold. leather of good quality, I sh'd also prefer; such as green, blew, or &ca., as may best suit the col'r of the outside. . . . On the Harness let my Crest be engraved.[49]

Thomas Jefferson, a compulsive collector of objects of aesthetic value, is an even better instance of such stylistic pursuits. His immense inner drive to attain consummate refinement and his antipathy toward the vulgarity of the coarse and the primitive translated into his passion for amassing art and perfecting his residence. His aim was to create at Monticello a sanctuary of elegance, shielded from the unpleasantness of slave cabins, rustic commoners, and the wilderness of nature outside—a genteel space into which he could emigrate. Even the service facilities of the house were ingeniously located under the house, below ground level and out of sight. After decades of efforts he achieved his goal of creating an imposing, aristocratic château, cluttered with innumerable pieces of elegant furniture, silverware, china, busts, and European engravings and paintings. The enormous debt resulting from his quest was testimony to the overriding power of this motivation.[50]

If such pedantry was inevitable, its one noticeable casualty was humor. That quality's rather conspicuous scarcity in the culture of the planter gentry says much about the nature of the legitimizing process. Among British urban high society, wit and humor were often more prized than even the merit of an argument; a mere scholar could produce solid facts, but a brilliant repartee or a charming joke could only come from a polished mind, capable of swiftly associating inconsonant ideas and identifying the comic ingredient. The writings of such prominent Virginians as William Fitzhugh, Robert "King" Carter, Landon Carter, George Washington, and Thomas Jefferson reveal a rather solid, matter-of-fact, businesslike style, where flashes of incisive, Swift-like humor are as rare as flowers in winter. It would be surprising if it was otherwise; meticulous attention to propriety is antagonistic to humor, which implies a certain irreverence toward the self and the world. The comical is most often that which departs from the norm; being able to laugh at one's own transgressions requires abundant confidence in one's style and identity. As the identity of the new American gentry was being forged, most could not afford this luxury. Certainly, being laughed at did not help, as Cooke found when he first published his satire on Maryland provincials. In subsequent editions of his poem, he had to omit the humorous "curse" on the colony at the end of the original version and insert an apologetic note that the account of Annapolis in the poem "was given Twenty Years ago, and does not resemble its present State."[51]

When humor did surface, it was usually targeted at those of lower rank, a method that allowed the colonial gentleman to play the role of a classifier, to affirm his own good style by pointing to its absence among others. Byrd, whose diaries are almost entirely devoid of humor, showed traces of playfulness in his 1728 description of backcountry North Carolina settlers. He obviously relished presenting them as country bumpkins who "flocked . . . to behold such rarities as they fancied us to be. The men left their beloved chimney corners, the good women their spinning wheels, and some, of more curiosity than the ordinary, rose out of their sick-beds to come and stare at us." The even more austere Landon Carter preferred sober realism to fancy witticisms; he revered his father for his ability as "a Solon to be sure in all his responses, especially as they were always made with [a] serious and unaffected gravity." Lightness of style seemed to him trivial; he found urbane British arrivals like Captain Edward Foy, secretary to Lord Dunmore, "rather more entertaining than sensible." George Washington was widely known to have been extremely sensitive to all situations that would make him feel awkward. His exceedingly rare humorous comments did not go beyond mild remarks that the hosts at a ball served "tea and coffee which the drinkers could not distinguish from hot water sweetened," or that Charles Willson Peale, who was painting his portrait, would fall "now and then under the influence of Morpheus." Humor is equally scarce in Jefferson's writings. We find a rare sample in his 1781 letter to James Madison in which, pointing to the danger posed by the presence of the British army in Virginia, he remarked that "we have no reason to believe they came here to Sleep."[52]

The charge of pedantry was leveled against the planter gentry by European elites throughout the eighteenth century. Robert Beverley was conscious of this problem in 1705, when he argued that in Virginia "all the better sort of People have been abroad, and seen the World, by which means they are free from that stiffness and formality, which discover more Civility, than Kindness."[53] In the last decades of the century, Chastellux provided one of the strongest commentaries on the cultural pedantry of the planter gentry. "I have often had occasion to observe," he noted in his account on November 29, 1780, "that there are more ceremonies than compliments in

America. All their politeness is mere form, such as drinking healths to the company, observing ranks, giving up the right of way, etc. But all this comes only from what they have been taught, none of it arises from feeling; in a word, politeness here is like religion in Italy, all in practice and nothing from principle."[54] But both Beverley and Chastellux were addressing readers in European salons. For the colonials, the exclusionary function of pedantry was mostly irrelevant; instead, strict autodidacticism and a rigorous, if sober, regard for the propriety of style were parts of an immense effort to create a polite environment, despite the lack of cultural roots and despite provincial rusticity. Faced with this task, meeting strict Chesterfieldian criteria of ease mattered little for the effectiveness of the American refining process, especially since there was no old aristocracy at hand to debate the nuances. Having achieved some of the elements of high style could already be counted as a major legitimizing success.

Admissible Ostentation

Ostentation was a vice eagerly used in England to caricature wealthy slaveholding provincials. But the applications of high styles within the sphere of colonial reality were very different. Conspicuous consumption of refined objects and styles, despite nominal condemnations, flourished as an effective means of validating rank. This divergence between colonial and metropolitan attitudes toward prominent display provides further testimony that select patterns of genteel style functioned successfully as cultural legitimizers on the provincial stage even when applied in ways not conforming to high criteria.

This divergence has been a source of misconceptions in colonial historiography, mostly occasioned by a focus on the supposedly imperfect colonial applications of metropolitan style and taste. Certainly, moderation was a prescribed standard that over the centuries cut across all attributes of gentility in Europe. It went back to the authority of Aristotle, who distinguished three states of feelings and actions: "excess, deficiency, and the observance of the mean.... As we call a person of the middle character gentle, let us name the observance of the mean GENTLENESS." Brathwaite urged the gentleman to seek "the golden meane," claiming that "moderation is a subduer of our desires to the obedience of Reason, and a temperate conformer of all our Affections, freeing them from too much subjection either of desires or feares." Francis Markham saw moderation as the ability "to containe many contrary wines in one bottell," which "makes a Man in the midst of a thousand perplexities to have a firme heart, and a quiet soule." This principle was very much alive at the time of the emergence of American planter gentry; a 1738 English epistle on gentility still saw this tenet as central, claiming that "in all Extreams, or Vice, or Folly's seen, But true Politeness holds the golden Mean."[55]

Some degree of spectacle, of course, had always been a part of early modern ruling class styles in Europe, and in that sense it was expected by both genteel peers and their subordinates. Its degrees of acceptability varied from the modesty of Dutch cities, through the more lavish Venice, to the dizzy heights of Richelieu's France; the limits were drawn by what was locally defined as legitimate. In early eighteenth-century English culture, the question of these limits gained much urgency. Display was emphasized as the old nobility and gentry—facing rivalry from the newly rich—wished to reassert their station symbolically, while parvenus did the same to validate their ambitions. As a result, most criticism was being leveled not at display as such but at illegitimate ostentation, condemning those who would "load their Fingers with Rings, at an unmerciful rate" or "bedaub their Cloath with Gold-lace, and Embroidery to that degree, that so much Richness would hardly become the highest rank of Nobility." Publications emphasized that "What is Splendor, Sumptuousness, and Magnificence in People of Quality, is Extravagance, Folly, and Impertinence in private Men" and lamented that often "a Sir gilds the most unbeseeming Behavior, and a Coronet dignifies Rusticity." True gentry, too, should pay less attention to display, for "the Mob knows well enough" that if quality be only "a Coach and Six, they will be apt to think themselves as good Men as their Masters." One author sternly warned that "for private Persons to go pompous, either in Equipage or Clothes, is but a vain-glorious Publication of their Grandeur" and pointed out that a true gentleman finds it "more agreeable to conceal than to make a needless Ostentation of his wealth."[56] It was in this context that the newly rich colonists received their share of reproaches for their relish in displaying high style. The West Indian planters, as usual, lead the way; a 1762 account of New World colonies in *The American Gazetteer* referred to them as living in "as much pomp and pleasure as any gentlemen in the world. They keep their coaches and fix, with a large retinue of servants; and have always exceeded other colonies in magnificence and luxury."[57]

But these were voices of the metropolitan elite. In the reality of colonial life the conspicuousness of various claims to polite style served the claimants well. These by no means involved only material display. For instance, the very language of various local public announcements, from marriage notices to epitaphs, often put an unabashedly pointed stress on the genteel attributes of the persons referred to. When on June 2, 1747, the *Maryland Gazette* announced the marriage of Alexander Hamilton to Margaret Dulany, it listed all the genteel assets of the bride—being born to a patrician family, consummate character, polite manners, and wealth: she was "Miss Margaret Dulany (Daughter of the Hon. Daniel Dulany, Esq.) a well accomplish'd and agreeable young Lady, with a handsome Fortune." Another typical notice, in the 1736 *Virginia Gazette*, ran: "Yesterday was fortnight Ralph Wormeley, of Middlesex County, Esq.; a young Gentleman of a fine Estate, was married to the celebrated Miss Salley Berkeley, a young Lady of great Beauty and Fortune." Stern warnings of courtesy book authors in England against gentlemen proclaiming themselves too blatantly "to be some-body" were certainly not heeded by William Byrd's family, who carved on his tombstone in Westover an epitaph that is a virtual inventory of genteel attributes. It lists Byrd's relationships with British aristocrats Sir Robert Southwell and Charles Boyle, earl of Orrery, the fact that he was "sent to England for his education," that he attained "a happy proficiency in polite and varied learning," that "he was introduced to the acquaintance of many of the first persons of his age," that he "visited the Court of France," that he had "a great elegance of taste and life," and that he was a "well-bred gentleman and polite companion." All the official functions—which, like titles of birth in England, bestowed honor on their bearer—were also duly cataloged. Similarly, the epitaph of Richard Lee II, who died in 1714, scrupulously listed the essentials defining his rank: a coat of arms ("Hic conditur corpus Richardi Lee, Armigeri"), office held and devotion to public duty shown ("In magistratum obeundo boni publici studiosissimi"), and polite education, including knowledge of the ancients ("in literis Graecis et Latinis et aliis humanioris literaturae disciplinis versatissimi"). That such an emphatic tombstone style was common in Virginia was indicated by a satirist's comment in 1769 on the local "Esquire" who "must know before his breath departs what Epitaph is to be left posterity concerning him . . . to inform the passengers that he had a father, a grandfather, and a great grandfather, who had some vain unprofitable title, and that they were born on one day, lived so many years, and died on another. This is no doubt genteel, and though it may be all true, his horse, when dead, might have the same Epitaph."[58]

A prime case of culturally successful ostentation was the planter gentry's remarkable propensity to use the language of titles. European theorists of gentility insisted on the strict exclusiveness of titles and pointed out that although using them was a part of good breeding, they properly fulfilled this role only if used among people of equal rank; to do otherwise would be "to put a Pygmy in Giant's Coat." Nor should inferiors address those above them by their titles, "for there is little pleasure in being Complemented by such, from whom we require Obedience and Fidelity."[59] In short, the value of titles in the legitimizing process was tremendous. They were not only easily applicable in everyday discourse, but they also forged equality among the gentry and separated them from the commoners.

Plantation gentry, both mainland and West Indian, applied these principles—having first tailored them to their own realities—with inordinate enthusiasm. European titles of nobility—largely inapplicable in the colonies—were replaced by the next best option available: military titles denoting officers' ranks in the militia. These quickly became ornaments of honor and functioned not only during periodic musters—which, of course, provided a unique opportunity for the local commissioned gentlemen to emphasize the desirable order of precedence in society—but in the relationships of everyday life. Virginian gentlemen routinely identified one another by their militia rank. Byrd as a rule referred in his writings to his neighbors and acquaintances in terms of military titles ("Major Mumford," "Col. Cock," "Major Mayo," etc.). That officers' titles were still a coveted source of prestige, if not of much actual power, in 1776 is evident from an entry in Landon Carter's diary: "For my resignation of my County Lieutenancy I gave for one good reason: That the County Lieutenant by the ordinance had not the appointment of any subaltern nor even a Serjant or a Drummer; and that from Experience I had learnt, that people who only took places for the sake of the feathers of distinction would be no controul but that of Native Indolence."[60]

The colonists did not seem to mind that in Britain this penchant to parade militia titles was portrayed as an obsession of upstarts. One author ridiculed it, noting that "they are all Colonels, Majors, Captains, Lieutenants and Ensigns, the last two being held in such disdain that they are looked upon as a Bungling Diver amongst a Gang of expert Pick-pockets." Kimber saw it as merely a case of the genteel pretensions of provincials: "Wherever you travel in Maryland (as also in Virginia and Carolina) your Ears are constantly astonished at the number of Colonels, Majors and Captains that you hear mentioned. In short, the whole country seems first to you a Retreat of Heroes." Reid thought that the propensity of Virginians to cling to every "title of respect" was ludicrous; he noted that every gentleman "is dubbed an Esquire and hugs himself upon the glorious appellation." Hamilton noticed this title-mania even in Rhode Island, where "there is great plenty of collonells, captains, and majors." Predictably, Oldmixon found the colonial preoccupation with titles excessive. He mocked the assumption of such honors by the Maryland officials who gathered in St. Mary's, the colony's tiny capital, for it caused "two Citizens to represent the rest in the Assembly, and the Government is by the Mayor, recorder, Aldermen and Common-Council; tho' true it is, so much Magistracy might have been spared . . . considering there is not above 60 houses in it."[61] However, comments of this sort did not deter the colonial gentry, for whom titles became preciously usable as a nomenclature of honor.

It should therefore not surprise us that colonial expressions of genteel pride as an aspect of honor also tended to be a bit ostentatious. One must realize that eighteenth-century noble pride was understood in the Aristotelian sense of the "greatness of soul." It did not necessarily imply vanity but pointed to the fact that someone was deserving of great things; ideally if a gentleman was able to hold a middle ground between humility and haughtiness, his pride was legitimate. Since inferiors were entitled to none, it was believed they could not take away the honor of a gentleman; duels were acceptable only between equals. "A poor man has no honour," exclaimed the disgusted Samuel Johnson on hearing of a duel between an earl and a commoner. A gentleman's proper carriage toward inferiors should be "between Pride and Familiarity," for without pride social boundaries would be obliterated, but with ostentatious pride the gentleman's dignity would be cheapened.[62] John Brown's immensely popular tract on manners, reprinted in America in 1758, attacked ostentation as the cause of the decline of the gentry, for "it is the Pride of Equipage, the Pride of Title, the Pride of Fortune, or the Pride of Dress, that have assumed the Empire over Souls and levelled Ambitions with Dirt."[63] But these were recommendations for those who already possessed titles, dress, and equipage and whose rank did not have to be validated. For the young colonial gentry, the shortage of approved cultural objects and styles, not their excess, was a major concern. The haughty American planter Barlow was censured for his suffering from a "want of humanity, and from pride, which cannot brook an intimate connection with the poor and unfortunate," but only on the pages of a London novel. The real planter was more likely to resemble Landon Carter, called in 1747 by his parish minister "very proud, haughty, imperious and fickle," wanting to extort from the pastor "mean, low, and humble obedience." Their confrontation began when Carter, on hearing the minister's sermon against pride, took it personally as an attack on the honor of his rank and, consequently, on his right to be proud as a gentleman. His sensitivity was inseparable from the colonial legitimizing process, which required both a more conspicuous manifestation of rank and a greater stress placed on inequality than would have been the case with the Johnsonian gentleman, whose honor was so well established and secure that it was above being affected by a commoner's intrusion. In all this, Carter's power was very real; the pastor was obliged to "preach out of doors in the yard for two years and a half."[64]

Hospitality: A Law We Cannot Repeal

Perhaps the most effective stylization taken from the fertile model of European gentility and applied to the plantation environment was hospitality. The colonial version of this social virtue did not necessarily represent the sophistication of the salon, with its stress on the delicate and the elaborate, but it was vastly successful in its antiprovincial significance, its compatibility with plantation life, and its ability to construct identity. Its attraction lay in the potential to happily blend elements of ease and entertainment with a serious pursuit of rank. Its entertainment value was highly coveted in the dispersed settlements of the mainland plantation region, while its desirable cultural meaning as a component of genteel virtue was well sanctioned by a long British tradition. Hospitality had become integral to the noble ethos because it derived from the venerable medieval idea of liberality as a Christian practice, involving the duty of a host to receive all comers, rich or poor, in his house. It therefore implied a central role for the head of the household, who dispensed hospitality in the form of food, lodging, and entertainment. It also offered a powerful cultural link between gentility and largesse because only the elite, by virtue of its affluence and breeding, was capable of such generosity. Thomas Hobbes had this link in mind when he wrote that "riches joined with liberality, is power; because it procureth friends, and servants."[65] In short, hospitality subtly but effectively expressed relationships of inequality in terms of honor—by distinguishing between inferiors, who were the recipients of hospitality as generosity or charity and were not expected to return the favor, and equals, who were expected to reciprocate and would be humiliated if the treatment received was a mere favor.

Hospitality as a distinctive aspect of lifestyle became exactly such a point of honor among colonial plantation elites. Robert Beverley advertised it in 1705 as Virginia's major attraction (and this time it was not a case of promotional bias), writing that "here is the most Good-nature, and Hospitality practis'd in the World, both toward Friends and Strangers. . . . This good Nature is so general among the People, that the Gentry when they go abroad, order their Principal Servant to entertain all Visitors, with everything the Plantation affords." Should anyone break out of this custom, "he has a mark of Infamy set upon him, and is abhorr'd by all." No wonder Byrd recorded in his diary on Sunday, December 7, 1740, that "after church came no company but only Bill Hardyman." Social gatherings provided a stage for communicating the various refined qualities so richly represented in the very notion of hospitality: generosity, graciousness, sociability, and gaiety. In 1711, at the annual Virginia governor's ball to honor the queen's birthday, the guests tried to outdo one another in polite manners. Governor Spotswood "was very gallant to the ladies and very courteous to the gentlemen"; "because the drive was dirty," he "carried the ladies into their coaches." Inspired by this show of courtesy, another guest, Daniel Wilkinson, "was so gallant as to lead the horses himself through all the dirt and rain to Mr. Blair's house."[66]

By midcentury, not only did hospitality become a fixture in the culture of the American planter gentry, but it gained a positive reputation in England. A narrative by a young gentleman from England of his 1737 visit to Carolina and Georgia is dense with recollections of his polite and generous reception. He recorded that he "reached Charles-Town the same night by twelve, calling at several Planters Houses by the Way, where we were handsomely received . . . after having crossed Ashley River, and two Branches of Stone River, took up my Lodgings at one Major Smith's, a very worthy Gentleman, where I was handsomely entertained. . . . About six miles to the South-East [of Jackson's Ferry, S.C.] I met with a beautiful Plantation there, belonging to Captain Peters, very much resembling a Gentleman's County Seat in England." He noted that another estate, owned by a Mr. Woodward, was "a fine old Plantation settled by his Grandfather, on the Head of the Ashepoo River . . . I stay'd at his House three days and met with a very hearty Welcome, and plenty of Wine, Punch, and good English Strong Beer." In Brunswick, "Mr. Roger More, hearing we were come, was so kind as to send fresh Horses for us to come up to his House, which he did and we were kindly received by him; he being the chief Gentleman in all Cape Fear." On Black River "we lodg'd . . . that Night at one Captain Gibbs's, adjoining to Mr. More's Plantation, where we met with very good Entertainment." The author concluded that "the Gentlemen in general, in this Country, are exceeding civil to Strangers, so that a Man, if he knows but the Nature of the Country, may go from one Plantation to another, for a Year or two, and keep his Horse and never cost him a farthing, and the Gentlemen will always be glad of his Company."[67]

By the 1770s hospitality among members of the Virginia elite had developed into a deeply rooted set of rituals inseparable from their honor; as such it became a mode of their cultural existence as gentry. This at times made it a bit more of a duty, even if a welcome one, than a mere relaxed diversion, as was the case with European urban elites. It became quite unacceptable, in terms of a gentleman's honor, to turn away a peer visitor, or not to entertain him personally. As one author noted, "That sordid Wretch who offends against this laudable Custom of his Country, is the Object of every ones Contempt." After the Sunday service, wrote Fithian to a friend, there would be "three quarters of an hour spent strolling round the Church among the Crowd, in which time you will be invited by several different Gentlemen home with them to dinner." The list of possibilities included "the Balls, the Fish-Feasts, the Dancing-Schools, the Christenings, the Cock-fights, the Horse-Races, the Chariots." He warned that "if you go much into company, you will find it extremely difficult to break away with any manner of credit till very late at night or in most cases for several days."[68] The plantation gentry's preoccupation with hospitality was so striking that some English authors tried to explain it scientifically—in accordance with the current fashion in cultural interpretation—by attributing it to the natural environment, claiming that the "climate and external appearance of the country conspire to make them indolent, easy and good-natured; extremely fond of society, and much given to convivial pleasures."[69] The real answer, however, lay in its highly effective legitimizing power. When Jefferson's pregnant daughter Martha complained about the incessant and exhausting flow of visitors through Monticello, her father argued that hospitality had become one of the most venerated "usages of our country" and represented "laws we cannot repeal."[70] This language leaves little doubt that hospitality was categorized as a matter of his honor as one of the Virginia gentry. By being able to define this virtue as exclusively and naturally theirs, members of the gentry could effectively claim their authoritative position in the hierarchy of culture.

The definitive validation of planter hospitality as a genteel attribute could only come from the metropolitan arbiters, and when it did, it was proof ultimate of success. While other colonial stylizations of life on genteel patterns were so often ridiculed in Britain, planter hospitality was widely recognized and acknowledged as a true mark of quality. One English visitor found that Maryland much resembled "old England" in that "all over the colony an universal Hospitality reigns: full Tables and open Doors, the kind Salute, the generous Detention speak somewhat like the old roast-Beef Ages of our Fore-fathers. . . . Strangers are sought after with Greediness, as they pass the Country, to be invited. . . . Every Comer is welcome." Another travel account pointed to the same tradition in its sister colony, noting that "such is the hospitality of the Virginia planters, that a stranger travelling in this country may be entertained at their house gratis; so that public inns in such a country are unnecessary." A traveling English aristocrat noted that the Virginians showed so much sociability that it "must deeply touch a person of any feeling and convince them that in this Country, Hospitality is every where practised."[71] Such exceptional recognition probably was helped by the contemporary perception in England that hospitality—once called by Brathwaite "a great relique of Gentrie"—was in a decline occasioned by luxury and the lure of cities which drew the gentry away from country lifestyles. Testimony that this view worked to the advantage of the American gentleman

Beautiful Order and Politeness

may be found in the remarks of the usually patronizing Oldmixon, who unequivocally praised Virginia, writing that "the Planters are almost all sociable; and as every Thing toward making their Friends welcome is cheaper than in England, so the Entertainments there are larger, the Reception more sincere, the Mirth of the Company more hearty than in most of our Gentlemens Houses, among whom Hospitality is so out of Fashion, that a Man who pretends to it is reckoned a sot or a Bubble, and the costly and pernicious Vices that were introduced in the Place of it, in the last Century, has banish'd it from that Country where it formerly flourish'd, to the eternal Praise of our Ancestors, and the Shame of their Posterity."[72]

What accounted for the phenomenal success of hospitality as compared to other aspects of genteel lifestyle? It seems that it was not only highly desirable on account of its potential for social legitimation but also that—unlike high art and literature—it could be readily transplanted to the plantation colonies once the planters were affluent enough to accommodate it. They may not have had the wealth of European aristocrats, but they had another huge asset—slavery. Large numbers of slaves who cooked, washed, cleaned, and served made the endless stream of guests visiting or staying at the plantation possible and paid for the leisure of their owners with their labor. Then there was space, a factor that strongly reinforced the attractiveness of hospitality. In the plantation region space imposed its own rules of social distance. One was that the wealthy, by virtue of being more mobile, had more opportunities to socialize. Another was that the gentry, deprived of urban life, situated at a great distance from the cultural metropolis, and curious for any information about the world, was starved of opportunities for the rituals of play and social contact. Hospitality could lighten this provincial burden. Through a specifically colonial combination of resources and aspirations, it became domesticated early as one of the central expressions of elite identity and prestige. It became a means and an end, a formula for articulating polite style, and a way of being a member of the gentry.

Genteel Style, Practical Mind-set

A survey of those patterns of European genteel taste and style which successfully functioned in eighteenth-century colonial American culture must lead to the observation that they represented an effective improvisation between the specific realities of plantation life and the ideal model. It was this improvisation that transformed many Old World forms of genteel lifestyle into a mold closer to popular culture. Furthermore, effective applications of such patterns involved a selection of those aspects of the ideal model which had utilitarian rather than abstract or theoretical connotations. This was rooted in the fact that in the first generation the new gentry usually retained some of the old hierarchy of values and tended to stress necessity and practicality rather than luxury, even if the economic need for practicality and frugality had disappeared. It was not easy for the members of this new gentry to put themselves in the place of old-wealth gentry and to understand that group's necessities. Instead, they were likely to initially perceive these necessities as impractical extravagances, for it was not immediately obvious that they were an expected, and even socially mandatory, part of the genteel lifestyle. This seems to have been more fully realized only in the second, and often the third, generation. The dispositions of the members of the first generation were, after all, derived from their own and their immediate ancestors' often commercial background and practical knowledge of the world before they were faced with the challenge of creating genteel lifestyles.[73]

A word of explanation about what is meant here by a "popular" orientation of the colonial elites' stylistic preferences. A European high aesthetic attitude toward material objects and art usually involved a scrupulous rejection of the vulgar, understood as that which was directly related to the practical, everyday experiences of life. In art the Europeans referred to "popular" representations, characterized by a low degree of formal transformation and by little ambiguity of meaning; the popular aesthetic was believed incapable of designs too formally refined. This view extended to other areas of culture. For instance, forms of popular entertainment usually implied collective participation in the festivities, while high forms of play implied distance rather than familiarity, just as strict norms of politeness tended to create barriers and social spaces. For colonials such norms carried great importance, but there was rarely a need for the requirements of good style to reach the rigid and formal heights of Europe in order to play their legitimizing role satisfactorily. Their own applications of select genteel styles—more direct, engaged, and fraternizing, with less patrician distance and more plebeian immediacy and congeniality—served their purpose equally well.

The well-known colonial preoccupation with horses serves as an exam-

Beautiful Order and Politeness

ple. Just as hospitality became one of the preferred and successful stylizations because of its unique compatibility with plantation reality, so did the various activities involving horses. For instance, the quarter race—a short, rapid dart, involving such unrefined actions as pushing or unseating opponents—was at the top of the list among Virginian entertainments claimed as genteel. It was only partly replaced by regular British-style races in the second half of the eighteenth century. Horses had enormous practical value in the region, but more importantly, they also epitomized patrician prestige, especially when quality was involved. Visitors to the colony were soon made aware that "the gentlemen of Virginia, who are exceedingly fond of horse racing, have spared no expence or trouble to improve the breed of them by importing great numbers from England." John Goode, owner of many prize horses, was so devoted to racing that he had two different courses constructed in the vicinity of his house. Gatherings related to horse races combined polite socializing with popular entertainment. Their local significance was manifest in the language of a race advertisement in the *Virginia Gazette* in 1737: "We have Advice from Hanover County, that on St. Andrew's Day, being the 30th of November next, there are to be Horse Races, and several Divisions for the Entertainment of Gentlemen and the Ladies, in the Old Field, near Capt. John Bickerton's, in that County (if permitted by the Hon. William Byrd, Esq., the Proprietor of the said Land)." The long list of "Diversions" that followed illuminates the peculiarly colonial mix of both genteel and popular forms of entertainment, with the balance in favor of the latter. They included runs, violin-playing contests, dinner and toasting, ballad singing ("the best Songster to have the prize, and all of them to have Liquor Sufficient to clear their Windpipes"), wrestling, dancing, and choosing "the handsomest young country Maid that appears in the Field."[74]

Horses validated landed prestige in another, peculiar way—by invoking the respectability of genealogy. Great pride was attached in the colonies to the pedigrees of the best horses; the more noble and blue-blooded the horse, the more prestige flowed to the owner. Colonel John Tayloe of Virginia was proud to have the walls of his dining room decorated with "twenty four of the most celebrated among the English Race Horses, Drawn masterly, & set in elegant gilt Frames." If we can rely on Fithian's narrative, at a dinner party he attended, the gentle folk debated heatedly about "the Excellence of each other's Colts" to the extent that one guest, Sally Panton, could hardly raise any other subject. "I wanted to hear her converse," he noted, "but poor Girl anything she attempted to say was drowned in the more polite & useful jargon about Dogs & Horses!" As an outsider to the colony, he was astonished at what he saw as a more respectful treatment given by the gentry to horses than to slaves; he thought it not surprising that some slaves would rebel in a "desperate attempt for gaining that Civility, & Plenty which tho' denied them, is here, commonly bestowed on Horses."[75]

Other forms of gentry lifestyle that illustrate the inclination toward the popular were cockfighting and dancing. The sport of cockfighting, in Europe considered a pastime suitable mainly for the commoners, did not carry such a stigma of vulgarity among the Virginia gentry, who participated in it widely and often with great passion. In the second half of the eighteenth century, cockfighting became a solidly established element of the gentry culture in the colony, with elaborate networks of patronage, betting, intercounty rivalries, and balls with music and dancing accompanying major games. Even John Carter of Shirley did not consider it below his rank of secretary of the colony to attend such matches. The colonists paid little heed to the fact that to members of European polite society such entertainments were distinctly ungenteel. Chastellux found this Virginia diversion, still commonplace in 1782, appropriate only for rustic, unsophisticated "countrymen, who are no more particular about the conveniences of life than they are in the choice of their amusements." A contemporary German aristocrat also found it "too cruel . . . to enjoy." Reid, complaining about the arrogant pride of Virginia gentlemen, asked dejectedly, "What wisdom can be learnt at a horse race or a cock-fight?"[76]

Dancing was another well-liked gentry diversion, but its style also was clearly more popular and less restrained by strict polite norms than among European elites. Predictably, European visitors pointed to what they saw as a lack of grace in the performances. One noted that Virginia gentlewomen—whom, unlike women of quality in Britain, he saw as "seldom accomplished" and "unequal to any interesting or refined conversation"—were "immoderately fond of dancing, and indeed it is almost the only amusement they partake of: but even in this they discover great want of taste and elegance, and seldom appear with that gracefulness and ease, which these movements are calculated to display." The willingness of colonial gentry to dance the jig rather than formal dances was seen as signifying a lack of refinement, because it appeared too spontaneous and informal, "without any method or regularity." Polite, formal dances were, of course, performed on various prominent occasions, but the colonists did not seem to show much enthusiasm for them. Performing the minuet at the beginning of a ball was often only a liturgical device of approved refinement, as everyone eagerly waited for the less docile country dances. This preference for spontaneity elicited comments that the planters tended to be too wild in their entertainments, sinning against the gentle virtue of moderation: "Some very odd customs they have at these Merry-makings; you would think all care was then thrown aside and that every Misfortune was buried in Oblivion . . . at set times nothing but Jollity and Feasting goes forward." But if we put aside the usual European highbrow complaints, dancing functioned in the colonies successfully as a local standard of genteel style. In Virginia the ability to dance was "a necessary qualification for a person to appear even decent in Company." One of Robert Carter's sons, Charles Carter of Cleve, even left precise instructions in his will that his sons and daughters were to be taught dancing. Reid noted in 1769 that in Virginia the ability to dance "is the principle characteristic of a fine gentleman, and no man can assume that title without it."[77]

This practical mind-set and a preference for more popular rather than formal aesthetics remained strong even among second-generation colonial gentlemen. Landon Carter, one of the wealthiest landowners in Virginia, was well known for his pronounced inclination toward useful and purposeful activities and pastimes, rather than those deemed too frivolous or abstract. For instance, theater was not for him a required genteel diversion; on the contrary, the play he was "dragged" to in Williamsburg in 1752 "surfeited" him "with Stupidity and nonsense." As Jack P. Greene has pointed out, literature made sense for the colonel only if it had some practical or didactic significance, preferably if it provided "agreeable instruction" or "some moral truth." This did not mean he was not well-read and perfectly capable of using a literary comparison, as he did, for instance, when he aptly likened his spoiled daughter-in-law to Lady Townley from one of Richard B. Sheridan's comedies. It was just that for him, as for so many others of his group, usefulness received higher priority in the hierarchy of values than art for art's sake. Unlike a European gentleman, in the plantation environment he did not have to suffer as much anxiety that such preferences could at times betray a commercial, ungenteel worldview.[78]

These utilitarian preferences were even more apparent in the evident lack of interest in high art. At first it might seem a little surprising that with so much attention devoted to achieving gentility, the link between noble virtue and the arts, so pronounced in Europe, was markedly weak or absent. Why such coolness to the arts amid so much enthusiasm for refinement? After all, it was art that the eighteenth century entrusted with the mission of creating ideal forms, an aspiration parallel to the model gentleman's ideal of perfection and beauty. Paintings that were not imported were often produced by way of imitation or simply copied from British engravings. The colonies developed practically no aesthetic theory. There was no market for artistic experiment with form and metaphor in pursuit of the sublime or the metaphysical; Sir Joshua Reynolds's *Third Discourse* on the ultimate, "divine" principles of art rarely if ever showed up on the bookshelves of the planter gentry. Even Byrd, who accumulated a library of 3,500 volumes in his residence at Westover, had almost no titles on art. Inventories of major eighteenth-century Virginia libraries show few literary works oriented exclusively toward amusement, revealing instead a striking predominance of books of utilitarian interest.[79] The reasons for this state of things must include the colonial gentry's lack of long traditions as a class and its decentralized, nonurban environment. Patronage as a form of supporting and promoting painters or writers was practically unknown, while in Europe it often involved the construction of monuments, buildings, and interiors and the creation of busts and portraits of both ancestors and the living in order to glorify the patron's good taste as well as family honor. Patronage of the arts and protection of men of literature, theater, and music had for centuries been considered one of the nobility's ethical obligations. Even the more sober, bourgeois elites, as in early modern Amsterdam, patronized art, especially painting, although with a preference for concrete themes, such as portraits, historical events, and biblical scenes.[80] In the nonurban cultures of plantation colonies this was not an option. Being knowledgeable about the latest developments in drama, poetry, or painting was expected and desired among the gentry, but it was not a sine qua non of their gentility, quite unlike British high society where the lack of such attributes would denote a gentle-

Beautiful Order and Politeness 167

man manqué. When the colonists did turn to art, a strong inclination toward the pragmatic was translated into selective preferences in terms of taste. For instance, paintings, if ordered at all, were mostly portraits, with expectations of simple realism.

Some insight into the problem of colonial artistic taste may be gained from the observations of John Singleton Copley, who gained much success as a portrait painter but decided to leave America for Europe. Copley noted in 1767 that if he returned to America, he would have to "Bury all my improvements among people entirely destitute of all just Ideas of the Arts and without any addition of Reputation to what I have presently gained." Reflecting on the taste for art among Americans, he noted that "the people generally regard it as no more than any other useful trade, as they sometimes term it, like that of a Carpenter tailor or shew maker, not as one of the most noble Arts in the World. Which is not a little Mortifying for me." Any support for his artistic pursuits would have to come from Europe, since in America "the Arts are so disregarded, I can hope for nothing, but what I receive from a thousand Leagues Distance." In the culture of colonial elites, paintings, whether portraits or engravings of prize racehorses, were primarily important as elegant embellishments of a gentleman's seat. William Byrd assembled a whole collection at Westover, including portraits of his family members and his various well-born friends in England, such as Sir Robert Southwell, the earl of Orrery, the marquis of Halifax, and the duke of Argyle.[81] It was almost as if the young colonial gentry was following the advice of Defoe, who in one of his didactic dialogues recommended the possession of paintings not so much for the sake of the sublime as to enhance the genteel status of the owner. "You want some good paintings," insisted one of his characters; "pictures are a noble ornament to a house. Nothing can set it off more." He made a similar observation on possessing a library; he did not prescribe what books it should contain but merely emphasized that "a gentleman should not be without it," for "'tis a handsome ornament."[82]

One of the most striking pieces of evidence of the colonial gentry's attitude toward aesthetics may be found in George Washington's arrangements in 1757 for the purchase of a painting for his residence. He wrote his factor in London for a "neat Lanskip, 3 feet by 21½ Inches—1 Inch Margin for a Chim'y." It was intended for a particular spot in the just remodeled west parlor at Mount Vernon (fig. 5). Except for the physical dimensions in feet and

5. A view of the front parlor at Mount Vernon, showing the "neat lanskip." (Courtesy of the Mount Vernon Ladies' Association)

inches, he gave no directions whatsoever as to the quality, style, or mood of the painting. Listing it together with other "sundry goods" such as windowpanes, wallpaper, tables, hinges, and locks left little doubt that its role as polite adornment transcended a purely artistic one.[83] Yet we might well say that it made the painting no less meaningful for the legitimizing process than if the invoice had quoted Joshua Reynolds's prescription for the sublime in art.

One of the notable exceptions to such attitudes—which only affirmed the general rule—was Jefferson, who came to see himself, especially during his stay in France, as both a fully legitimate arbiter and a patron of high art

Beautiful Order and Politeness

and culture for the new nation. He openly admitted to the somewhat ungenteel attribute of being "an enthusiast on the subject of the arts" but added that "it is an enthusiasm of which I am not ashamed, as it's object is to improve the taste of my countrymen, to increase their reputation, to reconcile to them the respect of the world." In 1785 when he learned in Paris that the Virginia Capitol was not going to be built according to his design (which he based on the plans of the Maison Carrée of Nîmes), he bitterly complained to Madison, writing that the Nîmes model was "noble beyond expression, and would have done honour to our country as presenting to travellers a morsel of taste in our infancy promising much for our maturer age." He argued that public money should be laid out for "something honorable, the satisfaction of seeing an object and proof of national good taste," rather than in a way that would bring upon Virginians "the regret and mortification of erecting a monument of our barbarism which will be loaded with execrations as long as it shall endure."[84]

Americans were not unique in their identity-driven pursuit of genteel style. To assert their authority, most emergent British colonial elites, as G. C. Bolton has observed, patterned themselves on the original model of the landed gentry; their common problem was a lack of historically shared high cultural dispositions as a group.[85] This was why the first generation of provincial gentry, carrying the main weight of the endeavor to refine and improve, made the greatest investment in the cultural capital of symbols and styles. This development was typified by the advancement from the crowded four-room wooden farmhouse of Captain Augustine Washington at Ferry Farm to his son's imposing residence at Mount Vernon. Among the most elegant possessions of Augustine, inventoried in 1743 when George was eleven, were—apart from a £2.10 looking glass—a set of "plate" including one soupspoon, eighteen small spoons, and seven teaspoons, a watch, and a sword, with a total value of £25.10. Aesthetic needs considered indispensable by his son George in 1768 ranged from fashionable English carriages to laced scarlet waistcoats.[86] The early phases of such development, even within one generation, usually focused on commanding objects of taste commensurate with growing wealth. During later, more established stages—and for the next generation—an aesthetic sensitivity to lifestyle served as a means of categorizing rank and quality, and was a vital component of the gentry's honor as a group.

Despite all the impediments of provincialism, the aesthetic sphere of the quest for gentility appears to have been the most immediately effective in its legitimizing outcomes. One major reason why a silver fork or a crest on the carriage door carried such power was that cultural history is inherently personal; we inhabit situations which in themselves are not separable from our immersion in them. Gentility—like wealth, gender, race, and other social categories—does not exist as a separate, objective, and somehow detached sphere of life, although we may describe it so upon reflection. Rather, they are all integral parts of the complex daily flow of human experience. Life takes place in everyday situations, and only when we take a broader view can we appreciate the power of these small gestures and objects to create meaning. It lies not in their ability merely to affirm a social order but in the substantial degree to which they actually constitute such an order. The colonial success of genteel stylization could indeed be used as evidence for Max Weber's assertion that whereas class is designated by the relationship to production and capital, prestige status is culturally defined by the consumption of goods as represented by exclusive styles of life.[87]

If we approach colonial applications of genteel style as improvised compromises between local reality and the metropolitan cultural model, the pursuit of such style must appear as an authentic, autonomous experience driving the legitimizing process. It is true that the model was incompletely applied, and that there was a peculiarly colonial pattern in this selectivity. If the eighteenth-century English gentleman was supposed to maintain a happy symmetry between keeping his head in the clouds and his feet on the ground, his counterpart in plantation America was much more disposed in his stylistic choices toward the practical, the solid, and the useful. Although this alleged deviation from the perfect standard has so often inspired critics—both contemporaries and historians—to denounce the whole process of validation by such means, the colonists succeeded quite well. They did so because for them the meaning of such refinement was being constructed not within the European cultural marketplace but within the colonial one, where they were the dominant elite. Moreover, the provincials' relentless determination not infrequently produced genuine achievements even when measured by demanding European standards. General Francisco de Miranda, well known for his interest in art, music, and literature, found the country residences of South Carolina gentry "handsome, comfortable, and spacious,

Beautiful Order and Politeness

reflecting thereby wealth, sound taste, and love for rural life." Julian Ursyn Niemcewicz, an aide to General Thaddeus Kosciuszko and a very discerning Polish gentleman, visited Mount Vernon in June 1798 and observed in his diary with much admiration and barely veiled surprise that so much refined taste was to be found so far from Europe. "In a word," he wrote, "the garden, the plantation, the house, the whole upkeep, proves that a man born with natural taste can divine the beautiful without having seen the model. The Gl. has never left America. After seeing his house and his gardens one would say that he had seen the most beautiful examples in England of this style."[88]

CHAPTER 5

Genteel Ethos on the Eve of the Revolution

> "We are descended from a people whose government was founded on liberty: our glorious forefathers of Great Britain made liberty the foundation of every thing. . . . We drew the spirit of liberty from our British ancestors; by that spirit we have triumphed over every difficulty."
>
> Edmund Randolph of Virginia, 1788

The Revolution put colonial gentility to its most severe test yet. The conflict also stood as the culmination of a cycle—begun in the early years of the century—in the colonial pursuit of this ambition. Members of the American gentry had not failed this test, but the reasons they ultimately remained victorious on the cultural battlefield were grounded not in their rejection of the genteel ethos but in their strong identification with it. It gave them the indispensable confidence and conviction of purpose and enabled them to pose an effective challenge to Britain in cultural terms, and not just politically. Just as Edmund Randolph, scion of one of the most prominent Virginia families, saw the heritage of liberty contained in the principles of British government as the main source of the strength that enabled Americans to attain victory in the Revolution, we should recognize that he and other leaders also drew energy and fortitude from the English genteel ethos, which successfully legitimized their authority as a ruling class and made personal liberty and independence of will central to their identity. When Randolph later was explaining his objections to the Constitution, he invoked such core components of this ethos as civic responsibility, honor, personal freedom, and probity of deportment: "Having obeyed the impulse of duty, having satisfied my conscience, and, I trust, my God, I shall appeal to no other tribunal: nor do I come a candidate for popularity; my manner

Genteel Ethos on the Eve of the Revolution 173

of life has never yet betrayed such a desire." He felt that these virtues substantiated his views so well that he saw no need for wider social acceptance or recognition. "Honors," he claimed, "when compared to the satisfaction accruing from a conscious independence and rectitude of conduct, are no equivalent."[1]

Let us now contrast this deeply internalized ethos with British rhetoric directed at Americans as the Revolutionary conflict developed in the 1770s. The English elite not only continued, as it had for so long, but even intensified its negative categorizations of Americans as inferiors and plebeians. A choice example revealing the cultural mechanism underlying the political conflict was Samuel Johnson's 1775 pamphlet on taxation. He began by ridiculing the American leaders as supposed "descendants of men who left all for liberty," who were now claiming that they had inherited "the right which their ancestors possessed, of enjoying all the privileges of Englishmen." They did inherit their ancestor's rights, he taunted them, and "can inherit no more," for "the colonists are descendants of men who either had no votes in elections, or who voluntarily resigned them for something, in their opinion, of more estimation." As a result, they had "exactly what their ancestors left them, not a vote in making laws." Such arguments came from the well of ingrained cultural labels attached by the British elite to the American colonists: their low social descent was now seen as precluding a title to liberties, and their duty as inferiors was to obey England: "A colony is to the mother-country as a member to the body." One of the most damaging of these labels—that of immorality epitomized in the practice of slavery—was reserved as a concluding argument. It pointed to the hypocrisy of the southern leaders of the Revolution, who themselves held slaves but relished using the concept of slavery as a metaphor for British tyranny. "If slavery be thus fatally contagious," ran the argument, "how is it that we hear the loudest yelps for liberty among the drivers of Negroes?" Perhaps, it was suggested, the Revolutionary leaders should decide "that the slaves should be set free, an act which, surely, the [American] lovers of liberty cannot but commend." Putting the political content aside, how would Randolph, with his intense pride as a gentleman and his deeply held belief that even a mention of abolishing slavery would be "dishonorable to Virginia," react to Johnson's arguments?[2] The answer offered to this question must be twofold. First, he, and others like him, employed certain genteel values, with which they strongly identified, to formulate the ideology of resistance to Britain. In this sense the Revolution may be said to have provided solid evidence that these values were indeed a source of strength for many colonial leaders. Second, for the American gentry the Revolution also became a catalyst for the first substantial transformation of the legitimizing pattern.

It is convenient to consider the latter point first. A common argument in the texts of patriot writers and intellectuals was that just as the old political system was being replaced, cultural dependence on Europe should also be terminated in order to forge a new identity for the nation.[3] Such statements, together with the accompanying invariably antiaristocratic rhetoric, may have led us to misread the cultural results of the quest for gentility and to dismiss the quest itself as irrelevant in the context of approaching democracy. A closer look at this rhetoric reveals that not only was the genteel canon not irrelevant but that there was a causal relationship between this canon and the Revolutionary conceptualizations of both anti-British arguments and America's emerging new self-image. What happened was that the ideal remained, but the legitimizing authority was changed. What was hitherto a one-way street from the metropolis to the provinces was reversed, so that the colonial elites could claim that they were the only remaining depositors of this ethos, since it was being perverted in Britain. Patriot gentlemen felt that the original, authentic model of British virtue, the "honour of our ancestors, the Antient Britons," now inhabited America, and that they were its rightful defenders. Admiral Howe might call them "rebellious barbarians," but Landon Carter now saw the English soldiers as no more than "slave tutored brutes," sent on a dishonorable mission against true liberty and noble rectitude. In other words, this inversion of the validating order largely preserved the core of the old genteel model and rejected only the dependence on British arbiters, while the model continued—with an increased intensity—to confer its legitimizing authority on the members of the American gentry.[4] Just as they justified their political opposition to England by invoking the British constitution, they repudiated London's contempt for their rights and for their title to the status of gentlemen that embodied those rights.

In this sense the Revolution only brought to the surface some of the tensions that had long been simmering. The new anti-British language had much to do with the American gentry's quiet loathing, accrued over decades, for European arrogance toward its civilizing ambitions. It is very significant that so many Revolutionary leaders from the South—and not only the South—were first-generation gentry, whose life experiences involved both the American success of their ambitions to achieve rank and refinement and the humiliation of metropolitan contempt. By the 1770s they were well established but still acutely conscious of their continuing dependence on Europe's cultural authority. As the new British policies after 1763 also began to undermine their political prominence, the old legitimizing mechanism, thus far merely frustrating, became insufferable. When this indignation surfaced, freed by the Revolution, it turned out to be excellent nourishment for cultural arguments against England. While Byrd could do little about the contempt he faced as a colonial from the London elite in 1723, Washington, who was equally inflamed by patronizing comments from the aristocratic Virginia governor Robert Dinwiddie and Maryland governor Horatio Sharpe, lived to find comfort and relief from such indignities in the language of Revolutionary republicanism. Old resentment surfaced anew but could now be effectively channeled. What had up to now been called a traditional colonial "respect and affection for Britain" and "fondness for its fashions" quickly became unfashionable. European definers of refinement suddenly appeared as nothing more than "pompous blockheads."[5] America now became a bulwark of true virtue; it was here that it would be defended and saved for posterity.

Among the chief tenets of this new rhetoric were arguments that European high society was corrupt, that this corruption was rooted in commercial greed and materialist luxury, that courtly, sophisticated refinement was vain and worthless, that true genteel virtue was now preserved in America, and that the old aristocracy was a "false" elite, while the American gentry fully deserved its title because it stood for true merit. Even a brief look at this list reveals two striking larger issues in this new discourse. One is that it contains a whole catalog of negative attributes formerly assigned by the metropolitans to the colonial gentry and therefore must be seen at least in part as a response to a century-long frustration of American ambitions. The other is that by placing the American gentry in a position superior to that of the old noble classes of Europe, it attempted to finally resolve the problem of legitimacy, hitherto unattainable for the colonials.

A century earlier an English author could claim that "the very Air" of the colonies corrupted even the most virtuous immigrants.[6] Now Thomas Paine assigned all corruption to the Old World and maintained that America by its very nature provided the proper atmosphere for true virtue: "Those who are conversant with Europe would be tempted to believe that even the air of the Atlantic disagrees with the constitution of foreign vices; if they survive the voyage, they either expire on their arrival, or linger away in an incurable consumption."[7] In this, he echoed the development of political discourse in the years leading up to the Revolution, with its frequent claims that the noble English constitution was declining due to political as well as moral and cultural corruption. Putting aside the well-known political aspects of these debates, the cultural argument was that the corruption of the British ruling classes—the same elite that thus far carried the little-questioned title to public virtue and refinement—was caused by luxury and wealth. To claim that Americans now defended true virtue was to kill two birds with one stone; it gave them a moral title to resist Britain, as well as a cultural title to legitimate virtue. It is no wonder that this argument gained such huge popularity among colonial and early republican elites.

The new Revolutionary role of genteel values also surfaced in the enthusiastic manner in which the old anticommercial bias of the landed ethos, so often used against colonial nouveaux riches, was now applied to the old country. According to Landon Carter, England's "declinsion," like that of Rome, was brought about by excessive power, resulting in "luxuries and extravagances of trade" and a growing "effeminacy" among the ruling class. The last epithet gained special prominence in the classically inspired republican rhetoric of the Revolutionaries. The highly gendered meaning of effeminacy, directly related to the exclusion of women from public life, was now ascribed both to British aristocracy and to cowardly, unpatriotic men in America; the conflict only intensified the old identification of masculinity with virtue, especially when it was understood as public spirit. Such a weakness, according to Carter, engendered "barbarity, servitude, and debauchery," vices that in the genteel ethos signified opposites to the virtues of politeness, liberty, and moderation. In contrast, the old idyllic image of the plantation as a genteel haven of uncorrupted simplicity and virtue could now be extended to all of America.[8]

Luxury became a Revolutionary code word not only for moral decline but also for affectation and enslavement to metropolitan fashion setters. The *Virginia Gazette* suggested that luxury was at the root of the whole conflict: "Luxury begot Arbitrary Power, Arbitrary Power begot Oppression." Aristocratic and delicate taste in the arts—which America, with its practical orientation, was wanting—was now depicted as not only superfluous but dangerous for the Republic for it represented nothing more than "sickly refinement" and a "false sentimental luxury."[9] Debunking monarchy and hereditary aristocracy became a sport from which Americans could draw peculiar comfort. Not only were former legitimizers assigned the vices of vanity, depravity, and arrogance, but even their old anti-American arguments involving cruelty to slaves and Indianization were conjured up; they were now declared ruthless masters, wanting to "enslave" America, worse than "brutes" who do not "devour their young" and worse than "savages" who "do not make war upon their families." Even American rusticity and provincialism were now blamed on London. They were portrayed as the result of a long dependence on Britain, which profited from the colonies to enrich itself so it could wallow in luxury and decadence, ignoring or looking down on America. From a revered arbiter of high culture, Britain descended to the status of the main "barrier between us and the polished world." When peace came in 1783, members of the local intellectual elite assembled at Washington College in Chester, Maryland, welcomed the end of English control, seeing it as an opportunity to finally expel provincialism from America, so that the country could become a "Land refin'd, Where once Ignorance sway'd th' untutor'd mind."[10]

Only with the assumption that the original European virtue now resided in America could the cosmopolitan Jefferson advise Americans to stay away from all things European. But such calls seem to have had the purpose of alleviating feelings of inferiority rather than of totally negating European culture. Americans rejected the extravagant magnificence of contemporary European high style to give the relative modesty of their country a sanction of noble quality. An American gentleman visiting the palace of Versailles in 1788 was stunned by its splendor but immediately claimed that America, where only merit was in esteem, was "more great because more virtuous." Such an assertion did not necessarily signify a major weakness of genteel identity on his part; to make this claim, he had to be confident of his own worth and honor. Aristocratic John Adams fervently believed that the virtuous American republic was safe from European-style depravity. "We, to be sure," he wrote, "are far remote from this. Many hundred years must roll away before we shall be corrupted."[11]

One of the outcomes of this cultural confrontation was the concept of an aristocracy of merit. It emerged at the intersection between continued American aspirations to gentility and the political ideology of the Revolution, as it developed in the debates over the role of hereditary aristocracy and monarchy. By assuming the corruption of virtue under the tyrannical system of Britain, members of the colonial gentry came to regard themselves as true defenders of the Montesquieuan link between honor and liberty. Long denied legitimacy by the European elite, they now reversed the comparison to deny it to the old European class. Such views were obviously morally beneficial for the American elite, since its dominant status was presented as deserved or earned rather than inherited. But this rhetoric of merit, however gratifying for the claimants, did not change the fact that they were still legitimizing their dominance. Neither was it a culturally novel idea, for the old genteel ethos had always stressed merit and birth as two sides of the same coin.

Jefferson saw great hope for post-Revolutionary America in his belief that "there is a natural aristocracy among men," the criteria of which—unlike those of the "artificial aristocracy" founded on wealth and birth—were "virtue and talents." Often portrayed as a major democratic departure from British tradition, this concept appears much more conservative when examined in the context of this discussion of gentility. This new Jeffersonian class was not merely conceived as a vessel of abstract refinement but—just like the old classes in Britain—was defined as possessing a title to govern; he called it a "precious gift of nature" which was "provided with virtue and wisdom enough to manage the concerns of society." In other words, two essential attributes of the old ethos—civic responsibility and a title to rule—were preserved; the difference was that Jefferson believed that common people would naturally elect such gentlemen to power. "May we not even say," he wrote, "that that form of government is the best which provides most effectually for a pure selection of these natural aristoi into the offices of government?" He even suggested that Virginians were more independent in their judgments than New Englanders, so that when they elected members of prominent gentry families like Randolphs or Burwells, they did so solely for their "great personal superiority over a common competitor."[12]

In his study of the American Revolution, Gordon Wood has suggested that its radicalism lay in the fact that "almost at a stroke the Revolution destroyed all the earlier talk of paternal and maternal government, filial alle-

Genteel Ethos on the Eve of the Revolution 179

giance, and mutual contractual obligations between the rulers and the ruled," and that "overnight, modern conceptions of public power replaced older archaic ideas." He links this shift to a parallel change in the very concept of gentility. The old system was to be replaced with political rulers who were "men of merit and talent," creating a "new moral and social order led by enlightened and virtuous men." It was to be accompanied by a general spread of civility, with "politeness, good manners, and elegance" as the "defining characteristics of the new society." At the heart of this concept of progress, Wood placed "the changing idea of a gentleman," which "now took a moral as well as social meaning, as gentility became republicanized," that is, purified of the old familial pride and ostentation. This meant that "new, man-made criteria of gentility—politeness, grace, learning, and character," instead of pedigree, were now to become dominant; the colonists were now "eager to create a new kind of aristocracy, based on principles that could be learned and were superior to those of birth and family, and even great wealth."[13]

My examination of legitimacy strongly supports Wood's emphasis on the importance of gentility, but it also suggests that some of the changes so central to his argument neither happened overnight, nor were they such a radical novelty. The concept of an "aristocracy of merit" was not a dramatically new departure but rather a new application of an old idea. It was not gentility that became republicanized but the old notion of a meritorious elite, a concept that had always been at the very core of the genteel ethos. It denoted persons of quality, unfettered by what were considered plebeian passions and prejudices, possessing a politeness that facilitated a harmonious society and maintaining a disinterested ability to serve the public good. Defoe used it as the basis for promoting attainable virtue, and it was crucial for the self-made colonial gentry. Neither placed stress (symbolic devices excepted) on birth and ancestry as a condition of quality, because it was precisely the hereditary criterion that made them vulnerable to attacks by the old elites. As a result, on the eve of the Revolution the colonial gentry not only did not have to take particular pains to reject heredity but was only too happy to articulate its abomination of that particular instrument, so long used in Britain to exclude it from legitimacy. This is why the open condemnations of heredity on the eve of the Revolution were not equivalent to a radically new "moral meaning" of being a gentleman in America. Consequently, the emergence of the idea of a "natural aristocracy of merit and virtue" was only a very partial modification of the old concept of the gentleman, while its message can be seen as rather more conservative than radical. After all, the "natural" element of the definition guaranteed that the elite of wealth maintained its position. The "aristocracy" element upheld the hierarchical, genteel-ungenteel dichotomy as a model of a desirably ordered society. The "merit" ingredient was to assure that the already refined and educated Americans would now be the new arbiters and definers of cultural legitimacy.

The ideas of public spirit and responsibility for the rest of society and a belief in the ability to rise above one's own private interest—all crucial elements of the old genteel ethos, and all emphasized anew by the Revolutionary gentry as parts of its own civic virtue—provide further examples of cultural self-perpetuation. The title and obligation to rule on behalf of the common people continued to be seen not only as an exclusive privilege for those ranked as gentry, that is, those who by their ownership of property were assumed to have a stake in the stability of society, but also as part of a larger natural order of things. "There can be no fixed and permanent government that does not rest on the fixed and permanent orders and objects of mankind," wrote John Francis Mercer in 1788 in the *Maryland Gazette*, and he elaborated that "the order of the GENTRY . . . is essential to a perfect government, founded on representation." It was to the title of gentry to represent society at large that George Mason, a great planter and slave owner in the Northern Neck of Virginia, was referring when he complained that in the House of Representatives, as designed by the Constitution, "there is not the substance, but the shadow only of representation. . . . The laws will, therefore, be generally made by men little concerned in, and unacquainted with their effects and consequences." When he spoke of republican government as "deriving from the great body of the society" and being incompatible with the power of "a favored class," the class he had in mind was "a handful of tyrannical nobles," not gentlemen of merit like himself.[14] Fear of hereditary aristocracy was no greater than the fear of "mobocracy." To undermine the assumption of the gentry's public spirit was to imperil the larger "order of mankind." Another Virginian gentleman, James Madison, expressed concern at the Constitutional Convention that the commoner class—dependent for lack of property and therefore incapable, in his view, of sufficient civic merit to govern—would soon grow perilously large, as "the proportion of those who will labor under all the hardships of life, and secretly sigh for a more equal distribution of its blessings . . . may in time outnumber those who are placed above the feelings of indigence." This could result in the subversion of order by new claims to power, a threat he saw as approaching, for "symptoms of a levelling spirit, as we have understood, have sufficiently appeared in certain quarters to give notice of the future danger.[15]

But even if we can agree that Revolutionary gentility had a conservative orientation, we still need to reconcile this with the egalitarian implications of republicanism. The explanation must rest on our understanding of gentility's modus operandi in eighteenth-century American culture. To illustrate this problem it is useful to refer once more to Richard Bushman's study of the emergence of polite society in America. In its first part, which deals with this period, he shows how genteel ideals of elegance and cultivation motivated wealthy colonials to express them in the world of material objects and concludes that what drove this refinement process was much more than mere emulation of cultural patterns from Europe. In his analysis gentility is a very broad and flexible ideal of personal refinement, at first available to the elite only and later, with the coming of nineteenth-century capitalism, to be shared by all wishing "to elevate human life" and raise themselves "to a higher plane." Improved style led to "a more satisfying life" because "gentility always aimed to form brilliant and harmonious societies, where people came together to perform for one another." His view of taste consistently follows this concept of gentility; taste "implied a mission for the refined to beautify the world, beginning with their own persons and radiating to all they possessed and influenced." This was why Washington spent every free moment on the "adornment of Mount Vernon" and "the beautification of his environment." Although he acknowledges the implications of taste for power, he shows that colonial emulation of high style was driven mainly by an enthrallment with the metropolitan elite's prominence. "Provincials paid heed to the English upper classes" because "their conspicuous wealth, their offices, their acknowledged eminence in society made them fascinating." But this positive, motivating force of gentility to create beauty, harmony, and smooth social relations was, in his view, seriously impaired by its "harsh" "judgmental and censorious" side. The tendency to discriminate, "to control nature and society for the sake of a beautiful appearance," was, according to Bushman, a "flaw at the core of gentility." He argues that its "damaging" power lay in the fact that taste divided people into the "better sort" and the "rude and ignorant." This antiegalitarian defect was the main reason why gentility ultimately proved to be "weak and superficial."[16]

Taken separately, all these arguments are true (except the last, for which Bushman's book, showing the enormously durable power of gentility, actually provides much contrary evidence), yet together they still leave us with an apparent contradiction between equality and exclusiveness. The preceding examination of legitimacy suggests that what made gentility so attractive was both the dream of achieving equality with members of the elite and the implication of inequality that such a superior station conveyed. Although on the surface it may appear somewhat paradoxical, and even strike us as a "flaw," discrimination was integral to gentility's cultural ontology, whether it involved excluding those uninitiated to good taste or those deemed not entitled to civic roles. The primary yearning of the newly wealthy claimants was to elevate themselves—above their own previous status, above their parents' earlier humble life, above their old milieu of origin in Britain, into what they saw as the higher categories of society. Their parents, as a rule, emigrated to America not to retain and preserve their old status but in the hope of economically and socially improving their lives. In contemporary British culture the ultimate model of such elevation was to achieve the position of a gentleman. Only there could one be equal among equals—while everyone else was made unequal, for nowhere did this equality extend to servants, slaves, women, or others classified as inferiors. In other words, while gentility equalized the elite, it sought to hierarchize the rest of society through its capacity to exclude and include. It was this rationale that drove young George Washington—eager to enter the genteel world opened to him through his brother Lawrence's marriage into the Fairfax family—when he diligently copied maxims on civility and decent behavior from Francis Hawkins's version of a French courtesy book. Their express purpose was not to please everyone but to develop a gentleman's ability to display appropriate manners in dealing with equals: "In your Apparel . . . keep to the Fashion of your equals"; with inferiors: "Let your Discourse with Men of Business be short and Comprehensive"; and with superiors: "In Pulling off your Hat to Persons of Distinction, as Noblemen, Justices, Churchmen &c make a Reverence, bowing more or less according to the Custom of the Better Bred, and Quality of the Person."[17]

There were thus two faces to gentility, one which glorified and honored equality, for members only, and one which insisted on inequality with inferiors, often treating them with patronizing contempt. The latter one is well known and documented; the former, with its potentially innovative implications for the future democratic culture of the new Republic, has not received much attention because it has been usual to depict the Revolution as a fundamental abandonment of old genteel inequalities in favor of an egalitarian democracy. As a result, the "aristocratic" element at the roots of American democracy—and especially its significance for the public articulation and propagation of the notions of liberty and equality—has been all too often selectively silenced. This element has not been appreciated because it seemed antithetical not only to democracy but also to the popular culture of common people, even though high culture in Europe was never hermetically sealed off from the popular culture, and both have always borrowed from each other, as was the case, for instance, with low, popular religious rituals built around themes defined by the high elites of the Catholic Church.

This analysis of the quest for legitimacy points to a different conclusion. Not only were republicanism and egalitarianism not antithetical to gentility, but, on the contrary, the colonial elite's seriousness in pursuing gentility (especially in the second half of the eighteenth century) and its success in achieving cultural maturity in terms of the genteel ethos contributed immensely to making equality a household word in America. This genteel pursuit involved both a cultivation and a jealous defense of liberty and equality for members of that class. As a result, when the Revolution elevated them to new authority, they themselves were able to sanction and impress egalitarian and libertarian ideas—as principles—on the public mind and ultimately help make them part of an otherwise inherently popular culture of America.

At the time of the Revolution, however, this sanctioning did not involve a pansocial application of such principles. It is well to bear in mind that for the elite, the meanings of liberty and its offspring equality did not yet carry a modern universal sense. They derived their power from the link between the honor of genteel rank and personal independence. It was precisely to this link that Montesquieu referred in *The Spirit of the Laws* when he observed that because such honor treats people "upon a level" and "knows not how to submit," it is intrinsically unsuited for despotic political systems. But Montesquieu—and many of his American followers such as, for instance,

Theophilus Parsons—separated two political interests by differentiating between two liberties: those of the common people and those of the elite, both deserving protection in the Constitution. Notably, the bicameral legislature, a standard in American republican theory, was an echo of such a view of differing interests of persons and property. Equality may have been declared a self-evident truth by Revolutionary leaders, but as J. R. Pole aptly observed, self-evident was not understood in a universal sense but referred to those who had the ability to perceive such truths, a criterion that, like property, was assumed to distinguish the gentry elite.[18] It may therefore be argued that the republican language of equality did not emerge as a result of a substantial rejection of the earlier model of gentility but derived in a large part directly from the notions of equality and liberty contained within this model. The Revolution only provided a forum to utilize the old notion of equality as an anti-British postulate and as an argument for self-government. The colonial gentleman, who saw himself as a citizen and bearer of public virtue, now asserted his rights to equality with those recognized as citizens in Britain. Richard Bland, a prominent member of the Virginia House of Burgesses and heir of a wealthy line of planters, used the postulate of the equality of citizens in his 1766 pamphlet to argue against the Stamp Act. George Mason, author of the Virginia Declaration of Rights, also invoked equality but was careful to reject its potential applications on the domestic scene.[19] Madison saw a threat to liberty in the prospect that people in the "common situation," who lacked the required disinterestedness, would claim more power: "the rights of property & the public liberty will not be secure in their hands."[20]

To strengthen their claims, Revolutionary gentlemen, wary of their long history of being denied recognition, reached for another legitimizing principle, articulated by Jefferson as an argument for the equality of Americans with Englishmen: natural rights. It was a powerful instrument, but like the notion of equality itself, its very power carried unforeseen risks for the dominant role of the gentry—it implied the equality of all people. The authors of the argument did not yet fully realize the danger inherent in the new language they were popularizing; nowhere did they state that they intended to diminish or abdicate their own power overnight with the victory of the Revolution. The more truly democratic cycle of qualitative change in the development of cultural legitimacy would come only during the following several decades, as Americans wrestled with new ideas and new reality. The larger society was ready for such a transformation; there were a number of other democratizing and egalitarian influences at work, from the strong individualism of pioneer immigrants to the appeals of churches and preachers to individual consciousness. A good indication that the gentry did not quite realize that it had helped bring the genie of equality out of the bottle may be found in the surprise at the widely disapproving reactions to the establishment in 1783 of the Society of Cincinnati, with its elite, hereditary membership and elaborate ceremonies and badges. The original members, including George Washington, at first saw it as perfectly appropriate for their class and for the exercise of influence due their class; twenty-seven members of the society took part in the Constitutional Convention.[21] But the seeds had been sown, and the soil was fertile for change.

The Revolution closed one long cycle in the American quest for genteel legitimacy. But two other time frames also emerge from the examination of this pursuit. One shows that the first- and, at times, second-generation gentry were the most intensely involved in the legitimizing process. The other reveals a remarkable continuity of the old genteel ethos across the eighteenth century and across British plantation colonies. As for the first pattern, it was no accident that so many of the Revolutionary leaders were first-generation gentlemen, for it was among this group that aspirations to virtue and refinement were most determined. The worldview of the second and third generations was different from that of the first, for whom ethos, taste, and lifestyle were crucial to its members' elevation to authority. Their sons and grandsons took their wealth and rank for granted and were not infrequently less scrupulous in their pursuit of propriety. Such was the difference between William Byrd II, with his untiring efforts to acquire complete gentility, and his less constrained son William who ran into debts through gambling and extravagance and eventually committed suicide. Such was the difference between Landon Carter, a second-generation Virginia gentleman, who—strongly opposed to extravagance and self-indulgence—was convinced that "extremes in any thing are bad," and his eldest son, Robert Wormeley, for whom self-control and moderation were only impediments to his passion for gambling. Such was the difference between the Virginia merchant and landowner Thomas Nelson, whose meteoric rise to prominence was sustained by the shrewd political and business activities of his two sons William and Thomas, and his grandsons, who decimated the family fortune by extravagant spending. And such was the difference between Robert Carter III and his son Robert Bladen, who did not feel obliged to strive for virtue and—to his father's vast disappointment—ruined his estate by drinking and gambling.[22]

The relatively unbroken continuity of the main tenets of the genteel ethos itself during the century preceding the Revolution seems less remarkable when we realize that this ethos was much more than a chapter in early modern British culture; it was a highly cosmopolitan and durable pattern, with roots in ancient history. What is extraordinary about it is that although it evolved over a long period of European history, many of its core values have often remained remarkably stable in the face of deep social and cultural changes. Homer's epics gave a precise description of virtues expected of Greek nobility, and his list must sound familiar: a long and noble family genealogy, a beautiful appearance, hospitality, the ability to speak and behave politely, courage as warrior, contempt for materialistic greed and commercial employments, ambition for fame and recognition (exemplified by Achilles' choice of honorable death over longer life), and elaborate deference shown to one another by the aristocracy. Aristotle changed this model only slightly, laying more stress on the courtly virtues rather than martial ones; his nobleman was to be of beautiful aspect, magnanimous, free of the need of making money or being too professional, of dignified demeanor, generous, and honest. It is not hard to trace many of these classical qualities in Castiglione's description of the ideal Renaissance gentleman; virtue, personal honor, fame, classical education, grace, ease, and a rejection of professionalism. By the early eighteenth century, many of these core values had developed into a lasting secular and international ethos which became a bridge between cultures in time and space, a phenomenon for which British America provided abundant evidence. One of its peculiarities was that it was uniquely effective in serving various dominant elites over centuries. It often endured long after its particular social base had disappeared, serving new elites and new purposes. For instance, in fifteenth-century England the displacement of the knight from his military and political position was followed by a revival of chivalric ideals, and it was not merely a case of idealizing a lost world but of using the old ethos to legitimize a newly emerging nationalism. In America the landed model of gentility retained substantial legitimizing power long after the Revolution, and not only in the South but also—in a different variant—in New England. In Boston, for instance, members of the early nineteenth-century merchant elite acquired country estates to emphasize their membership in the class of ruling gentry. It mattered little that they were mostly profit-oriented merchants; they took up agriculture as disinterested dilettantes and pictured themselves as frugal, sober, and industrious gentlemen, in positive contrast with what they considered their more luxury-inclined and lazy southern counterparts.[23]

Approaching colonial gentility through the issue of cultural legitimacy has shown that this gentility was far more coherent, successful, and durable than we have been told. It played at least four highly effective roles in the plantation colonies: it validated the power of the historically new elite, it provided the members with the group identity they lacked, it helped stabilize and structure a still fluid society, and it made possible the accomplishment of personal improvement and refinement in a provincial setting. After all, when the founders—coming from various, often very different colonies and background experiences—met at the First Continental Congress in Philadelphia, gentility was probably the most powerful element that united them as a social class and implied certain common interests and assumptions. The role of provincialism in the success of this pursuit has been especially unappreciated. While in Britain tensions over legitimacy sprang from a rivalry between old elites and new aspirants, in the colonies a greater enemy was the provincial syndrome: lack of tradition, absence of models, rustic environment, chaotic social world, and metropolitan condescension. The gentry's protracted struggle with this adversary activated powerful ambitions, sustained by firm, self-imposed discipline. I have tried to show that the complicated story of this quest cannot be reduced to simple class formation or to purely idealistic attempts to achieve beauty and harmony. Genteel style did not merely "reinforce the established social order" in the colonies, as is sometimes suggested, but was in itself a major mode of creating and maintaining such an order.[24]

To do all this, colonial gentility could not have been artificial or fragile. Armed with historian's hindsight, one is tempted to see it as a mere facade, a colorful but artificial fantasy, with the colonists making sense of the harsh, crude, and often savage reality by invoking a noble ideal and constructing around it an elaborate social play to deceive themselves. But they were not just playing, on the colonial stage, roles written for them elsewhere. The reality of this stage was primary to their efforts, and the roles were chosen when they satisfied specific local needs.[25] Only when we realize that it was a play staged by people who were not dreamers and utopians but sober businessmen, calculating traders, and shrewd politicians do we become aware that this diligent and persevering pursuit of improvement provided a major driving motivation for their behavior. They evolved their own blend of gentility—less concerned with pedigrees and the sublime in art and more pragmatic, enterprising, materialistic, possessive, and irreverent. In Jefferson's own words, they were "fiery, voluptuary, indolent, unsteady, independent, zealous for their liberties, but trampling on those of others." An English visitor confirmed this view, noting that "they are haughty and jealous of their liberties, impatient of restraint, and can scarcely bear the thought of being controuled by any superior power."[26] This gentility was not of the salon type, but neither was it brittle; it was strong enough in its cult of independence and liberty to provide a solid base of values and ideas when the Revolution called for taking a stand. These values originally came from the well-stocked arsenal of English culture, the only such warehouse that hitherto had supplied genteel legitimacy. Defoe, although extremely proud of his commercial success, could not be expected to rest his ambition for social elevation on the honor of the merchant and had little choice but to strive for gentility. His imperatives help us understand that a European-style gentleman in the woods of Virginia was far from being an anomaly.

The reason why it has so often been presented as an anomaly has had much to do with the influence of exceptionalism on American historiography. Exceptionalism as an insistence on American uniqueness—a concept going back culturally as far as the early Puritans and intellectually to Tocqueville and Crèvecoeur—was largely responsible for the preoccupation of colonial historians with the Revolution and with democratic ideas, at the expense of writing transnational history or applying what Braudel called the *longue durée* perspective.[27] At the same time, in the past several decades exceptionalism, as well as its remaining residue in recent studies of colonial America, has in itself been a form of pursuing legitimacy, whether historians were validating the national past or were reacting to the long rivalry with Europe over cultural identity. While the more radical forms of the exceptionalist interpretation have now been abandoned, it has managed to perpetuate an assumption which could perhaps be labeled—in a Gramscian fashion—false consciousness. It has been used to denote a worldview actually, though nonreflectively, held by a social group but remaining in theoretical contradiction with the group's supposedly objective interests and socioeconomic realities. A notion of this sort, in a very broad sense, has been and still is being applied even by some of the most distinguished historians as an analytical tool to argue that colonial gentility was an impediment to achieving cultural maturity. For example, let us return again to the studies of Jack P. Greene. He has called the craving of the colonial gentry for British styles "a clear rejection of many of the most manifest and basic tendencies in American society." Like earlier scholars, he drew attention to the apparent contradiction between the gentry's tenacious Anglophilia and the reality of colonial life and suggested that the result was an undue dependence on an idealized image of English society and culture. Since local conditions of life did not make it possible to live up to those standards, the situation "inevitably created deep social and psychological insecurities, a major crisis of identity." The colonist's attention to British roots "made him so dependent psychologically upon them for a sense of his own identity and a model of his society that it was impossible for him to develop either his own cultural models or distinctive status symbols."[28]

Similarly, in his study of William Byrd, Kenneth Lockridge characterized British culture—and specifically its model of the gentleman to which Byrd, like so many of his Virginian contemporaries, intensely aspired—as highly restrictive, confining the Virginian until he "learned to fly" by stretching its norms, that is, until he moved beyond the British model to "express the virtue of cheerful gentlemen amidst potential democratic chaos of America." To do so, he first had to abandon "his former, brittle self" as well as his "stiff compulsiveness" in pursuing "a rigid code of behavior" to be "a proper gentleman." Both Byrd and Landon Carter bore a "terrible cultural burden" as "adapters of a foreign model of perfection." This approach is consistent with Lockridge's larger view of colonial culture, in which the pursuit of English gentility could only have been a lost cause, since "all legitimacies were vulnerable in early America. Too artificial, too obvious, or too untried, every principle of social or political authority was eroded by the colonists' skepticism or by other principles also striving for acceptance."[29]

I have tried to offer a different perspective on this problem by arguing that members of the colonial planter elite saw their lives through the concepts of genteel ethos and style, concepts which were not foreign and, despite all the obstacles, did provide a central ingredient for the very dynamic of their existence. As such, they proved much more effective and functional than we have been made to believe. Furthermore, without the success of the genteel quest in the construction of the provincial elite, gentility could not have become both a cultural catalyst and an intellectual resource for Revolutionary ideology.

The trouble with exceptionalism, in all its incarnations, was that it prompted the wrong questions by placing the center of analytical gravity on the differences between America and Europe from the earliest times. But when we move beyond such queries, it becomes possible to say that the exceptionalists were right—for the wrong reasons. Through a peculiar twist of history, America did create in the late eighteenth century something highly unique. Because it had achieved conformity with the European genteel ethos, the late colonial gentry acquired the confidence, authority, and sense of public mission necessary to take over the role of cultural arbiters, capable of allocating values and taste for the wider—though still to a large extent based on a hierarchy of dependencies—society. In consequence, this gentry, when elevated to new prominence on the wings of the Revolution, was able to effectively popularize and legitimize for the generality of Americans a language of liberty and equality taken from its own otherwise elitist and exclusive ethos and make it available, if not yet fully applicable, to those whom it did not originally embrace. The inherently popular culture of immigrants, by definition a society of uprooted people, absorbed and domesticated these ideas readily (just as later, with the mass production of consumer goods, it embraced elements of genteel taste) because they could play the same role as they did earlier in constructing colonial gentry: that of a cultural means of improvement and elevation of status. This was a dramatic development—even if at this stage it involved only sections of society—when we consider that in Europe these same ideas retained their exclusive character for much longer, as is abundantly substantiated by Tocqueville's observations made in the 1830s. In the United States they soon became "Americanized" and came to serve as instruments of building a distinct national identity. The immigrant society found in them a common denominator reflecting both their pioneer experience and their ambitions for better life, as well as a way of making sense of their society, the members of which often had little in common.

The long-term pattern that emerges here is one of ambition to lift oneself up from humbler origins and to advance to a better existence and a higher social station, a process defined differently in each phase by a specific compromise between the economic and cultural means of those involved and the current yardsticks of such advancement. To view what happened in the first decades of independence in terms of a decline from the Revolutionary leaders' high expectations of a virtuous republic and an enlightened, disinterested public-minded citizenry into the individualism, competitiveness, and private interest of market society is to look only from the heights of Mount Vernon or Monticello.[30] In reality, there was much striking cultural continuity. Gentry ideals of liberty and equality were adopted and transformed by ordinary people who, unlike the elite, did not have the luxury of a comfortable material base to make disinterestedness and abstract idealism feasible, but who—like the new gentry earlier—were eager to elevate themselves to the condition of respectability. One of the reasons why the common folk would soon accept these ideas was because they were so forcefully introduced into the public consciousness by the Revolutionary gentry. They were so attractive because—stripped of their aristocratic underpinnings—they carried the promise of full citizenship and liberation from humble and dependent status. They could also be readily used as antielitist weapons, as shown in the outburst over the Society of Cincinnati. The Declaration of Independence soon became mythologized in American culture, and the mass of ordinary people who would never have studied Jefferson's theories of political philosophy of natural order would become very familiar with the core meaning of the concepts of liberty and equality. Ultimately, the wide and popular sanctioning of such notions by the Revolutionary gentry helped create a society diametrically different from the one imagined by them. Though quite unforeseen by the recently legitimized legitimizers, this was to be perhaps the most original legacy of the long struggle between determined ambition and the limitations of provincial life.

Notes

ABBREVIATIONS
AB   Andrew Burnaby, *Travels through the Middle Settlements in North America in the Years 1759 and 1760* (Ithaca, N.Y., 1968).
ASD   Maude H. Woodfin, ed., *Another Secret Diary of William Byrd of Westover, 1739–1726: With Letters and Literary Exercises, 1696–1726* (Richmond, 1942).
CEG   Daniel Defoe, *The Compleat English Gentleman*, ed. Karl D. Bülbring (London, 1891).
GP   Carl Bridenbaugh, ed., *Gentleman's Progress: Itinerarium of Dr. Alexander Hamilton, 1744* (Chapel Hill, N.C., 1948).
GW   John C. Fitzpatrick, ed., *The Writings of George Washington from the Original Sources, 1745–1799* (Washington, D.C., 1931–44).
LC   Jack P. Greene, ed., *The Diary of Colonel Landon Carter of Sabine Hall, 1752–1778* (Charlottesville, Va., 1965).
LD   Louis B. Wright and Marion Tinling, eds., *William Byrd of Virginia: The London Diary (1717–1721) and Other Writings* (New York, 1958).
MDC   Marquis de Chastellux, *Travels in North America in the Years 1780, 1781, and 1782*, ed. Howard C. Rice, Jr. (Chapel Hill, N.C., 1963).
OLD   John Oldmixon, *The British Empire in America* (London, 1741; rept. New York, 1969).
SD   Louis B. Wright and Marion Tinling, eds., *The Secret Diary of William Byrd of Westover, 1709–1712* (Richmond, 1941).
TC   Alexander Hamilton, *The History of the Ancient and Honorable Tuesday Club*, ed. Robert Micklus (Chapel Hill, N.C., 1990).
VMHB   *Virginia Magazine of History and Biography*
WF   Richard B. Davis, ed., *William Fitzhugh and His Chesapeake World, 1676–1701: The Fitzhugh Letters and Other Documents* (Chapel Hill, N.C., 1963).
WMQ   *William and Mary Quarterly*

INTRODUCTION

1. *MDC* 2:442, 431; Samuel Johnson, *A Dictionary of the English Language* (London, 1755; rept. New York, 1979).

2. Jefferson to Chastellux, Paris, Sept. 2, 1785, in Julian P. Boyd et al., eds., *The Papers of Thomas Jefferson* (Princeton, N.J., 1950), 8:467–72. Jefferson devoted considerable space in his *Notes on the State of Virginia* to refuting the theories of Buffon and Raynal about the

inferiority of Americans (C. Vann Woodward, *The Old World's New World* [New York and Oxford, 1991], 11–14).

3. See Susan R. Stein, *The Worlds of Thomas Jefferson at Monticello: Catalogue of Exhibition at Monticello, April 13–December 31, 1993* (New York, 1993); Washington to Isaac Heard, May 2, 1792, *GW* 32:31–33; Ralph L. Ketcham, ed., *The Political Thought of Benjamin Franklin* (Indianapolis, 1965), 229.

4. Kenneth Lockridge, *The Diary and Life of William Byrd II of Virginia, 1674–1744* (Chapel Hill, N.C., 1987), 166.

5. Quoted in Jack P. Greene, "A Fortuitous Convergence: Culture, Circumstance, and Contingency in the Emergence of the American Nation," in *Imperatives, Behaviors, and Identities: Essays in Early American Cultural History* (Charlottesville, Va., 1992), 301.

6. See Richard L. Bushman, *The Refinement of America: Persons, Houses, Cities* (New York, 1992); ; Cary Carson, Ronald Hoffman, and Peter J. Albert, eds., *Of Consuming Interests: The Style of Life in the Eighteenth Century* (Charlottesville, Va., and London, 1994). Gordon Wood's *The Radicalism of the American Revolution* (New York, 1992) captures the links between late colonial political developments and sociocultural circumstances.

CHAPTER 1
THE PROBLEM

1. Richard L. Bushman, "American High-Style and Vernacular Cultures," in Jack P. Greene and J. R. Pole, eds., *British Colonial America: Essays in the New History of the Early Modern Era* (Baltimore and London, 1984), 348.

2. Wood, *Radicalism*, 367. As late as 1962 Richard Hofstadter, arguing for a more prominent role for cultivated elites in American culture and politics, noted that by the age of Andrew Jackson, "the estrangement of training and intellect from the power to decide and to manage had been completed" (*Anti-Intellectualism in American Life* [New York, 1962], 171).

3. For instance, in Fitzgerald, *Tender Is the Night* (New York, 1934).

4. Johan Huizinga, *America: A Dutch Historian's Vision from Afar and Near*, trans. Herbert H. Rowen (New York, 1972), 174, 180–81.

5. Jacques Maritain, *Reflections on America* (Garden City, N.Y., 1958), 78, 45.

6. Leavis quoted in C. W. E. Bigsby, "Europe, America, and the Cultural Debate," in Bigsby, ed., *Superculture* (Bowling Green, Ohio, 1975), 10; Czeslaw Milosz, *Visions from San Francisco Bay* (Manchester, Eng., 1982), 39.

7. Jean Baudrillard, *America*, trans. Chris Turner (London and New York, 1988), 76 (identity), 67 (barbarians), 7 (primitiveness), 58 (Los Angeles), 60 (manners), 33–34 (smile), 94 (ease), 98 (transcendence), 101 (New York), 98 (unculture), 14 (Wisconsin).

8. Matthew Arnold, *Culture and Anarchy* (Cambridge, 1971), 18–19.

9. Philip Alexander Bruce, *The Social Life of Virginia in the Seventeenth Century* (Richmond, 1907), 36.

10. Howard Mumford Jones, *O, Strange New World: American Culture, the Formative Years* (New York, 1965), 115.

11. Louis B. Wright, *South Carolina: A Bicentennial History* (New York, 1976), 100; Wright, *The Cultural Life of the American Colonies, 1607–1763* (New York, 1962), 19;

Wright, *The American Heritage History of the Thirteen Colonies* (New York, 1967), 311; Thomas J. Wertenbaker, *Patrician and Plebeian in Virginia: or The Origin and Development of the Social Classes of the Old Dominion* (New York, 1958), 54, 73.

12. Jefferson to Adams, Oct. 28, 1813, in Lester J. Cappon, ed., *The Adams-Jefferson Letters: The Complete Correspondence between Thomas Jefferson and Abigail and John Adams* (Chapel Hill, N.C., 1959), 2:338.

13. Arthur Schlesinger Jr., *The Birth of the Nation: A Portrait of the American People on the Eve of Independence* (New York, 1969), 145; Wright, *Cultural Life of the American Colonies*, 6; Charles S. Sydnor, *Gentlemen Freeholders: Political Practices in Washington's Virginia* (New York, 1966), 60.

14. Carl and Jessica Bridenbaugh, *Rebels and Gentlemen: Philadelphia in the Age of Franklin* (London, Oxford, and New York, 1968), 176, 369–70, 172, 205.

15. Wright, *Cultural Life of the American Colonies*, 154.

16. Bridenbaugh, *Rebels and Gentlemen*, 366; *GP*, caption to illustrations following p. 48.

17. Daniel J. Boorstin, *The Americans: The Colonial Experience* (New York, 1958), 150. Cf. J. R. Pole, "Daniel J. Boorstin," in *Paths to the American Past* (New York, Oxford, 1979), 299–334.

18. On validation, see Pierre Bourdieu, Jean-Claude Chamboredon, and Jean-Claude Passeron, *The Craft of Sociology: Epistemological Preliminaries*, ed. Beate Krais, trans. Richard Nice (Berlin, 1991), vii.

19. Jack P. Greene, "Search for Identity: An Interpretation of the Meaning of Selected Patterns of Social Response in Eighteenth-Century America," *Journal of Social History* 3 (1970): 212, 205; Greene, *The Intellectual Construction of America: Exceptionalism and Identity from 1492 to 1800* (Chapel Hill, N.C., 1993), 129. Greene observes that this "imitation" was an expression of genuine needs but still sees it as a desperate effort, leading to undue dependence ("Search," 211).

20. Lockridge, *Diary and Life*, 151, 153, 143, 134, 49, 65; Lockridge, *Settlement and Unsettlement in Early America* (Cambridge, Eng., 1981), 105; Stephanie Grauman Wolf, *As Various as Their Land: The Everyday Lives of Eighteenth-Century Americans* (New York, 1994), 30; Richard Waterhouse, *A New World Gentry: The Making of a Merchant and Planter Class in South Carolina, 1670–1770* (New York and London, 1989), 106–8, 196; Cary Carson, "The Consumer Revolution in Colonial British America: Why Demand?" in Carson et al., *Of Consuming Interests*, 675; Maaja A. Stewart, "Inexhaustible Generosity: The Fictions of Eighteenth-Century British Imperialism in Richard Cumberland's 'The West Indian,'" *Eighteenth Century: Theory and Interpretation* 37 (1996): 49–50.

21. Gloria Main, *Tobacco Colony: Life in Early Maryland, 1650–1720* (Princeton, N.J., 1982), 37, 159.

22. Such a bipolar view is taken by James Horn in his *Adapting to a New World: English Society in Seventeenth-Century Chesapeake* (Chapel Hill, N.C., 1994), 433.

23. Pierre Bourdieu in an interview with Beate Krais, in Bourdieu et al., *Craft of Sociology*, 259.

24. Maria Ossowska, *Etos rycerski i jego odmiany* (The chivalric ethos and its varieties)

(Warsaw, 1973), 7; Clifford Geertz, "Ethos, World View, and the Analysis of Sacred Symbols," in *The Interpretation of Cultures: Selected Essays* (New York, 1973), 127 (for Geertz's interpretive theory of culture, see ibid., chap. 7); see also Michael Kammen, "Extending the Reach of American Cultural History: A Retrospective and a Prospectus," in *Selvages and Biases: The Fabric of History in American Culture* (Ithaca, N.Y., and London, 1987), 118–53.

25. On culture, see Eric R. Wolf, *Anthropology* (New York, 1974), 53–55; Norbert Elias, *Power and Civility*, trans. Edmund Jephcott (New York, 1982), 230.

26. Pierre Bourdieu, *Distinction: A Social Critique of the Judgement of Taste*, trans. Richard Nice (Cambridge, Mass., 1984); Pierre Bourdieu and Jean-Claude Passeron, *Reproduction in Education, Society, and Culture*, trans. Richard Nice (London, 1990). For an exposition of Bourdieu's theories, see Richard Jenkins, *Pierre Bourdieu* (London, 1992). For Stephen Greenblatt's theory, see especially his *Shakespearean Negotiations: The Circulation of Social Energy in Renaissance England* (Oxford, 1988) and *Marvelous Possessions: The Wonder of the New World* (Oxford, 1991), and Jan R. Veenstra, "The New Historicism of Stephen Greenblatt: On Poetics of Culture and the Interpretation of Shakespeare," *History and Theory* 34 (1995): 174–98.

27. Max Weber, "Die 'Objektivität' sozialwissenschaftlicher und sozialpolitisher Erkenntnis," in *Gesammelte Aufsätze zur Wissenschaftslehre* (Tübingen, 1973), 162. On subjectivity in humanistic studies, see Raymond Martin, "The Essential Difference between History and Science," *History and Theory* 36 (1997): 1–14.

28. Lockridge, *Settlement and Unsettlement in Early America*, 90, 92–93, 107 (he also pursues this view in *The Diary and Life of William Byrd*); Richard Waterhouse, "The Development of Elite Culture in the Colonial American South: A Study of Charles Town, 1670–1770," *Australian Journal of Politics and History* 28 (1982): 400. Certain elements of this approach are also present in Jack P. Greene, *Landon Carter: An Inquiry into the Personal Values and Social Imperatives of the Eighteenth-Century Virginia Gentry* (Charlottesville, Va., 1967).

29. See Florian Znaniecki, *Cultural Reality* (Chicago, 1919), 23.

30. James M. Ostrow, *Social Sensitivity: A Study of Habit and Experience* (New York, 1990), 28, 33. On cultural persistence, see Alfred L. Kroeber, *Anthropology: Culture Patterns and Processes* (New York, 1963), 154–55.

31. Joyce Appleby, "The Agrarian Myth in the Early Republic," in *Liberalism and Republicanism in the Historical Imagination* (Cambridge, Mass., 1992), 260–61.

32. Ernst Cassirer, *An Essay on Man: An Introduction to a Philosophy of Human Culture* (New York, 1953), 142–76; Edmund Husserl, *Ideas: General Introduction to Pure Phenomenology*, trans. B. Gibson (New York, 1931).

33. Word examples from *CEG*, 258, 267, 268, 261, 257, 178, 13–15. On invisible realities and social domination, see Maurice Godelier, "Infrastructures, Societies, and History," *Current Anthropology* 19 (1978): 763–68.

34. A. G. Roeber, "'The Scrutiny of the Ill Natured Ignorant Vulgar': Lawyers and Print Culture in Virginia, 1716–1774," *VMHB* 91 (1983): 4, 390; Hunter D. Farish, ed., *Journal*

and Letters of Philip Vickers Fithian, 1773–1774: A Plantation Tutor of the Old Dominion (Williamsburg, Va., 1957), 111.

35. Pierre Bourdieu, "Symbolic Power," in Denis Gleeson, ed., *Identity and Structure: Issues in the Sociology of Education* (Driffield, Eng., 1977), 117; Erving Goffman, "The Nature of Deference and Demeanor," *American Anthropologist* 58 (June 1956): 477.

36. On symbolic power, see Pierre Bourdieu, *Language and Symbolic Power*, ed. John B. Thompson, trans. Gino Raymond and Matthew Adamson (Oxford, 1991), 23.

37. See Toivo Miljan, "Culture, Political Culture, and Legitimacy," in Miljan, ed., *Culture and Legitimacy* (Waterloo, Ont., 1982), 1–6; *Oxford English Dictionary*.

38. Bushman, *Refinement*, 183–85, 447, 183.

39. On sumptuary laws, see John Sekora, *Luxury: The Concept in Western Thought, Eden to Smollett* (Baltimore and London, 1977), 52–62.

40. Martin H. Quitt, "Immigrant Origins of the Virginia Gentry: A Study of Cultural Transmission and Innovation," *WMQ*, 3d ser., 25 (1988): 653–54, 631. For the role of the gentry in early modern Britain, see Lawrence Stone, *The Crisis of Aristocracy, 1558–1641* (Oxford, 1965); Lawrence Stone and Jeanne C. Fawtier Stone, *An Open Elite? England, 1540–1880* (Oxford, 1986); J. H. Hexter, "Storm over the Gentry," in *Reappraisals in History* (London, 1961); G. E. Mingay, *English Landed Society in the Eighteenth Century* (London, 1963) and *The Gentry: The Rise and Fall of a Ruling Class* (London, 1978). On the term *gentry*, see P. R. Coss, "The Formation of the English Gentry," *Past and Present* 147 (1995): 38–64.

CHAPTER 2
GENTILITY: A TRANSATLANTIC ASPIRATION

1. Stone, *Crisis of Aristocracy*, 258.

2. H. J. Habbakkuk, "England," in Albert Goodwin, ed., *The European Nobility in the Eighteenth Century* (New York, 1967), 15–17; Lawrence Stone, *The Causes of the English Revolution, 1525–1642* (New York, 1972), 110–13; J. G. A. Pocock, *The Machiavellian Moment: Florentine Political Thought and the Atlantic Republican Tradition* (Princeton, N.J., 1975), 425. See also Roy Porter, *English Society in the Eighteenth Century* (Harmondsworth, Eng., 1982); Keith Wrightson, *English Society, 1580–1680* (London, 1982).

3. Richard Grassby, "Social Mobility and Business Enterprise in Seventeenth-Century England," in *Puritans and Revolutionaries: Essays in Seventeenth-Century History Presented to Christopher Hill*, ed. Donald Pennington and Keith Thomas (Oxford, 1978), 361; Stone and Fawtier-Stone, *An Open Elite?* 8, 278; P. J. Cain and A. G. Hopkins, "Gentlemanly Capitalism and British Expansion Overseas: The Old Colonial System, 1688–1850," *Economic History Review*, 2d ser., 39 (1986): 501–25; John Brewer, J. H. Plumb, and Neil McKendrick, *The Birth of the Consumer Society: Commercialization in Eighteenth-Century Britain* (London, 1979).

4. *The Compleat English Gentleman* was first published in 1891. On Defoe, see Paula R. Beckschneider, *Daniel Defoe: His Life* (Baltimore and London, 1989).

5. A. L. Morgan, "The Individual Style of the English Gentleman," in Michael Jones, ed., *Gentry and Lesser Nobility in Late Medieval Europe* (New York, 1986), 16.

6. See James Horn, "Cavalier Culture? The Social Development of Colonial Virginia," *WMQ*, 3d ser., 48 (1991): 238–45.

7. The argument certainly seems supported by developments in postrevolutionary Russia or in the English Revolution. On the reproduction of societies, see Bourdieu and Passeron, *Reproduction in Education*; on Cromwell, see Peter Laslett, *The World We Have Lost: England before the Industrial Age* (New York, 1973), 42.

8. Fernand Braudel, *The Wheels of Commerce*, trans. Siân Reynolds (New York, 1979), 2:471–72, 464.

9. Kenneth Prewitt and Alan Stone, *The Ruling Elites: Elite Theory, Power, and American Democracy* (New York, 1973), 2; Wood, *Radicalism*, 24–25, 30, 40; David Castronovo, *The American Gentleman: Social Prestige and the Modern Literary Mind* (New York, 1991), 18. On the reverence for equality in twentieth-century Princeton, see Maritain, *Reflections on America*, 79.

10. Carole Shammas, *The Pre-Industrial Consumer in England and America* (Oxford, 1990), 151 n.8.

11. *OLD* 1:425.

12. [William Darrell], *The Gentleman Instructed in the Conduct of a Virtuous and a Happy Life* (London, 1723), 14–15; *TC* 2:166.

13. John Adams to Joseph Hawley, Nov. 25, 1775, in Jack P. Greene, "The Constitution of 1787 and the Question of Southern Distinctiveness," in *Imperatives*, 331.

14. See Richard Beale Davis, *Intellectual Life in the Colonial South, 1588–1763* (Knoxville, Tenn., 1978) and *A Colonial Southern Bookshelf: Reading in the Eighteenth Century* (Athens, Ga., 1979).

15. For the focus on elites who occupy institutional positions of power rather than on the cultural roles of elites, see Gaetano Mosca, *The Ruling Class* (New York, 1939); Vilfredo Pareto, *Sociological Writings*, ed. S. E. Finer (London, 1966); C. Wright Mills, *The Power Elite* (New York, 1956). For elite theory, see Michael G. Burton and John Higley, "Invitation to Elite Theory: The Basic Contentions Reconsidered," in G. William Domhoff and Thomas R. Dye, eds., *Power Elites and Organizations* (Newbury Park, Calif., 1987), 219–38.

16. Thomas Hobbes, *Leviathan, or The Matter, Forme, and Power of a Commonwealth Ecclesiastical and Civil*, ed. Michael Oakeshott (New York, 1962), 72. On elite self-perpetuation, see Robert Michels, *Political Parties: A Sociological Study of the Oligarchical Tendencies of Modern Democracy* (New York, 1962).

17. Aubrey Land, "Economic Base and Social Structure: The Northern Chesapeake in the Eighteenth Century," *Journal of Economic History* 25 (1965): 643; Richard S. Dunn, *Sugar and Slaves: The Rise of the Planter Class in the English West Indies, 1624–1713* (New York, 1973), 266.

18. Greene, "Colonial South Carolina and the Caribbean Connection," 83.

19. David W. Jordan, "Political Stability and the Emergence of a Native Elite in Maryland," in Thad W. Tate and David L. Ammerman, eds., *The Chesapeake in the Seventeenth*

Century: Essays on Anglo-American Society and Politics (New York, 1979), 264; Carole Shammas, "English-Born and Creole Elites in Turn-of-the-Century Virginia," ibid., 274–96. On patronage, see Donnell M. Owings, *His Lordship's Patronage: Offices of Profit in Colonial Maryland* (Baltimore, 1953). For southern colonial sociocultural development, see Jack P. Greene, *Pursuits of Happiness: The Social Development of Early Modern British Colonies and the Formation of American Culture* (Chapel Hill, N.C., 1988), 81–100. On the links between the economy and the emergence of the elite in the Chesapeake, see Allan Kulikoff, *Tobacco and Slaves: The Development of Southern Cultures in the Chesapeake, 1680–1800* (Chapel Hill, N.C., and London, 1986). On the gentry of the upper Valley, where a similar hierarchic and deferential culture developed, see Albert H. Tillotson, Jr., *Gentry and Common Folk: Political Culture on a Virginia Frontier, 1740–1789* (Lexington, Ky., 1991).

20. William Byrd, "A Progress to the Mines," *LD*, 624; Sydnor, *Gentlemen Freeholders*, 64; Louis B. Wright, *The First Gentlemen of Virginia: Intellectual Qualities of the Early Virginia Ruling Class* (San Marino, Calif., 1940), 170; Louis Morton, *Robert Carter of Nomini Hall* (Williamsburg, Va., 1945), 21–29; Bernard Bailyn, "Politics and Social Structure in Virginia," in James M. Smith, ed., *Seventeenth-Century America* (Chapel Hill, N.C., 1959), 111; Greene, *Pursuits of Happiness*, 93; Kulikoff, *Tobacco and Slaves*, 7–10, 259–63; David H. Fischer, *The Revolution of American Conservatism: The Federalist Party in the Era of Jeffersonian Democracy* (New York, 1965), 220. Trevor Burnard has argued that kinship among the Chesapeake elite was less important than genteel behavior and style ("A Tangled Cousinry? Associational Networks of the Maryland Elite, 1691–1776," *Journal of Southern History* 41 [1995]: 17–44), but even though exclusiveness of birth was practiced on a much lesser scale than in Europe, family networks were nevertheless a powerful social glue among the planter elite.

21. Rachel N. Klein, *Unification of a Slave State: The Rise of the Planter Class in the South Carolina Backcountry, 1760–1808* (Chapel Hill, N.C., 1990), 33; James T. Flexner, *George Washington: The Forge of Experience, 1732–1775* (Boston, 1965), 188–91; Philip H. Burch, Jr., *Elites in American History: The Federalist Years to the Civil War* (New York, 1981), 49; Marvin R. Zahniser, *Charles Cotesworth Pinckney* (Chapel Hill, N.C., 1967), 134.

22. Aubrey Land, "Genesis of a Colonial Fortune," *WMQ*, 3d ser., 7 (1950): 255–69.

23. Shammas, *Pre-Industrial Consumer*, 163, 166–68, 59–60, 104, 185. In fact, even the 1798 government survey of houses in the United States still showed that only about 15 percent were of nonwood construction and had several rooms with differing functions, a stairway, a brick chimney, and glass windows (ibid., 167). For Maryland, see Gregory A. Stiverson, *Poverty in a Land of Plenty: Tenancy in Eighteenth-Century Maryland* (Baltimore, 1977), 56–84. See also Lois Green Carr and Lorena S. Walsh, "Inventories and the Analysis of Wealth and Consumption Patterns in St. Mary's County, Maryland, 1658–1777," *Historical Methods* 13 (1980): 81–104.

24. Andrew Burnaby, who traveled through the American colonies in 1759–60, felt that the country was full of tension and instability and that "were they left to themselves, there would soon be a civil war from one end of the continent to the other" (*AB*, 113). Historians have increasingly been using the notion of chaos as a descriptive and analytical category in studying the colonial scene; Bernard Bailyn has focused extensively on the confusion, con-

troversy, and change as central elements that characterized early colonial American culture (*The Peopling of British North America: An Introduction* [New York, 1988], 58, 48).

25. Baltasar Gratian, *The Compleat Gentleman*, trans. T. Saldkeld (London, 1730), 137–38.

26. Anthony Ashley Cooper, earl of Shaftesbury, *An Inquiry concerning Virtue, or Merit*, ed. David Walford (Manchester, Eng., 1977), 83, 17; *New England Magazine*, Aug. 1758, 19; Bourdieu, *Distinction*, 56.

27. Francis Markham, *The Booke of Honour* (London, 1625), 48.

28. *Examiner*, no. 41 (May 10, 1711), in Frank H. Ellis, ed., *Swift vs. Mainwaring: The Examiner and The Medley* (Oxford, 1985), 418. See also John F. Ross, *Swift and Defoe: A Study in Relationship* (Berkeley, Calif., 1941).

29. Michael Shinagel, *Daniel Defoe and Middle-Class Gentility* (Cambridge, Mass., 1968), 47, 76, 73–74.

30. *WF*, 194 and n.2, 7–9, 246; Wright, *First Gentlemen of Virginia*, 287, 191; Fithian, *Journal*, 116.

31. Washington Genealogy and Washington to Isaac Heard, May 2, 1792, Washington to Hannah Fairfax Washington, March 24, 1792, *GW* 32:26–33, 11; bookplates, Flexner, *Washington*, 240.

32. *Autobiography*, in Merrill D. Peterson, ed., *Thomas Jefferson: Writings* (New York, 1984), 3. On legitimizing agencies, see Bourdieu, *Reproductions*, 18.

33. Anthony R. Wagner, *English Genealogy* (Oxford, 1960), 327.

34. George Alsop, "Character of the Province of Maryland," in Clayton C. Hall, ed., *Narratives of Early Maryland* (New York, 1910), 367; *TC* 1:238.

35. *OLD* 2:124.

36. [Lord Adam Gordon], "Journal of an Officer who Travelled in America and the West Indies in 1764 and 1765," in *Travels in the American Colonies*, ed. Newton D. Mereness (New York, 1961), 404–5, 398.

37. *CEG*, 258, 257, 259, 262, 275.

38. Ibid., 262, 13; Swift, *Examiner*, May 10, 1711, in Ellis, *Swift vs. Mainwaring*, 419.

39. *CEG*, 4; John Tutchin, *The Foreigners: A Poem* (London, 1700), 11.

40. [Daniel Defoe], *The True-Born Englishman: A Satyr* (London, 1701), 13.

41. [Darrell], *Gentleman Instructed*, 8; Gratian, *Compleat Gentleman*, 15.

42. *CEG*, 3–4, 167, 4.

43. Ibid., 64, 177, 38, 239, 98, 105, 129 149, 93. Defoe recounted that when he had mentioned to a certain prominent gentleman the lack of learning among his class in comparison to those of Scotland, of Holland, and Germany, "he laugh and told me it was because they were all poor and universally had the advance of their fortunes in view, which the English gentry had not" (ibid., 118).

44. Ibid., 231, 114–15, 198–99, 201, 228, 201, 203.

45. Hugh Jones, *The Present State of Virginia* (London, 1724), 83–94; Lawrence E. Cremin, *American Education: The Colonial Experience, 1607–1783* (New York, 1970), 527.

46. Washington to Jonathan Boucher, July 9, 1771, *GW* 3:50; Fitzhugh to George Mason, May 17, 1695, *WF,* 335.

47. *The Letterbook of Eliza Lucas Pinckney, 1739–1762,* ed. Elise Pinckney (Chapel Hill, N.C., 1972), 182; *TC* 1:404, 409.

48. *TC* 1:218–19.

49. Baldassare Castiglione, *The Book of the Courtier* (1561), trans. Sir Thomas Hoby (London, 1974), 33–34, 31–32, 23.

50. Arthur B. Ferguson, *The Indian Summer of English Chivalry: Studies in the Decline and Transmission of Chivalric Idealism* (Durham, N.C., 1960), 200–202; Coquault quoted in Braudel, *Wheels of Commerce* 2:485; [Defoe], *True-Born Englishman,* 6.

51. Aug. 20, 1714, Donald F. Bond, ed., *The Spectator* (Oxford, 1965), 4:593–94; *CEG,* 3.

52. Arthur Wellesley Secord, ed., *Defoe's Review* (New York, 1938, facs.), no. 38, 2:149.

53. *Examiner,* no. 16 (Nov. 16, 1710), in Ellis, *Swift vs. Mainwaring,* 35–36.

54. Edmund Morgan, *American Slavery, American Freedom: The Ordeal of Colonial Virginia* (New York and London, 1975), 261.

55. Shinagel, *Daniel Defoe,* 79.

56. Ellis, *Swift vs. Mainwaring,* 418.

57. Charles Lamb to Walter Wilson, Dec. 16, 1822, in Laura Ann Curtis, ed., *The Versatile Defoe: An Anthology of Uncollected Writings by Defoe* (Totowa, N.J., 1979), 377.

58. William Penn, *Some Fruits of Solitude, in Reflections and Maxims Relating to the Conduct of Human Life* (London, 1706), 73; Aphra Behn, *The Widdow Ranter* (London, 1690), 3; John Brown, *An Estimate of the Manners and Principles of the Times* (Boston, 1758), 58. On the relation between genteel and commercial mentality, see Maria Ossowska, *Bourgeois Morality,* trans. G. L. Campbell (London and New York, 1986), chap. 5.

59. *The Conscious Lovers,* in Shirley S. Kenny, ed., *The Plays of Richard Steele* (Oxford, 1871), 358–59.

60. From Franklin's notes dated April 4, 1769, and Franklin to Benjamin Vaughan, July 26, 1784, in Ketcham, *Political Thought of Franklin,* 229, 365–66.

61. March 2, 1711, *Spectator* 1:10–11.

62. *OLD* 1:424, 2:125. On Oldmixon, see Richard S. Dunn, "Seventeenth-Century English Historians of America," in Smith, *Seventeenth-Century America,* 222–24.

63. David Hackett Fischer, *Albion's Seed: Four British Folkways in America* (New York and Oxford, 1989), 216; Quitt, "Immigrant Origins," 630.

64. *LD,* 9; *SD,* Oct. 17, 1710, 224; *Letters of Robert Carter, 1720–1727: The Commercial Interests of a Virginia Gentleman,* ed. Louis B. Wright (Westport, Conn., 1970), 42, 53; Fithian, *Journal,* 79; Pinckney, *Letterbook,* 34. An exemplary career of this kind was that of Charles Carroll of Maryland; see Ronald Hoffman, "'Marylando-Hibernus': Charles Carroll the Settler, 1660–1720," *WMQ,* 3d ser., 45 (1988): 207–36. See also R. B. Sheridan, "The Rise of a Colonial Gentry: A Case Study of Antigua, 1730–1775," *Economic History Review,* 2d ser., 13 (1960–61): 342–55.

65. *LC*, 397, 467, 350.

66. John Bartram, *Diary of a Journey through the Carolinas, Georgia, and Florida from July 1, 1765, to April 10, 1766*, ed. Francis Harper (Philadelphia, 1942), 30.

67. Klein, *Unification of a Slave State*, 31–36.

68. July 2, 1736, *VMHB* 9 (1901): 124; T. H. Breen, *Tobacco Culture: The Mentality of the Great Tidewater Planters on the Eve of the Revolution* (Princeton, N.J., 1985), 124–59; Flexner, *Washington*, 279–80. One writer alleged as early as 1676 that the proprietary elite in Maryland "have made Merchandize of the land" ("Complaint from Heaven with a Huy and Crye and a Petition out of Virginia and Maryland," in W. H. Browne, ed., *Archives of Maryland* [Baltimore, 1883–1972], 5:140).

69. *LC*, 910, 373; *The Beauties of the Spectators, Tatlers, and Guardians* (Dublin, 1767), 1:90.

70. *The Gentleman's Library, Containing Rules of Conduct in All Parts of Life*, 4th ed. (London, 1744), 43.

71. For Defoe's argument that business values should be sanctioned as compatible with gentility because a landed gentleman had to be a businessman to be effective, see *CEG*, 103, 244–45. On the relationship between property, citizenship, and political participation, see Jack P. Greene, "All Men Are Created Equal: Some Reflections on the Character of the American Revolution," in *Imperatives*, 248.

72. Pocock, *Machiavellian Moment*, 428, 430–31.

73. [George Berkeley], *A Proposal for the Better Supplying of Churches in Our Foreign Plantations* (Dublin, 1725), 8.

74. [Joseph] Morgan, *The Nature of Riches* (Philadelphia, 1732), 17; *CEG*, 89; Sekora, *Luxury*, 116–17.

75. Fitzhugh to George Mason, July 21, 1698, *WF*, 361. For Landon Carter's commercial mentality, see *LC*, 706, 703.

76. June 27, 1729, quoted in Pierre Marambaud, *William Byrd of Westover, 1674–1744* (Charlottesville, Va., 1971), 59.

77. Brown, *Estimate*, 22.

78. *CEG*, 219, 222; Byrd, "The Female Creed," in *ASD*, 463, 449; *LC*, 1102; *TC* 1:54–55, 405. Kenneth A. Lockridge, in his *On the Sources of Patriarchal Rage: The Commonplace Books of William Byrd and Thomas Jefferson and the Gendering of Power in the Eighteenth Century* (New York, 1992), has shown how tensions arose as men in a predominantly male, patriarchal culture were forced to compete for women and were not infrequently torn between exercising what he calls gendered mastery and the de facto power of women.

79. *GW* 2:386; Thomas Jefferson, *Notes on the State of Virginia*, ed. William Peden (Chapel Hill, N.C., 1955), 135. On the consumer revolution and the pursuit of gentility in colonial America, see Kevin M. Sweeney, "High-Style Vernacular: Lifestyles of the Colonial Elite," in Carson et al., *Of Consuming Interests*, 1–58.

80. *The Journal of John Harrower: An Indentured Servant in the Colony of Virginia, 1773–1776*, ed. Edward Miles Riley (Williamsburg, Va., 1963), 76; Daniel Defoe, *The History and Remarkable Life of the Truly Honourable Colonel Jacque* in *The Works of Daniel Defoe*, with intro. by G. H. Maynadier (New York, 1904), 6:242–43.

81. *CEG*, 19.
82. [Richard Allestree], *The Gentleman's Calling* (London, 1705), 57; Penn, *Fruits of Solitude*, 91–93.
83. *WF*, 287, 297; [William Gooch], *A Dialogue between Thomas Sweet-Scented, William Oronoco, Planters, Both Men of Good Understanding, and Justice Love-Country, Who Can Speak for Himself* (Williamsburg, Va., 1732), 11, 14, 17.
84. *GP*, 25; *LC*, 103.
85. Christopher Hill, "Robinson Crusoe," *History Workshop: A Journal of Socialist Historians* 10 (1980): 16; Karl Marx, *Capital*, trans. Samuel Moore and Edward Aveling (Chicago, 1921), 88–91. On Defoe's conservatism, see Manuel Schonhorn, *Defoe's Politics: Parliament, Power, Kingship, and "Robinson Crusoe"* (Cambridge, Eng., 1991).
86. Daniel Defoe, *The Further Adventures of Robinson Crusoe* (Oxford, 1927), 80, 200.
87. *LC*, 840.
88. Byrd to Charles Boyle, earl of Orrery, July 5, 1726, *VMHB* 32 (1924): 27. Byrd was quite familiar with *Robinson Crusoe*; see *LD*, 546.
89. Izard to Jefferson, June 10, 1785, "The Letters of Ralph Izard," *South Carolina Historical and Genealogical Magazine* 2 (1901): 197.

Chapter 3
The Curse of Provincialism

1. On rusticity in Virginia as a function of communication with England, see Richard D. Brown, *Knowledge Is Power: The Diffusion of Information in Early America, 1700–1865* (New York and Oxford, 1989), 42–64.
2. *OLD* 1:424.
3. Byrd to Minionet, Feb. 21, 1722/23, *ASD*, 379–80; "Inamorato L'Oiseaux," ibid., 276–82. Byrd concluded that "without the Ladys, a schollar is a Pedant, a Philosopher a Cynick, all morality is morose, & all behaviour either too Formal or too licentious."
4. Byrd to John Boyle, July 28, 1730, Marion Tinling, ed., *The Correspondence of the Three William Byrds of Westover, Virginia, 1684–1776* (Charlottesville, Va., 1977), 1:432.
5. Byrd to Sabina, March 28, 1718, *ASD*, 337.
6. [Edward Ward], *A Trip to New England with a Character of the Country and People, Both English and Indian* (London, 1699), 10.
7. Richard Thornton, "A Happie Shipwreck or the Losse of a Late Intended Voyage by Sea" (1629), in *Colonizing Expeditions to the West Indies and Guiana, 1623–1667* (London, 1925), 170.
8. Alsop, "Character of the Province of Maryland," 379.
9. Jaspar Dankers and Peter Sluyter, *Journal of a Voyage to New York and a Tour in the Several of the American Colonies*, ed. C. Murphy (Brooklyn, 1967), 220–21; Dalby Thomas, *An Historical Account of the Rise and Growth of the West India Colonies* (London, 1690), 1.
10. [Thomas Hodges], *Plantation Justice* (London, 1701), 10, 4–5.

11. [Ward], *Trip to New England*, 7.

12. *A Short View of the Smuggling Trade Carried Oon by the British Northern Colonies in Violation of the Acts of Navigation* (London, 1750), 1, 3.

13. Josiah Child, *A Discourse about Trade* (London, 1690), 187, 171; [Edward Ward], *A Trip to Jamaica with a True Character of the People and Island* (London, 1700), 13; Ebenezer Cooke, *The Sot-Weed Factor* (1708), Maryland Historical Society Fund Publications, no. 36 (Baltimore, 1900), 12; Ebenezer Cooke, *Sot-Weed Redivivus: or the Planter's Looking-Glass* (London, 1730), 11. On Oldmixon's use of Child's treatise as a source, see *OLD* 1:xxviii.

14. *American Magazine* (Philadelphia), Jan. 1740–41, 6–7.

15. *GP*, 14–15; Fithian, *Journal*, 9, 27, 46.

16. [Ward], *Trip to Jamaica*, 16; *OLD* 1:425.

17. [Berkeley], *Proposal*, 3–5; Isaac Maddox, *A Sermon Preached before the Incorporated Society for the Propagation of the Gospel in Forreign Parts* (London, 1734), 27.

18. Sharpe to Lord Baltimore, June 6, 1754, *Archives of Maryland* 6:68.

19. Jack P. Greene, "Travails of an Infant Colony: The Search for Viability, Coherence, and Identity in Colonial Georgia," in *Imperatives*, 133; Waterhouse, "Development of Elite Culture," 395, 393.

20. Charles Leslie, *A New and Exact Account of Jamaica, Wherein the Antient and Present State of That Colony, Its Land, Trade, etc., Are Described*, 3d ed. (Edinburgh, 1740), 37–39; Richard Beale Davis, ed., "The Colonial Virginia Satirist: Mid-Eighteenth Century Commentaries on Politics, Religion, and Society," *Transactions of the American Philosophical Society*, n.s., 57, pt. 1 (1967): 57; Charles Woodmason, *The Carolina Backcountry on the Eve of the Revolution: The Journal and Other Writings of Charles Woodmason, American Itinerant*, ed. Richard J. Hooker (Chapel Hill, N.C., 1953), 52–53, 38.

21. Edward Kimber, "Observations in Several Voyages and Travels in America: Extracts from the *London Magazine* 14 and 15 (1745–1746)," comp. Ruth Kimber, 35, John Carter Brown Library, Providence, R.I.; Edward Kimber, *The History of the Life and Adventures of Mr. Anderson* (London, 1782), 222, 39.

22. [Thomas Tryon], *Friendly Advice to Gentlemen Planters of the East and West Indies* (London, 1684), 96, 60.

23. Hans Sloane, *A Voyage to the Islands Madera, Barbados, Nieves, S. Christopher, and Jamaica* (London, 1701–25), 1:xxvii–xxix; Dunn, *Sugar and Slaves*, 277–78, 281.

24. Aphra Behn, "The History of the Royal Slave," in *The Novels of Mrs. Aphra Behn* (London, 1913), 62; [William King], *Useful Transactions for the Months of May, June, July, August, and September* (London, 1707), 33–34, 40, 33; [Ward], *Trip to Jamaica*, 15; Cooke, *The Sot-Weed Factor*, 22. Nor was drinking the main shortcoming of the local dignitaries; they were all shown as uneducated simpletons, and only one judge "of all the Bench" could claim title to being able to write his name (Cooke, *Sotweed Redivivus*, 7). For the popularity of rum in New England around 1700, see [Ward], *Trip to New England*, 10.

25. Henry Hulton, [Autobiographical Memoir, 1784–1785], 65, John Carter Brown Library, Providence, R.I.

26. Rodney M. Baine, *Robert Munford: America's First Comic Dramatist* (Athens, Ga., 1967), 57–72.

27. W. J. Rorabaugh, *The Alcoholic Republic: An American Tradition* (New York and Oxford, 1979), 10, 64.

28. Eve Kornfeld, "Encountering 'the Other': American Intellectuals and Indians in the 1790s," *WMQ*, 3d ser., 52 (1955): 287–314. Edward W. Said in his *Culture and Imperialism* (New York, 1993), 50, stresses the essentially "contrapuntal" manner of creating identities, invariably requiring opposites.

29. Bernard W. Sheehan, *Savagism and Civility: Indians and Englishmen in Colonial Virginia* (Cambridge, Eng., 1980), 2–5; [Edward Kimber], *A Relation or Journal of a Late Expedition to the Gates of St. Augustine, on Florida: Conducted by the Hon. General Oglethorpe* (London, 1744), 16–17; Woodmason, *Carolina Backcountry*, 121; *Rudiments of Taste in a Series of Letters from a Mother to Her Daughters* (Philadelphia, 1790), 45. Such treatment of Indians was well established by the later seventeenth century. William Byam spoke of the necessity for the English inhabitants of the colony of Surinam in 1667 "to defend themselves against ye Indians, wilde Beasts and all other Vermins" ("An Exact Narrative of the State of Guyana and of the English Colony in Surinam. . . . By William Byam," Feb. 1667, in *Colonizing Expeditions*, 218). On the savage-civil dichotomy, see also Robert F. Berkhofer, *The White Man's Indian: Images of the American Indian from Columbus to the Present* (New York, 1978).

30. Klein, *Unification of a Slave State*, 51; William Stith, *The History of the First Discovery and Settlement of Virginia* (London, 1753; rept. New York and London, 1969), 45, 54; Cotton Mather, *Things for a Distress'd People to Think upon* (Boston, 1696; rept. Gainesville, Fla., 1970), 11; William Byrd, "History of the Dividing Line," in *LD*, 564, 573.

31. *OLD* 1:328, 419, 435; [Berkeley], *Proposal*, 20.

32. [James MacSparran], *America Dissected* (Dublin, 1753), 9–10; Kimber, "Observations," 40.

33. Lester C. Olson, *Emblems of American Community in the Revolutionary Era: A Study in Rhetorical Iconology* (Washington, D.C., and London, 1991), 77–78, 80, 114–15, 87, 79. In the next two paragraphs I rely heavily on this study. On the stereotype of the savages, see Berkhofer, *White Man's Indian*, 4, 15.

34. *LC*, 80; Thomas Moffat to Ezra Stiles, March 18, 1776, John Carter Brown Library, codex Eng. 2.

35. Thomas Paine, *Common Sense*, in Moncure D. Conway, ed., *The Writings of Thomas Paine* (New York, 1967), 3:86–87; Olson, *Emblems of American Community*, 150, 238–51, illus. nos. 14, 15.

36. See Christopher Hill, *The World Turned Upside Down: Radical Ideas during the English Revolution* (Harmondsworth, Eng., 1978). See also E. A. Wrigley, *Population and History* (London, 1969), 78–80; Perez Zagorin, *A History of Political Thought in the English Revolution* (London, 1965), 37.

37. Edwin Sandys to Robert Naunton, Jan. 28, 1620, Noel Sainsbury, ed., *Calendar of State Papers, Colonial Series, 1574–1660, America and West Indies* (London, 1860—), 23;

Jones, *Present State of Virginia*, 118. Samual Hartlib's utopia, *A Description of the Famous Kingdome of Macaria* (London, 1641), intended to inspire the revolutionary parliament to improve Britain, depicted a wealthy and stable nation with a special "Councell for New Plantations," which saw to it that "every yeere, a certaine number shall be sent out" of the "surplusage of people."

38. *Gentleman's Library*, 165; George Birkbeck Hill, ed., *Boswell's Life of Johnson* (Oxford, 1924), 4:18.

39. George Berkeley, *The Querist* (Glasgow, 1751), 51–52; Edmund Morgan, *American Slavery, American Freedom*, 324–25; Francis Hutcheson, *A System of Moral Philosophy* (London, 1755; rept. New York, 1968), bk. 3:202.

40. [Samuel Hartlib], *Parliament's Reformation* (London, 1646), 5; Klaus E. Knorr, *British Colonial Theories* (Toronto, 1964), 49; Child, *Discourse about Trade*, 169; Abbot E. Smith, *Colonists in Bondage: White Servitude and Convict Labor in America, 1607–1776* (Chapel Hill, N.C., 1947), 91–92, 111–15, 142–43, 94.

41. Joseph Redington and Richard A. Roberts, eds., *Calendar of Home Office Papers in the Reign of George III, 1760–1775* (London, 1878–99; rept. Nendeln, 1967), 4:11. Bernard Bailyn observed that the early colonies were considered such a distant periphery, so remote and primitive "that merely sending people there would be punitive" (Bailyn, *Peopling of America*, 121).

42. *Canary-Birds Naturaliz'd in Utopia: A Canto* (London, 1709), 24.

43. Cooke, *The Sot-Weed Factor*, 15; Abbot Smith, *Colonists in Bondage*, 140.

44. *OLD* 1:526.

45. William W. Hening, comp., *The Statutes at Large, Being a Collection of All the Laws of Virginia* (New York, 1823), 2:510; *LC*, 80; [Mac Sparran], *America Dissected*, 12.

46. [MacSparran], *America Dissected*, 5, 9.

47. *Some Modest Observations upon Jamaica* (London 1727), 19; *Virginia Gazette* quoted in Abbot Smith, *Colonists in Bondage*, 130.

48. Daniel Defoe, *The Fortunes and Misfortunes of the Famous Moll Flanders*, ed. G. A. Starr (London, 1971), 339–40, 86–87.

49. *Boswell's Life of Johnson*, 5:78, 2:312, 27. The title of James MacSparran's 1753 description of British America captured some of the accumulated negatives: *America Dissected, Being a Full and True Account of All the American Colonies, Shewing, the Intemperance of the Climates, Excessive Heat and Cold, and Sudden Violent Changes in Weather, Terrible and Mischivious Thunder and Lightning, Bad and Unwholesome Air, Destructive to Human Bodies, Badness of Money, Danger from Enemies, but Above All the Danger to the Souls of the Poor People That Remove Thither*. On sixteenth-century European images of America, see Greene, *Intellectual Construction of America*, 8–33.

50. [Darrell], *Gentleman Instructed*, 19.

51. *GP*, 185–86.

52. Dunn, *Sugar and Slaves*, 77; *A Discourse of the Duties on Merchandize* (London, 1695), 10–12; [Ward], *Trip to Jamaica*, 16.

53. [Ward], *Trip to New England*, 12, 16; [Ward], *Trip to Jamaica*, 16.
54. Thomas Southerne, *Oronooko: A Tragedy* (London, 1694), 9–11, 14, 64.
55. Behn, *Widdow Ranter*, 3, 5, 6, 12, 23.
56. Davis, "Colonial Virginia Satirist," 48, 53, 56.
57. *AB*, 23–24.
58. Edmund Burke, *Account of European Settlement in America* (London, 1759), 141–44.
59. *OLD* 1:138, 141; Burke, *Account of European Settlement*, 210.
60. Kimber, *History of the Life and Adventures of Mr. Anderson*, 12–13, 18, 23; James Ramsay, *An Essay on the Treatment and Conversion of African Slaves in British Sugar Colonies* (1784), quoted in Frank J. Klingberg, *The Anti-Slavery Movement in England: A Study in English Humanitarianism* (1926; rept. Hamden, Conn., 1968), 62.
61. *MDC* 2:437, 384, 426, 441, 391.
62. Jones, *Present State of Virginia*, i, 116, 43–44, 32, 114.
63. Ebenezer Cooke, "The History of Colonel Nathaniel Bacon's Rebellion in Virginia," in *The Maryland Muse* (Annapolis, 1731), 1–5.
64. Robert Beverley, *History and Present State of Virginia* (London, 1705), bk. 4:60–61; John Lawson, *The History of Carolina* (London, 1714), 5; Greene, "Changing Identity in the British West Indies," 31, 41–42; Howard Mumford Jones, "The Colonial Impulse: An Analysis of the 'Promotion' Literature of Colonization," *Proceedings of the American Philosophical Society* 90 (1946): 131.
65. Carter to William Dawkins, Feb. 23, 1720, to Thomas Evans, Feb. 23, 1720, *Letters of Robert Carter*, 80–82, 83. See also Michael Kugler, "Provincial Intellectuals: Identity, Patriotism, and Enlightened Peripheries," *Eighteenth Century: Theory and Interpretation* 37 (1996): 156–72.
66. *The Examination of Doctor Benjamin Franklin, before an August Assembly, Relating to the Repeal of the Stamp Act* (Philadelphia, 1766), 3.
67. Cooke, *The Sot-Weed Factor*, 14.
68. Pinckney, *Letterbook*, 19, 26, 180–81; William Byrd to Ann Taylor Otway, June 30, 1736, *Correspondence of the Three William Byrds* 2:481–83. Johnson's *Dictionary* defined a *colony* as "a body of people drawn from the mother country to inhabit some distant place," and *provincial* as "not of the mother country; rude; unpolished."
69. Robert Carter to William Dawkins, Feb. 23, 1720/21, to John Carter, July 13, 1720, *Letters of Robert Carter*, 8, 81.
70. *TC* 2:253, 145.
71. Beverley, *History and Present State of Virginia*, bk. 4:58, 2:40, 1:preface.
72. Byrd to John Boyle, Feb. 2, 1726/27, in Marambaud, *William Byrd*, 147.
73. Greene, "Changing Identity in the British West Indies," 57–59; James Grainger, *The Sugar Cane: A Poem in Four Books with Notes* (London, 1764), 109, 114–15. Outside visitors also saw the parallels between plantation reality and classical patterns; in reflecting on the life of a Mr. Bull, a wealthy planter, "owner of a great number of Negroes," who "lived in tran-

quility, surrounded by his slaves and his flocks, until Arnold and Philips invaded Virginia," Chastellux asked, "Does this not recall to mind the ancient patriarchs emigrating with their family and flocks?" (*MDC*, 425–26).

74. Henry Darnall, *A Just and Impartial Account of Transactions of the Merchants in London for the Advancement of the Price of Tobacco* (Annapolis, 1728), 12.

75. Robert Micklus, "'The History of the Tuesday Club': A Mock-Jeremiad of the Colonial South," *WMQ*, 3d ser., 40 (1983): 60; Cooke, *The Sot-Weed Factor*, 19; *AB*, 46–47.

76. *TC* 1:xvi; Waterhouse, "Development of Elite Culture," 395–96.

77. Dorothy Ann Lipson, *Freemasonry in Federalist Connecticut* (Princeton, N.J., 1977), 46, 61.

78. See Steven C. Bullock, *Revolutionary Brotherhood: Freemasonry and the Transformation of the American Social Order, 1730–1840* (Chapel Hill, N.C., 1996). See also Bernard Vincent, "Les frères fondateurs: enquête sur le rôle de la franc-maçonnerie dans la Revolution américaine," *Les oubliés de la Revolution américaine* (Nancy, 1990), 137–66; Margaret Jacob, *The Radical Enlightenment: Pantheists, Freemasons, and Republicans* (London, 1981); J. A. Leo Lemay, ed., *Deism, Masonry, and the Enlightenment: Essays Honoring Alfred Owen Aldridge* (Newark, Del., 1987).

79. *The Constitutions of the Free-Masons: Containing the History, Charges, Regulations, etc. of That Most Ancient and Right Worshipful Fraternity* (Philadelphia, 1734), 45–46, 48, 55–56, 59, 93.

80. *OLD* 1:408–9; *AB*, 4–5.

81. Davis, "Colonial Virginia Satirist," 48.

82. Wylie Sypher, *Guinea's Captive Kings: British Anti-Slavery Literature of the XVIIIth Century* (1942; rept. New York, 1969), 22.

83. Morgan Godwyn, *Trade Preferr'd before Religion* (London, 1685), 1, 17, 6, 16. The planters were not oblivious to such attacks; Ralph Wormeley's library contained Godwyn's book (Marambaud, *William Byrd*, 174).

84. [Henry Pitman], *A Relation of the Great Sufferings and Strange Adventures of Henry Pitman* (London, 1689), 12.

85. [Tryon], *Friendly Advice*, 77, 86, 96, 165, 208–9; [Thomas Tryon], *The Country-Man's Companion* (London, 1684), 97.

86. Sloane, *Voyage to the Islands*, lvii; *A Letter from a Merchant of Jamaica to a Member of Parliament in London* (London, 1729), 28, 31, 8–9, 31; Leslie, *New and Exact Account of Jamaica*, 4, 41–42.

87. Sypher, *Guinea's Captive Kings*, 106–37; Klingberg, *Anti-Slavery Movement in England*, 64–65.

88. Thomas Bluett, *Some Memoir of the Life of Job, the Son of Solomon the High Priest of Boonda in Africa; Who Was a Slave about Two Years in Maryland* (London, 1734), 18–32, 60–63.

89. Kimber, "Observations," 38, 29–30. See also "Eighteenth-Century Maryland as Portrayed in the 'Itinerant Observations' of Edward Kimber," *Maryland Historical Magazine* 44 (1951): 329.

90. John Woolman, *Some Considerations on the Keeping of Negroes* (Philadelphia, 1754), 15; Davis, "Colonial Virginia Satirist," 57; *MDC* 2:439; Richard Cumberland, *The West Indian: A Comedy. As It Is Performed at the Theatre Royal in Drury Lane* (London, 1771), 3, 6; Philip Greven, *The Protestant Temperament: Patterns of Child-Rearing, Religious Experience, and the Self in Early America* (New York, 1977), 265.

91. *AB*, 22, 111, 22, 111, 110.

92. *OLD* 1:127, 339–40; Kimber, "Observations," 29; *Some Modern Observations upon Jamaica. . . . By an English Merchant* (London, 1727), 16; *OLD* 1:453; Fithian, *Journal*, 161.

93. *CEG*, 18, 257; Jones, *Present State of Virginia*, 37; *MDC* 2:397–98. See also Margaret T. Hodgen, *Early Anthropology in the Sixteenth and Seventeenth Centuries* (Philadelphia, 1964), esp. 354–426. Jefferson, who suggested that Africans were innately inferior to Europeans, reflected a similar mentality (although in an ambiguous way, since he did attack slavery as an institution) and even contributed to it by his scholarly authority (David S. Wiesen, "The Contribution of Antiquity to American Racial Thought," in John W. Eadie, ed., *Classical Traditions in Early America* [Ann Arbor, Mich., 1976], 201).

94. Grainger, *Sugar Cane*, 109, 135, 133, 130–31, 157, 136, 127–29; Sypher, *Guinea's Captive Kings*, 260.

95. James Oakes, *The Ruling Race: A History of American Slaveholders* (New York, 1982), 22, 31, 12.

96. Eugene Genovese, *The Political Economy of Slavery* (New York, 1967), 13–31; Oakes, *Ruling Race*, xii and chap. 1.

97. *LC*, 865, 840–41.

98. *OLD* 1:xv–xviii; Edmund Burke, *Reflections on the Revolution in France*, ed. Sidney Lee (London, 1905), 68; Edmund Burke, *A Philosophical Enquiry into the Origin of Our Idea of the Sublime and Beautiful*, ed. James T. Boulton (London, 1958), 134, 116.

99. *Examination of Doctor Benjamin Franklin*, 12; Benjamin Rush to Ebenezer Hazard, Oct. 1768, L. H. Butterfield, ed., *Letters of Benjamin Rush* (Princeton, N.J., 1951), 1:68–69.

CHAPTER 4
BEAUTIFUL ORDER AND POLITENESS

1. Bourdieu, *Distinction*, 6.

2. *Rudiments of Taste*, 61.

3. Jasper Tregagle to the editors, *Royal Magazine* (London), May 1762, 232; Gratian, *Compleat Gentleman*, 206. See also Timothy Dykstal, "The Politics of Taste in the *Spectator*," *Eighteenth Century: Theory and Interpretation* 35 (1994): 46–63.

4. Giovanni Della Casa, *A Renaissance Courtesy Book: Galateo of Manners and Behaviors*, ed. J. E. Springarn (London, 1914), 126. See also John E. Mason, *Gentlefolk in the Making: Studies in the History of English Courtesy Literature and Related Topics from 1531 to 1774* (1935; rept. New York, 1971); Ruth Kelso, *The Doctrine of the English Gentleman in the Sixteenth Century* (Urbana, Ill., 1929).

5. *OLD* 1:428, 537.

6. *GP*, 8, 23, 146.

7. Fithian, *Journal*, 29.
8. [Gordon], "Journal of an Officer," 375, 379.
9. *TC* 2:253.
10. Instructions to Charles Calvert, *Archives of Maryland* 15:16.
11. Braudel, *Wheels of Commerce* 2:463.
12. *WF*, 382, 362; Byrd's order, Aug. 8, 1690, in *VMHB* 26 (1918): 391.
13. Aug. 24, 1711, *SD*, 393; Wright, *First Gentlemen of Virginia*, 73.
14. *Royal Magazine*, May 1762, 301.
15. [Thomas Tryon], *Some General Considerations Offered Relating to Our Present Trade* (London, 1698), 7.
16. Carson, "Consumer Revolution"; Elias, *Power and Civility*, 254–55; *Royal Magazine*, May 1762, 230.
17. *Gentleman's Magazine*, Jan. 1738, 84, 28–29; *Remarks on the Common Topics of Conversation in Towns, at the Meeting of the Parliament* (London, 1725 [misprint for 1735]), 36–37.
18. *GP*, 55; *LC*, 728.
19. Washington quoted in Bushman, *Refinement*, 183; *LD*, 567; *GP*, 7.
20. William Byrd, "A Progress to the Mines," in *LD*, 624; *OLD* 1:382.
21. See Lois Green Carr and Lorena S. Walsh, "Changing Lifestyles and Consumer Behavior in Colonial Chesapeake," in Carson et al., *Of Consuming Interests*, 59–166.
22. *Gentleman's Library*, 373.
23. *CEG*, 258.
24. Swift, *Examiner*, no. 41 (May 10, 1711), in Ellis, *Swift vs. Mainwaring*, 419.
25. *New England Magazine of Knowledge and Pleasure* (Boston), no. 3 (1759), 44.
26. Henry Peacham, *The Compleat Gentleman: Fashioning Him Absolute in the Most Necessary and Commendable Qualities concerning Minde and Bodie That May Be Required in a Noble Gentleman* (London, 1622), 3, 16; Gratian, *Compleat Gentleman*, 19; Jan. 21, 1712, *Spectator* 2:591.
27. John Mason, *Self-Knowledge: A Treatise Showing the Nature and Benefit of That Important Science* (Worcester, Mass., 1789), 54.
28. *New England Magazine of Knowledge and Pleasure*, no. 3 (1759), 44; ibid., Aug. 1758, 19, 27; *Boston Weekly Magazine*, March 9, 1743, 14; *Gentleman's Magazine*, March 1734, 131; Fithian, *Journal*, 70.
29. John Trumbull, "The Progress of Dullness," in Edwin T. Bowden, ed., *The Satiric Poems of John Trumbull* (Austin, Tex., 1962), 75, 56–58; Bushman, *Refinement of America*, 188.
30. Sept. 18–25, 1710, *SD*, 232–34; Fithian, *Journal*, 161; Pinckney, *Letterbook*, 34. On Carolinian gentry, see George C. Rogers, *Charleston in the Age of the Pinckneys* (Columbia, S.C., 1969).
31. Grace Galloway to Betsey Nickleson, Oct. 18, 1758, Galloway MSS, Huntington Library.

32. *LC,* 790, 905.

33. *TC* 1:352.

34. [William Dawson], *Poems on Several Occasions: By a Gentleman of Virginia* (Williamsburg, Va., 1736), 7, 13, 21; William K. Boyd, ed., *William Byrd's Histories of the Dividing Line* (Raleigh, N.C., 1929), 29. For the *Maryland Gazette,* see, for instance, the elegies for Elisabeth Young (Oct. 13, 1730) and Charles Calvert (March 8, 1734).

35. Charles Leslie, *New History of Jamaica* (London, 1740), quoted in Errol Hill, *The Jamaican Stage, 1655–1900* (Amherst, Mass., 1992), 20; *OLD* 2:127.

36. *GW* 2:331, 320–21.

37. To William Pulteney, June 1761, Montagu MSS, Huntington Library; Hugh Morrison, *Early American Architecture: From the First Colonial Settlements to the National Period* (New York, 1952), 357; Flexner, *Washington,* 246–27. See also Thomas T. Waterman, *The Mansions of Virginia, 1706–1776* (Chapel Hill, N.C., 1946).

38. [James Miller], *Of Politeness: An Epistle to the Right Honourable William Stanhope, Lord Harrington* (London, 1738), 19.

39. John Adams, *Poems on Several Occasions* (Boston, 1745), 33.

40. Richard Brathwaite, *The English Gentleman: Containing Sundry Excellent Rules or Exquisite Observations, Tending to Direction of Every Gentleman, of Selecter Ranke and Qualitie* (London, 1630), 457–60; Della Casa, *Renaissance Courtesy Book,* preface; Gratian, *Compleat Gentleman,* 156; [Jonathan Swift], *A Complete Collection of Genteel and Ingenious Conversation . . .* (London, 1738), xv.

41. R. K. Root, ed., *Lord Chesterfield: Letters to His Son and Others* (London, 1984), 13; *TC* 1:320. On European traditions of cultivation and refinement, see Elias, *Power and Civility* and *The History of Manners,* trans. Edmund Jephcott (New York, 1978).

42. *Virginia Gazette,* Feb. 18–25, 1736; *TC* 1:140, 137–38.

43. Kimber, *History of the Life and Adventures of Mr. Anderson,* 21; Fischer, *Albion's Seed,* 359.

44. *AB,* 30; Kimber, "Observations," 38; *GP,* 123.

45. Sloane, *Voyage,* quoted in Dunn, *Sugar and Slaves,* 286; Jędrzej Kitowicz, *Opis obyczajów za panowania Augusta III* (A description of manners in the reign of Augustus III) (Warsaw, 1985), 239.

46. Leslie, *New and Exact Account of Jamaica,* 35–36.

47. Kimber, "Observations," 36.

48. *LD,* 513–24; Lockridge, *Diary and Life,* 135.

49. *GW* 2:488–89.

50. See Stein, *Worlds of Jefferson at Monticello;* Jack McLaughlin, *Jefferson and Monticello: The Biography of a Builder* (New York, 1988); Robert F. Dalzell Jr., "Constructing Independence: Monticello, Mount Vernon, and the Men Who Built Them," *Eighteenth-Century Studies* 26 (1993): 543–80.

51. See author's note at the end of Cooke, *The Sot-Weed Factor.*

52. Byrd, "History of the Dividing Line," *LD,* 546; *LC,* 316, 837; Flexner, *Washington,*

236, 317; Jefferson to Madison, April 6, 1781, in James Morton Smith, ed., *The Republic of Letters: The Correspondence between Thomas Jefferson and James Madison, 1776–1826* (New York, 1995), 1:184. Hamilton had a theory explaining this aversion to frivolities: upstart gentlemen were too "pragmatical," and their humor was "a dull form and precise Starchness" (*TC* 1:251, 106).

53. Beverley, *History and Present State of Virginia*, bk. 4:71.

54. *MDC* 1:127.

55. Aristotle, *Nichomachean Ethics*, trans. H. Rackham (Cambridge, Mass., 1962), 103; Brathwaite, *English Gentleman*, 135–36; Markham, *Booke of Honour*, 52; [Miller], *Of Politeness*, 18.

56. Della Casa, *Renaissance Courtesy Book*, 49; *Gentleman's Library*, 63; [Darrell], *Gentleman Instructed*, 7; Gratian, *Compleat Gentleman*, 15; Abbé Ancourt, *The Lady's Preceptor, or, A Letter to a Young Lady of Distinction upon Politeness* (London, 1743), 63, 67. Braudel suggested that ostentatious luxury was typical of societies which were not based on money, or where money was slow in appearing, forcing the ruling class to rely on display rather than on "the silent support of money" (*Wheels of Commerce* 2:491).

57. *The American Gazetteer, Containing a Distinct Account of All the Parts of the New World* (London, 1762), [2].

58. Announcement quoted in the introduction to *GP*, xvii–xviii; *Virginia Gazette*, Nov. 12–19, 1736; *LD*, 11; Edmund Jennings Lee, ed., *Lee of Virginia, 1642–1892: Biography and Genealogical Sketches of the Descendants of Colonel Richard Lee* (Philadelphia, 1895), 77; Davis, "Colonial Virginia Satirist," 66.

59. Della Casa, *Renaissance Courtesy Book*, 63, 72.

60. *LD*, 615, 613, and passim; *LC*, 985. As Rhys Isaac has observed, militia roles were not only associated with both the arms-bearing gentry and yeomanry of England but also—for the classically educated elites—with the farmer-soldiers of Rome (*The Transformation of Virginia, 1740–1790* [Chapel Hill, N.C., 1982], 109).

61. [Ward], *Trip to Jamaica*, 16, 13; Kimber, "Eighteenth-Century Maryland," 326; Davis, "Colonial Virginia Satirist," 56; *GP*, 100; *OLD* 1:336–37. Jack P. Greene has suggested that the Barbadian title-mania may have been linked—just as their fortified residences were—to the underlying fear of being assaulted by their dejected slaves ("Changing Identity in the British West Indies," 23). It seems more likely that this infatuation with military appellations was mainly inspired by the provincial craving for genteel status and a semblance of an ordered, hierarchical society.

62. Aristotle, *Nichomachean Ethics*, 213; *Boswell's Life of Johnson* 3:189; [William Ramsey], *The Gentleman's Companion, or, A Character of True Nobility and Gentility* (London, 1672), 88.

63. Brown, *An Estimate*, 34.

64. William Kay to Bishop of London, June 14, 1752, William Stevens Perry, ed., *Historical Collections Relating to the American Colonial Church* (Hartford, 1870; rept. New York, 1969), 1:389–90. See also Isaac, *Transformation of Virginia*, 143–44.

65. Hobbes, *Leviathan*, 72. See also Felicity Heal, "The Idea of Hospitality in Early Modern England," *Past and Present* 102 (1984): 66–93. See also Daniel Blake Smith, *Inside the Great House: Planter Family Life in Eighteenth-Century Chesapeake Society* (Ithaca, N.Y., 1980).

66. Beverley, *History and Present State of Virginia*, bk. 4: 76; *ASD*, 117; *SD*, 297.

67. *A New Voyage to Georgia, by a Young Gentleman* (London, 1737), 27–30, 46, 30–31.

68. Beverley, *History and Present State of Virginia*, bk. 4:71, 76; *ASD*, 117; Fithian, *Journal*, 167–68, 165. On Virginian hospitality, see Jack P. Greene, "The Hopefullest Plantation: Virginia, 1584–1660," in *Douglas Southall Freeman Historical Review*, Spring 1996, 66–68.

69. *AB*, 21.

70. Jefferson quoted in McLaughlin, *Jefferson and Monticello*, 269.

71. Kimber, "Observations," 29; *American Gazetteer*, vol. 3, unpaginated; [Gordon], "Journal of an Officer," 405.

72. Brathwaite, *English Gentleman*, 333; *OLD* 1:429.

73. On such a "delay" of taste, see Bourdieu, *Distinction*, 375–76. See also Alan Gallay, *The Formation of a Planter Elite: Jonathan Bryan and the Southern Colonial Frontier* (Athens, Ga., and London, 1989); Harold F. Davis, *The Fledgling Province: Social and Cultural Life in Colonial Georgia, 1733–1776* (Chapel Hill, N.C., 1976).

74. *AB*, 14; on Goode, see Baine, *Robert Munford*, 60; *Virginia Gazette*, Sept. 30–Oct 7, 1737. For an example of the genteel exclusiveness of racing, see Jane Carson, *Colonial Virginians at Play* (Williamsburg, Va., 1965), 109–10. On the role of horse races, see T. H. Breen, "Horses and Gentlemen: The Cultural Significance of Gambling among the Gentry of Virginia," *WMQ*, 3d ser., 34 (1977): 239–57.

75. Fithian, *Journal*, 95, 177, 190, 187.

76. Isaac, *Transformation of Virginia*, 102–4 (for John Carter); *MDC* 2:386; Baron von Closen quoted in Jane Carson, *Colonial Virginians at Play*, 159; Davis, "Colonial Virginia Satirist," 57.

77. *AB*, 26; Kimber, "*Observations*," 36; Fithian, *Journal*, 33; Morton, *Robert Carter*, 212; Davis, "Colonial Virginia Satirist," 57.

78. *LC*, 103, 17, 646; see also ibid., 907.

79. Irma B. Jafee, "Ethics and Aesthetics in Eighteenth-Century American Art," in Paul J. Korshin, ed., *The American Revolution and Eighteenth-Century Culture* (New York, 1986), 157; Kevin J. Hayes, *The Library of William Byrd* (Madison, Wis., 1996); Wright, *First Gentlemen of Virginia*, 154.

80. Peter Burke, *Venice and Amsterdam: A Study of Seventeenth-Century Elites* (London, 1974), 86–87.

81. Copley to [R. Bruce, 1767?], Guernsey Jones, ed., *Letters and Papers of John Singleton Copley and Henry Pelham, 1739–1776* (Boston, 1914), 64–66; Wright, *First Gentlemen of Virginia*, 330, 324.

82. *CEG*, 124–25, 136.

83. *GW* 2:23.

84. Jefferson to Madison, Sept. 20, 1785, *Republic of Letters*, 384–85.
85. G. C. Bolton, "The Idea of Colonial Gentry," *Historical Studies* 13, no. 51 (1968): 307. On the theory of dispositions, see Bourdieu, *Distinction*, 477–79.
86. Flexner, *Washington*, 14, 287, 282.
87. E. Goffman, "The Nature of Deference and Demeanor," *American Anthropologist* 58 (June 1956): 473–502; Geraint Parry, *Political Elites* (New York, 1969), 69–70. See also Ostrow, *Social Sensitivity*, 73–74, 79–80; Bourdieu, "Symbolic Power," 112–19.
88. John S. Ezell, ed., *The New Democracy in America: Travels of Francisco de Miranda in the United States, 1783–84*, trans. Judson P. Wood (Norman, Okla., 1963), 17; Julian Ursyn Niemcewicz, *Under the Vine and Fig Tree: Travels through America in 1797–1799, 1805, with Some Further Account of Life in New Jersey*, trans. and ed. Metchie J. E. Budka (Elizabeth, N.J., 1965), 98.

CHAPTER 5
GENTEEL ETHOS ON THE EVE OF THE REVOLUTION

1. Jonathan Elliot, ed., *The Debates in the Several State Conventions on the Adoption of the Federal Constitution* (Washington, D.C., 1854), 3:24, 650; epigraph to this chapter, ibid., 53–54.
2. Samuel Johnson, "Taxation No Tyranny," in Donald J. Greene, ed., *The Yale Edition of the Works of Samuel Johnson* 10 (New Haven and London, 1977): 413, 431, 425, 454; Elliot, *Debates*, 598.
3. For examples of such voices, see Greene, *Intellectual Construction of America*, 183–87.
4. *LC*, 1086–87.
5. Flexner, *Washington*, 110–12; *The Examination of Doctor Benjamin Franklin*, 3; Gordon Wood, *The Creation of the American Republic, 1776–1787* (Chapel Hill, N.C., 1969), 100.
6. [Hodges], *Plantation Justice*, 10.
7. Thomas Paine, "The Magazine in America," in *Writings of Thomas Paine*, 15.
8. *LC*, 1086–87; Ruth H. Bloch, "The Gendered Meanings of Virtue in Revolutionary America," *Signs: Journal of Women in Culture and Society* 3 (1987): 57. See also Ruth H. Bloch, "Untangling the Roots of Modern Sex Roles: A Survey of Four Centuries of Change," ibid., 4 (1978): 237–52. On the appeal to plantation gentry of Adam Smith's idea of the superiority of agrarian economy, see Forrest McDonald, *Novus Ordo Seclorum: The Intellectual Origins of the Constitution* (Lawrence, Kans., 1985), 129.
9. Kenneth Silverman, *A Cultural History of the American Revolution: Painting, Music, Literature, and the Theatre in the Colonies and the United States from the Treaty of Paris to the Inauguration of George Washington, 1763–1789* (New York, 1976), 505, 511.
10. Paine, *Common Sense*, in *Writings of Thomas Paine*, 86, 96; Wood, *Creation*, 104; Silverman, *Cultural History*, 444.
11. Wood, *Creation*, 47; Adams to Jefferson, Nov. 15, 1813, *Adams-Jefferson Letters* 2:400.

12. Jefferson to Adams, Oct. 28, 1813, *Adams-Jefferson Letters* 2:338–39.
13. Wood, *Radicalism*, 187, 189–90, 194–96.
14. J. R. Pole, ed., *The American Constitution, For and Against: The Federalist and Anti-Federalist Papers* (New York, 1987), 85, 126, 198.
15. June 26, 1787, Max Farrand, ed., *The Records of the Federal Convention of 1787* (New Haven, 1937), 1:422–23.
16. Bushman, *Refinement*, 403 (emulation), xiv (harmony), 96–97 (beautification), 405 (metropolis), xiv (harshness), 99 (flaw), 182–83 (divisiveness), 99 (weakness); see also *SD*, 273.
17. Charles Moore, ed., *George Washington's Rules of Civility and Decent Behavior in Company and Conversation* (Boston, 1926), 11, 9, 7. A vivid example of how a breakdown in exclusivenss devalued honor is to be found in the huge inflation of titles in early modern France; for instance, the Order of St. Michel, founded in 1469 and limited to 36 knights, by the 1580s numbered in the thousands—with the result that those with any pride had to publicly demonstrate disdain for the title's now debased honor (Robert R. Harding, *Anatomy of a Power Elite: The Provincial Governors of Early Modern France* [New Haven, 1979], 81–82). On the monopoly of legitimacy, see also Bourdieu and Passeron, *Reproduction in Education*, 18–19.
18. Montesquieu, *The Spirit of the Laws* (1748), trans. Thomas Nugent (Chicago, 1952), 12; J. R. Pole, *Political Representation in England and the Origins of the American Republic* (London, 1966), 420–21; J. R. Pole, *The Pursuit of Equality in American History* (Berkeley, Calif., 1978), 13–59, 52.
19. Richard Bland, *An Inquiry into the Rights of the British Colonies* (Williamsburg, Va., 1766), 13–24; Willi Paul Adams, *The First American Constitution: Republican Ideology and the Making of State Constitutions in the Revolutionary Era*, trans. Rita and Robert Kimber (Chapel Hill, N.C., 1980), 171–75. Even the radical Thomas Paine did not extend the principle of equality to social conditions or political prerogatives in America.
20. Records of the Federal Convention, Aug. 7, 1787, in J. R. Pole, ed., *The Revolution in America: Documents on the Internal Development of America in the Revolutionary Era* (London, 1970), 569.
21. Pole, *Equality*, 58.
22. *Correspondence of the Three William Byrds* 2:603–14; *LC*, 52–56, 505; Emory G. Evans, "The Rise and Decline of the Virginia Aristocracy in the Eighteenth Century: The Nelsons," in Darrett B. Rutman, ed., *The Old Dominion: Essays for Thomas Perkins Abernethy* (Charlottesville, Va., 1964), 62–78; Morton, *Robert Carter*, 226.
23. Ossowska, *Etos*, 21–48, 100–104; Ferguson, *Indian Summer*, 224; Maurice Keen, *Chivalry* (New Haven, 1984), 36, 46, 145; Tamara T. Thornton, *Cultivating Gentlemen: The Meaning of Country Life among the Boston Elite, 1785–1860* (New Haven, 1989), 21–22. The cosmopolitan character of gentility contributed significantly to the integration of the modern Europe of manners. In 1785 the Reverend William Coxe could travel from London to Warsaw in Poland and immediately recognize the "elegance and luxury" of his hosts' houses,

which "happily blended the English and French modes," and showed "good taste" (William Coxe, *Travels in Poland, Russia, Sweden, and Denmark* [London, 1802], 166).

24. Bushman, *Refinement*, xv. See also John H. Elliott, "Colonial Identity in the Atlantic World," in Nicholas Canny and Anthony Pagden, eds., *Colonial Identity in the Atlantic World* (Princeton, N.J., 1987), 3–13.

25. Kenneth Lockridge suggests such a primarily conscious adoption of gentility, writing that, while at Felsted School in England, young William Byrd "seized on the project of becoming a perfect gentleman" (*Diary and Life*, 21).

26. Jefferson to Chastellux, Sept. 2, 1785, Boyd, *Papers of Thomas Jefferson* 8:468; *AB*, 24. On the arrogance of Virginians, see Jan Lewis, *The Pursuit of Happiness: Family and Values in Jefferson's Virginia* (Cambridge, Eng., 1985), 106–34.

27. See Ian Tyrell, "American Exceptionalism in an Age of International History," *American Historical Review* 96 (1991): 1031–55.

28. Greene, "Search for Identity," 212, 205, 217.

29. Lockridge, *Diary and Life*, 151, 153, 134, 49, 157, 65.

30. See Joyce Appleby, "The Radical Recreation of the American Republic," *WMQ*, 3d ser., 51 (1994): 679–83, and Jack P. Greene, "All Men Are Created Equal: Some Reflections on the Character of the American Revolution," in *Imperatives*, 236–67.

Index

Adams, John, 34, 177
Adams, John (clergyman), 144
Addison, Joseph, 39, 57, 62
Alcoholism, colonial, 85–87
Alsop, George, 47, 80
American Gazetteer, 153
American Magazine, 82
Anarchiad, 101
Annapolis, 109
Antigua, 130
Aristocracy: attacked by Revolutionary planter-gentlemen, 49; French proposal to wear ribbons by, 131; of merit, 178–80
Aristotle: on moderation and gentility, 152; on aristocracy, 186
Armstrong, Marmaduke, 133
Arnold, Matthew, 9, 11

Bacon, Francis, 92
Bacon, Nathaniel, 59, 104, 135
Bacon, Thomas, 109
Baltimore, Charles Calvert, lord, 131
Barbados, 48, 62, 80, 97, 108, 115
Baudrillard, Jean, 7, 10–11
Behn, Aphra, 61; *Oronooko*, 61, 115; *Widdow Ranter*, 99–100
Berkeley, George, bishop of Cloyne, 66, 83, 88
Berkeley, William, 59, 66
Beverley, Robert, the elder, 45
Beverley, Robert, 104, 107, 151, 158
Bishop, Robert, 112
Bladen, Robert, 186
Bland, Richard, 184

Bluett, Thomas, 116
Bolling, Mary, 103
Bolton, C. G., 170–71
Bordley, John Beale, 109
Boston, 187
Bourdieu, Pierre, 18, 20–21, 128
Brathwaite, Richard, 144, 152–53
Braudel, Fernand, 32, 188
Breen, T. H., 65
Bridenbaugh, Carl and Jessica, 13
Brown, John, poet, 67, 156–57
Bruce, Philip Alexander, 11
Burke, Edmund, 101, 124
Burnaby, Andrew, 109, 118
Bushman, Richard, 181–82
Byrd, William I, 63, 76, 132
Byrd, William II, 30, 33, 34, 37, 63, 132, 155, 175, 189; on luxury, 67; on effeminacy, 68; as patriarch, 73, 120–21; faces condescension on London, 77–79; on Indians, 88; on colonial isolation, 107; on provincialism, 108, 135; on Edenton, N.C., 135; visited by Governor Spotswood in Westover, 139–40; commonplace book of, 140; poetry of, 141; rigid daily schedule, 148–49; humor of, 151; epitaph of, 154; library of, 166
Byrd, William III, 185

Carghill, Cornelius, 86
Carolina, 76, 79, 158–59; North, 151; South, 171
Carroll, Charles, 34
Carson, Cary, 133
Carter, Charles of Cleve, 165

Carter, John, 45, 164
Carter, Landon, 33, 34, 63–64, 65, 68, 107, 189; as slaveowner, 123–24; on foreign styles, 140; his lack of humor, 151; his pride, 157; his propensity for the useful, 165; on British army, 174; on Britain's declension, 176; on ideal of moderation, 185
Carter, Robert, 36, 37, 63, 105, 107
Carter, Robert III, 186
Cassirer, Ernst, 23
Castiglione, Baldassare, 28, 56, 186
Cave, Edward, 139
Charleston, S.C., 7, 12, 64, 83–84
Chastellux, chevalier de, 1, 102, 117, 120, 151–52, 164
Chesterfield, Philip Dormer Stanhope, earl of, 144–45
Child, Sir Josiah, 81, 92
Cincinnati, Society of, 185, 191
Closen, Baron von, 164
Cock-fights, 159, 164
Cole, Charles, 145–46
College of Willliam and Mary, 54
Continental Congress, First, 187
Convicts sent to the Chesapeake, 70, 90–96
Cooke, Ebenezer, 82, 86, 104, 106, 109, 150–51
Copley, John Singleton, 167
Coquault, Oudard, 56
Coverley, Sir Roger de, 57
Crèvecoeur, Michel-Guillaume Jean de, 188
Culture, concept of, 19; methodology of studying, 20–27
Cumberland, Richard, 117

Daingerfeld, William, 70
Dancing and gentility, 164–65
Darnall, Henry, 108–9
Darrell, William, 33
Dawkins, William, 105
Dawson, William, 140–41
Declaration of Independence, 191
Defoe, Daniel, 28, 30, 43, 188; his model of virtue, 50–58; on education, 52, 54; his *Review*, 58, 59–60; on commercial virtues, 56–57; attacks on, 58–59; his *Complete English Tradesman*, 60; his *True-Born Englishman*, 60; on luxury, 66; on effeminacy, 67–68; *Moll Flanders*, 70, 95–96; on social hierarchy, 70–71;

Colonel Jacque, 70; *Robinson Crusoe*, 72–73; on plebeians, 119; assails vulgar style of the newly rich, 137; on art as genteel ornament, 167; on aristocracy of merit, 179
Della Casa, Giovanni, 144
Dinwiddie, Robert, 175
Dulany, Margaret, 55

Edenton, N.C., 135
Effeminacy and gentility, 67–68, 176
Elias, Norbert, 133–34
Elites, new, 28–29, 31, 32
Ethos, cultural, 19–20
European highbrow attitudes to American culture, 9–11
Examiner, 59
Exceptionalism in American historiography, 8, 18, 188–89, 190

Ferriar, J., 115
Fielding, Henry, 22
Fielding, Sir John, 92
Fithian, Philip, 23, 163
Fitzgerald, Scott, 9
Fitzhugh, William, 45, 54–55, 67, 71, 76, 131
Fletcher, Andrew, 91
Franklin, Benjamin, 2, 61–62, 105–6, 109, 125
Freeport, Sir Andrew, of the Spectator Club, 57

Generosity as genteel virtue, 1, 157–58
Genovese, Eugene, 123
Gentility: debate on its role in American culture, 3, 189; aspirations to in Britain and America, 28–75; and new elites, 28–38; as means of social demarcation, 38–43; and pedigrees, 43–50; Defoe's attempt to expand traditional model of genteel ethos to include new elites, 50–61; and merit, 51–52; and commercial values, 74; colonial gentility dismissed by metropolitan elites, 76–126, and taste, 127–36; and hospitality, 157–61; and cult of equality, 181–85; social uses account for continuity of much of its ethos since antiquity, 186–87
Gentleman, cultural models of, 4, 17, 21, 26, 39
Gentleman, Francis, 115

Index

Gentleman's Magazine, 134, 139
Gentry: American colonial planter, and Anglophilia, 14, 16; power of, 34–35; wealth of, 35, 37; kinship bonds, 35–36; rise of, 37–38; and their commercial roots, 61–69; and conservatism of the adopted landed model, 69–75; its pursuit of taste, 134–71; and social hierarchy, 70–71; and slavery, 111–24; ritualized manner of entering church, 130; practical inclinations in their stylistic pursuits, 161–71; Revolution as ultimate test of their aspirations, 172–85
Georgia, 83, 93, 158–59
Godwyn, Morgan, 112
Gooch, William, 71
Goode, John, 163
Gordon, Lord Adam, 48, 130
Goudey, Robert, 64
Grainger, James, 108, 121–22
Gramsci, Antonio, 189
Gratian, Baltasar, 127, 128, 138
Green, Jonas, 109
Greene, Jack P., 15, 36, 104–5, 165, 189
Gucht, Michael von der, 43
Guiana, British, 80

Hamilton, Dr. Alexander, 15, 33, 47, 55, 154; on effeminacy, 68; on social classes, 72; on genteel simplicity, 107; on provincialism of American gentry, 109, 140; on elegance, 129; on plebeian lack of taste, 130–31; on propriety of taste for different social ranks, 134; on pedantry, 145; on militia titles, 156
Hammond, LeRoy, 64
Harley, Robert, 58
Harrower, John, 70
Hartlib, Samuel, 91–92
Hawkesworth, John, 115
Hawkins, Francis, 182
Heard, Sir Isaac, 46
Heraldry, 43–50; pursuit of by Virginians, 44–47; false heraldry, 47; and gentility, 48–49, 55; coats of arms in Virginia, 132
Hobbes, Thomas, 34
Homer on genteel virtues, 186
Horses, 162–63
Hospitality in plantation America, 157–61
Howe, William, viscount, 174
Huizinga, Johan, 9

Hulton, Henry, 86
Husserl, Edmund, 23
Hutcheson, Francis, 91

Indians, 47, 87–88, 147
Inkle, 114
Izard, Ralph, 74

Jamaica, 82, 84, 85, 119, 141, 147, 148
James I, king, 30, 47, 92
Jamestown, 62
Jefferson, Thomas, 33, 34, 177, 191; and heraldry, 46–47; his rigid schedule, 148; and landed gentry model, 68–69; and Monticello, 103, 150; on hospitality as duty of gentry, 160; as patron of art, 168–69; his opinion of Virginia gentry, 188
Johnson, Samuel, 1, 41, 81, 96, 156, 173
Jones, Howard Mumford, 11
Jones, Hugh, 54, 91, 103, 110, 119

Kershaw, Joseph, 64
Kimber, Edward: on illiteracy in Maryland, 84–85; on Indians, 87, 88; on slavery, 102, 116–17; on use of titles in Chesapeake, 156
Kosciuszko, Thaddeus, 171
Kulikoff, Alan, 36

Lamb, Charles, 60
Language as symbolic form of cognition, 23
La Rochefoucauld-Liancourt, duc de, 102
Lawson, John, 104
Leavis, F. R., 10
Lee, Richard, colonel, 132
Lee, Richard II, 154
Leeward Islands, 147
Legitimacy, cultural, 7, 15, 24–27
Leslie, Charles, 114, 141
Levellers, 90
Library Society, 109
Ligon, Richard, 115
Lockridge, Kenneth, 4, 16, 149, 189
Luxury, 66–67, 176

MacSparran, James, 88
Maddox, Isaac, dean of Wells, 83
Madison, James, 34, 109, 180–81, 184
Maritain, Jacques, 9
Markham, Francis, 41, 153
Marx, Karl, 72

Maryland, 82, 86, 88, 93, 106, 116, 147, 150–51, 156, 160
Maryland Gazette, 154, 180
Mason, George, 34, 180, 184
Mason, John, 138
Masons, 109–10
Mather, Cotton, 88
McIntosh, Alexander, 64
Meade, David, 1
Mercer, John Francis, 180
Militia titles, use of, 155–56
Milne, John, 134
Milosz, Czeslaw, 10
Miranda, Francisco de, 170–71
Mocquet, Jean, 115
Moffat, Thomas, 89
Montesquieu, Charles Louis de Secondat de, 178, 183
Monticello, 2, 103, 150, 191
More, Thomas, 56
Morgan, Joseph, 66
Mount Vernon, 143, 167, 171, 191
Munford, Robert, 86

Nelson, Thomas, 185
Nelson, Thomas, Jr., 185–86
Nelson, William, 185–86
New England, 81
New History, 31
Niemcewicz, Julian Ursyn, 171
Nomini Hall, 45
Nouveau riche, colonial, 97–103

Oakes, James, 123
Offley House, 102
Oglethorpe, James, general, 116
Oldmixon, John, 48, 62, 77, 88, 110, 115, 119, 138, 141, 156, 161
Olson, Lester, 90
Oronooko, 115
Ostentation, and gentility, 152–57
Ostrow, James, 22
Otis, James, 89

Paine, Thomas, 89–90, 175–76
Parsons, Theophilus, 184
Patriarchalism, 120–24
Peacham, Henry, 138
Peale, Charles Willson, 151
Pedigree as criterion of gentility, 41–49; claims to by Defoe, 43; Defoe's view of, 50–51, 60; Swift's view of, 137–38; claims by Virginia planter elite, 152
Penn, William, 71
Perry, Micajah, 65
Phips, William, 101
Pinckney, Charles, 36
Pinckney, Eliza Lucas, 55, 63, 106, 140
Pinckney, Thomas, 36
Pitman, Henry, 112
Pitt, Sir William, 125
Pocock, J. G. A., 29
Pole, J. R., 184
Poland, gentry of, 147–48
Prewitt, Kenneth, 32
Pulteney, William, earl of Bath, 143

Quakers, 129, 141
Quitt, Martin, 26–27

Ramsay, James, 102, 115
Randolph, Edmund, 34, 36, 172–73
Reid, James, 100–101, 111, 117, 156, 164
Reynolds, Sir Joshua, 166, 168
Rochambeau, Jean Baptiste Donatien de Vimeur, comte de, 1
Rockingham, marquis of, 89
Rosegill, 45
Royal Magazine, 128, 133–34
Rush, Benjamin, 125

Sabine Hall, 107
Sandys, Sir Edwin, 90–91
Schlesinger, Arthur, 13
Shaftesbury, Anthony Ashley Cooper, earl of, 39, 41
Shammas, Carole, 32
Sheehan, Bernard, 87
Shenandoah Valley, 135
Sheridan, Richard B., 165
Slavery, and identity of American plantation gentry, 111–18
Sloane, Sir Hans, 85, 113–14, 147
Southerne, Thomas, 98–99, 115
Spectator, 39, 57, 62, 115, 138
Spengler, Oswald, 9
Spotswood, Alexander, 158
St. Andrew's Society, 109
St. Cecelia's Society, 109
St. Christopher (St. Kitts), 108

Index

Steele, Richard, 39, 61, 62, 115, 138
Stone, Allen, 32
Sumter, Thomas, 36, 64
Surinam, British, 85
Swift, Jonathan, 42; attacks Defoe, 59; on Irish emigrants to America, 82; ridicules upstart gentry, 137–38
Sydnor, Charles, 13

Talleyrand, Prince Charles Maurice, 102
Taste: and legitimacy, 128–29; and economy, 129–30; and social ranks, 130, accumulating objects of, 136–37; ability to appreciate, 136–37, lack of, 138–39; popular versus elite, 162
Tatler, 65
Tayloe, John, 163
Thomas, Sir Dalby, 80
Thornton, Richard, 80
Tocqueville, Alexis de, 9, 188, 190
Tregagle, Jasper, 134
Trumbull, John, 139
Tryon, Thomas, 112–13
Tuesday Club of Annapolis, 87, 109
Tutchin, John, 51, 60
Tyler, John, 146

Versailles, palace of, 177
Virgil, 57
Virginia: its colonial gentry, 1–2, 33, 88, 109, 118; British negative notions of, 103–4; Chastellux on its provincialism, 102–3; civility in, 151; wealth of, 116, 119; slavery, 120; views on gentility of planters, 1–2, 48, 99–100; design of its Capitol, 169

Virginia Gazette, 145, 154, 163, 176
Washington, Augustine, 169
Washington, George, 1, 2, 33, 36, 175, 185; and his coat of arms, 45–46; on education, 54; commonplace book, 140; orders fashionable supplies, 141–42; refurbishes Mount Vernon, 143; orders stylish carriage, 149–50; has servants wear livery, 146; rigid daily schedule, 148; lack of humor, 151; purchases a painting, 167–68; and his rules of civility, 182
Washington, Lawrence, 182
Washington College, 177
Waterhouse, Richard, 16, 83
Weber, Max, 21–22, 170
Wertenbaker, Thomas, 12
Westover, 154, 166
Whistler, Henry, 97
White, John, 92
Widdow Ranter, 61, 99–100
Wigs, as part of genteel dress code, 148
Wilkinson, Daniel, 158
William I, king, 51
William of Orange, king, 51
Williamsburg, 110–11
Wolf, Stephanie G., 16
Wood, Gordon, 32, 178–79
Woodmason, Charles, 76, 84, 87
Woolman, John, 117
Women, fallen, emigrate to America, 82–83
Wormeley, Ralph II, 45
Wormeley, Robert, 185
Wright, Louis B., 12
Wythe, George, 34

Yarico, 114

www.ingramcontent.com/pod-product-compliance
Lightning Source LLC
Chambersburg PA
CBHW022011300426
44117CB00005B/139